"A very timely and eminently engaging book for all those who care deeply about the church's mission in our day. Again and again, I found myself nodding in agreement as the authors made a key point from Scripture or noted the missional relevance of a given biblical passage. I highly recommend this book, not just as food for thought, but more importantly, as a call to obedient, biblically informed action."

  —**Andreas Köstenberger,** Senior Professor of New Testament and Biblical Theology, Director of PhD Studies, Southeastern Baptist Theological Seminary

"In what appears to be a growing tension over what the mission of the church encompasses, DeYoung and Gilbert bring a remarkably balanced book that can correct, restore, and help regardless of which way you lean or land on all things 'missional.' I found the chapters on social justice and our motivation in good works to be especially helpful. Whether you are actively engaging the people around you with the gospel and serving the least of these or you are hesitant of anything 'missional,' this book will help you rest in God's plan to reconcile all things to himself in Christ."

  —**Matt Chandler,** Lead Pastor, The Village Church, Highland Village, Texas

"Christ is the greatest message in the world, and delivering it is the greatest mission. But are we losing our focus? Are we being distracted, sometimes even by good things? Zealous Christians disagree sharply today over the church's proper ministry and mission. Kevin DeYoung and Greg Gilbert bring us back to first things in an age of mission creep and distraction. Offering balanced wisdom, this book will give us not only encouragement but discomfort exactly where we all need it. It's the kind of biblical sanity we need at this moment."

  —**Michael Horton,** J. Gresham Machen Professor of Systematic Theology and Apologetics, Westminster Seminary California

"Kevin DeYoung and Greg Gilbert have written an important book on an important topic. Fair, keenly observant, startlingly honest, this book is replete with careful exegetical work. Verses are not merely cited; they are considered in context. The length of an idea is considered, all the way from its expression in the local church back to its source in Scripture. The result is a book that is nuanced and clear, useful and enjoyable to read, and that is no small gift from two young pastor-theologians who have already become reliable voices. Open this book and you'll want to open your Bible and open your mind on everything from justice to capitalism, from mercy to love."

  —**Mark Dever,** Senior Pastor, Capitol Hill Baptist Church, Washington, DC

"DeYoung and Gilbert clear the fog that has settled over the nature of the church's mission. Their tone is gracious, the style is accessible, but most importantly this book is marked by fidelity to biblical revelation and the gospel of Jesus Christ. The authors have succeeded in what they exhort us to do: they have kept the main thing as the main thing."
—**Thomas R. Schreiner,** James Buchanan Harrison Professor of New Testament Interpretation, The Southern Baptist Theological Seminary

"Among the many books that have recently appeared on mission, this is the best one if you are looking for sensible definitions, clear thinking, readable writing, and the ability to handle the Bible in more than proof-texting ways. I pray that God will use it to bring many to a renewed grasp of what the gospel is and how that gospel relates, on the one hand, to biblical theology and, on the other, to what we are called to do."
—**D. A. Carson,** Research Professor of New Testament, Trinity Evangelical Divinity School

"DeYoung and Gilbert provide clarity to some of the most complex contemporary issues facing the church. Focusing us squarely on the redemptive nature of the gospel, they ultimately point us not only to the church's mission, but to practical ways to understand and live it. The result is a book that will be of great help to pastors, missiologists, theologians, and practitioners."
—**M. David Sills,** Faye Stone Professor of Christian Missions and Cultural Anthropology, Director of the Doctor of Missiology Program and Great Commission Ministries, The Southern Baptist Theological Seminary

"DeYoung and Gilbert have put us in their debt with their clear, biblical, theological, and pastoral exposition of the mission of God's people. That mission, which they rightly understand within the story line of the whole Bible, is summarized in the Great Commission and involves gospel proclamation and disciple making. This superb book will encourage its readers 'to go into the world and make disciples by declaring the gospel of Jesus Christ in the power of the Spirit and gathering these disciples into churches, that they might worship and obey Jesus Christ now and in eternity to the glory of God the Father.'"
—**Peter O'Brien,** Emeritus Faculty Member, Moore College, Sydney, Australia

What Is the *Mission* of the Church?

What Is the *Mission* of the Church?

MAKING SENSE *of* SOCIAL JUSTICE, SHALOM, *and the* GREAT COMMISSION

KEVIN DEYOUNG AND **GREG GILBERT**

WHEATON, ILLINOIS

What Is the Mission of the Church? Making Sense of Social Justice, Shalom, and the Great Commission

Copyright © 2011 by Kevin DeYoung and Gregory D. Gilbert

Published by Crossway
        1300 Crescent Street
        Wheaton, Illinois 60187

Published in association with the literary agency of Wolgemuth & Associates, Inc.

Cover design: Faceout Studio, www.faceoutstudio.com

Cover photo: Shutterstock

Interior design and typesetting: Dawn Premako

First printing 2011

Printed in the United States of America

Trade paperback ISBN: 978-1-4335-2690-9
ePub ISBN: 978-1-4335-2693-0
PDF ISBN: 978-1-4335-2691-6
Mobipocket ISBN: 978-1-4335-2692-3

Library of Congress Cataloging-in-Publication Data
DeYoung, Kevin.
What is the mission of the church? : making sense of social justice, shalom, and the Great Commission / Kevin DeYoung and Greg Gilbert.
   p. cm.
Includes bibliographical references and index.
ISBN 978-1-4335-2690-9 (tp)
   1. Mission of the church. 2. Social justice—Religious aspects—Christianity. I. Gilbert, Greg, 1977–
II. Title.
BV601.8.D48 2011
262'.7—dc23
                                   2011017072

Crossway is a publishing ministry of Good News Publishers.

LB	23	22	21	20	19	18	17	16	15	14	13	12	11
14	13	12	11	10	9	8	7	6	5	4	3	2	1

To Collin, Josh, Justin, and Tullian—
thanks for sharpening us, laughing with us,
and sharing your Crazy Bread.

Contents

PART 3: UNDERSTANDING WHAT WE DO AND WHY WE DO IT

Acknowledgments

IT'S FUN TO WRITE acknowledgments because saying "thank you" is enjoyable. But it's also difficult because we can't possibly say thank you to everyone we should. Here's an abbreviated list.

We are grateful for all the good people at Crossway who have been excited about this book and eager to make an interesting concept into an attractive read.

We appreciate Andrew Wolgemuth for always being in our corner and providing thoughtful counsel and support.

We love our churches—University Reformed Church and Third Avenue Baptist Church. It is a privilege to be in mission with and through you.

A thousand thanks to Justin Taylor. You are a great friend, editor, thinker, and encourager. It's not an exaggeration to say this project would not have happened without you.

We're glad to have good friends like Collin, Tullian, Josh, and Justin, who sharpen us and make us laugh.

Thanks to Mark Dever, D. A. Carson, and Tim Keller for reading through the manuscript and providing invaluable feedback. Many others read through portions of the manuscript. The book is stronger because of good push-back from a lot of smart people. Of course, we don't claim their support for every jot and tittle.

Lastly, we thank our families. We love you deeply, but still not as well as we should.

PART 1

Understanding Our Mission

CHAPTER 1

A Common Word in Need of a Careful Definition

If everything is mission, nothing is mission.
—STEPHEN NEILL

IF YOU'RE READING THIS BOOK, you're probably a Christian. And if a Christian, you probably take some kind of interest in the church. And if you've been involved in a church, you've probably wondered from time to time, "What arc we trying to accomplish anyway?" Maybe as a pastor you've asked yourself, "With everyone interested in their own program and passionate about their own cause, are we even aiming at the same thing?" Maybe as a Christian businessman or stay-at-home mom you've thought, "I know we are supposed to glorify God. But under that big umbrella, what does God want our church to be doing?"

At their root, these questions all ask the same thing: *What is the mission of the church?*

The question is deceptively complex and potentially divisive. For starters, what do we even mean by *mission?* And if that can be settled, we then face more difficult questions. Is the mission of the church *discipleship* or *good deeds* or both? Is the mission of the church the same as the mission of God? Is the mission of the church distinct from the responsibilities of individual Christians? Is the mission of the church a continuation of the mission of Jesus? If so, what was his mission anyway?

Related to these questions are others: What should be the church's role in pursuing *social justice?* Are we right to even use that phrase, and what do we mean by it? Does God expect the church to change the world, to be about the work of transforming its social structures? What about the *kingdom?* How do we build the kingdom of God? Or are we even capable of building the kingdom? How does the kingdom relate to the *gospel?* How does the gospel relate to *the whole story line of the Bible?* And how does all of this relate to *mission?*

Despite all these questions, there is a lot that evangelicals can agree on when it comes to mission: the gospel is, at the very least, the good news of Jesus's death and resurrection; proclamation is essential to the church's witness; heaven and hell are real; people are lost without Jesus; bodies matter as well as souls; and good deeds as the fruit of transformed lives are not optional. But if we are to find a lasting and robust agreement on mission praxis and mission priorities, we must move past generalities and build our theology of mission using the right categories and the right building blocks. In other words, as we grasp key concepts like kingdom, gospel, and social justice, we will be better able to articulate a careful, biblically faithful understanding of the mission of the church. And just as important, we'll be able to pursue obedience to Christ in a way that is more realistic, freeing, and, in the long run, fruitful.

What Is Mission?

Before going any further in answering the question posed in this book's title, we should acknowledge the difficulty in the question itself. A big part of the problem in defining the mission of the church is defining the word *mission*. Because *mission* is not a biblical word like *covenant* or *justification* or *gospel*, determining its meaning for believers is particularly difficult. We could do a study of the word *gospel* and come to some pretty firm biblical conclusions about "What is the Gospel?"—and we will, later in this book![1] But *mission* is a bit trickier. On the one hand the Latin verb *mittere* corresponds to the Greek verb *apostellein*, which occurs 137 times in the New Testament. So mission is not exactly extrabiblical. But as a noun, *mission* does not occur in the Bible, which makes the question of this book more difficult.

The answer to the question, "What is the mission of the church?" depends, to a large degree, on what is meant by "mission." One could make a case that *glorifying God and enjoying him forever* is the mission of the church, because that is our chief end as redeemed believers. Someone else might argue that *loving God and loving neighbor* is the best description of our mission, because those are the greatest commandments. And someone else might borrow from the nineteenth-century hymn and argue that *trust and obey* is the essence of our mission, because that is the great call of the gospel message. In one sense we would be foolish to argue with any of these answers. If mission is simply a synonym for living a faithful Christian life, then there are dozens of ways to answer the question, "What is the mission of the church?"

But isn't it wise to aim for a more precise definition of such a common word? We've never met a Christian who was against mission. In fact, every church we've ever known would say they are passionate about mission. So shouldn't we try to be clear

---

[1]See also Greg Gilbert, *What Is the Gospel?* (Wheaton, IL: Crossway, 2010), and D. A. Carson, "What Is the Gospel?—Revisited," in *For the Fame of God's Name: Essays in Honor of John Piper*, ed. Sam Storms and Justin Taylor (Wheaton, IL: Crossway, 2010), 147–70.

what we are all for? Christians have long seen the importance of carefully defining other theological words like *Trinity*, *essence*, and *inerrancy*.[2] Theology will not go far without careful attention to distinctions and definitions. So why not work toward a definition of *mission*? Christians often talk about mission trips, mission fields, and mission work, so it would seem to be a good idea at least to attempt to define what we are talking about. Granted, word meanings can change, and it may not be possible to rein in the definition of *mission* after fifty years of expansion. But it seems to us that a more precise definition is necessary, if for no other reason than the conviction that Stephen Neill's quip is spot-on: "If everything is mission, nothing is mission."[3]

But where to start with a definition? In his influential book *Transforming Mission*, David Bosch rightly argues, "Since the 1950s there has been a remarkable escalation in the use of the word 'mission' among Christians. This went hand in hand with a significant broadening of the concept, at least in certain circles."[4] It used to be that *mission* referred pretty narrowly to Christians sent out cross-culturally to convert non-Christians and plant churches. But now *mission* is understood much more broadly. Environmental stewardship is mission. Community renewal is mission. Blessing our neighbors is mission. Mission is here. Mission is there. Mission is everywhere. We are all missionaries. As Christopher Wright puts it, disagreeing with Stephen Neill's quote, "If everything is mission . . . *everything is mission*."[5] The ambiguity of the term *mission* is only augmented

---

[2]Jonathan Edwards, in his famous treatise *The End for Which God Created the World*, went so far as to distinguish between a *chief* end, an *ultimate* end, an *inferior* end, and a *subordinate* end. See John Piper, *God's Passion for His Glory: Living the Vision of Jonathan Edwards* (Wheaton, IL: Crossway, 2006).

[3]Quoted in Keith Ferdinando, "Mission: A Problem of Definition," *Themelios* 33, no. 1; http://thegospelcoalition.org/publications/33–1/mission-a-problem-of-definition.

[4]David J. Bosch, *Transforming Mission: Paradigm Shifts in Theology of Mission* (Maryknoll, NY: Orbis, 1991), 1.

[5]Christopher J. H. Wright, *The Mission of God's People: A Biblical Theology of the Church's Mission* (Grand Rapids: Zondervan, 2010), 26; emphasis added. The disagreement, however, should not be exaggerated. Neill allows for a broad scope of Christian activities, but would place these within a correct theology of the *church* and a correct theology of

by the recent proliferation of terms like *missional* and *missio Dei*. It's no wonder Bosch concludes a few pages later, "Ultimately, mission remains undefinable."[6]

But perhaps a common definition is not yet a lost cause. Before giving up on a definition, Bosch acknowledges that *mission*, at least in traditional usage, "presupposes a sender, a person or persons sent by the sender, those to whom one is sent, and an assignment."[7] Though his broader theology of mission is quite different from what we will propose in this book, and though he doesn't like many of the ways this traditional understanding was employed, Bosch is on to something here. At its most basic, the term *mission* implies two things to most people: (1) being sent and (2) being given a task. The first point makes sense because *mission* comes from a Latin word (*mittere*) meaning "to send." The second point is implied in the first. When sent on a mission, we are sent to *do something*—and not *everything*, either, but rather we are given a particular assignment. On a street level, people basically know what mission means. For example, the old TV show *Mission: Impossible* always involved a specific goal that Peter Graves was supposed to accomplish. Companies spend millions every year honing their "mission statements," and fast-food restaurants even post "Our Mission" on the wall to assure us they're fanatically focused on serving us the best burgers in town. Even in the world around us, everyone understands that a mission is that primary thing you set out to accomplish. Most every organization has *something*, as opposed to other things, that it does and must do, and it understands that thing to be its mission. We think the same is true of the church.

In his study of mission in John's Gospel, Andreas Köstenberger proposes a working definition along the same lines: "Mission is the specific task or purpose which a person or group seeks

---

ministry. In other words, mission is not everything, but that doesn't mean the church does only one thing. Thanks to David Reimer for drawing our attention to this point.
[6]Ibid., 9.
[7]Ibid., 1.

to accomplish."[8] Notice again the key concepts of being sent and being given a task. Likewise, John Stott has argued that mission is not everything the church does, but rather describes "everything the church is sent into the world to do."[9] We are convinced that if you ask most Christians, "What is the mission of the church?" they will hear you asking, "What is the specific task or purpose that the church is *sent into the world to accomplish?*" This is our working definition of *mission* and what we mean to ask with the title of this book.

A Correction to the Correction

Our sincere hope is that this book can be a positive contribution to the mission discussion so prevalent and so needed in the evangelical world. We want to be positive in tone. We want to build up rather than tear down. But inevitably, a fair amount of our work in these chapters will be corrective as well.

Some of what we want to correct is an overexpansive definition that understands mission to be just about every good thing a Christian could do as a partner with God in his mission to redeem the whole world.[10] But we are *not* antimissional.[11] More and more, *missional* simply means being "on mission"—conscious of how everything we do should serve the mission of the church, being winsome and other-centered and Good Samaritan–like with those outside the community of faith, and having a sanctified strategy

---

[8]Andreas J. Köstenberger, *The Missions of Jesus and the Disciples according to the Fourth Gospel: With Implications for the Fourth Gospel's Purpose and the Mission of the Contemporary Church* (Grand Rapids: Eerdmans, 1998), 199. The full quotation reads, "Mission is the specific task or purpose which a person or group seeks to accomplish, involving various modes of movement, be it sending or being sent, coming and going, descending and ascending, gathering by calling others to follow, or following."
[9]John R. W. Stott, *Christian Mission in the Modern World: What the Church Should Be Doing Now!* (Downers Grove, IL: InterVarsity, 1975), 30.
[10]For example, Reggie McNeal says "the missional church is *the people of God partnering with God in his redemptive mission in the world.*" *Missional Renaissance: Changing the Scorecard for the Church* (San Francisco: Jossey-Bass, 2009), 24.
[11]We hope it goes without saying that we are not anti-our brothers in the Acts 29 and Redeemer networks. This book is not written to critique them, and we are confident they share our desire to make gospel proclamation and discipleship central in the mission of the church.

of being intentional and "attractional" for those who don't know Christ. It is often shorthand for "get out of your holy huddle and go engage your community with the gospel." We are all for that. Every Christian should be. We are not out to tar and feather any Christian who dares put -*al* on the end of *mission*. Even less do we want to cast aspersions on many of our friends who happily use the word and usually mean very good things by it.

Nevertheless, it is not wrong to probe the word *missional.* It's a big trunk that can smuggle a great deal of unwanted baggage. Being suspicious of every mention of the word is bad, but raising concerns about how the word is sometimes used is simply wise.

With that in mind, we register a few concerns about how missional thinking has sometimes played out in the conversation about the church's mission:

1. We are concerned that good behaviors are sometimes commended but in the wrong categories. For example, many good deeds are promoted under the term *social justice*, when we think "loving your neighbor" is often a better category. Or, folks will talk about transforming the world, when we think "faithful presence" is a better way to describe what we are trying to do and actually can do in the world. Or, sometimes well-meaning Christians talk about "building the kingdom" or "building *for* the kingdom," when actually the verbs associated with the kingdom are almost always passive (*enter, receive, inherit*). We'd do better to speak of living as citizens of the kingdom, rather than telling our people that they build the kingdom.

2. We are concerned that in our newfound missional zeal we sometimes put hard "oughts" on Christians where there should be inviting "cans." You *ought* to do something about human trafficking. You *ought* to do something about AIDS. You *ought* to do something about lack of good public education. When you say "ought," you imply that if the church does not tackle these problems, we are being disobedient. We think it would be better to invite individual Christians, in keeping with their gifts and

calling, to try to solve these problems rather than indicting the church for "not caring."

3. We are concerned that in all our passion for renewing the city or tackling social problems, we run the risk of marginalizing the one thing that makes Christian mission Christian: namely, making disciples of Jesus Christ.

Before we go any farther down the missional-corrective road, though, perhaps it would be helpful to make clear at the outset what we do and do not want to accomplish with this book.

We do *not* want:

- Christians to be indifferent toward the suffering around them and around the world
- Christians to think evangelism is the only thing in life that really counts
- Christians who risk their lives and sacrifice for the poor and disadvantaged to think their work is in any way suspect or is praiseworthy only if it results in conversions
- Christians to retreat into holy huddles or be blissfully unconcerned to work hard and make an impact in whatever field or career to which the Lord calls them
- Christians to stop dreaming of creative, courageous ways to love their neighbors and impact their cities

We want to underline all those bullet points, star them, mark them with highlighter, and write them on our hearts. It's far too easy to get our heads right, but our hearts and hands wrong.

Having said all that, however, here's some of what we *do* want:

- We want to make sure the gospel—the good news of Christ's death for sin and subsequent resurrection—is of first importance in our churches.

- We want Christians freed from false guilt—from thinking the church is either responsible for most problems in the world or responsible to fix these problems.
- We want the crystal-clear and utterly unique task of the church—making disciples of Jesus Christ to the glory of God the Father—put front and center, not lost in a flurry of commendable concerns.
- We want Christians to understand the story line of the Bible and think more critically about specific texts within this story.
- We want the church to remember that there is something worse than death and something better than human flourishing. If we hope only for renewed cities and restored bodies in this life, we are of all people most to be pitied.

In correcting certain aspects of some missional thinking, we realize that missional thinking itself is striving to correct abuses of traditional missiology. Both corrections may be necessary at times. Hopefully no evangelical would say (or think), "Ah, let it all burn up. Who cares about food and water for the poor? Who gives a rip about HIV? Give 'em the gospel for the soul and ignore the needs of the body." This is what missional thinking is *against.* And similarly, we hope no evangelical would say (or think) the opposite: "Sharing the gospel is offensive and to be avoided. As long as the poor have job training, health care, and education—that's enough. The world needs more food, not more sermons." This is what we trust missional thinking is *not for.*

A Prayer for Humility and Understanding

The truth is that both sides have some important things to say to one another, and we should be careful in our mutual correction not to overcompensate. At their best, missional thinkers

23

are warning the church against a careless, loveless indifference to the problems and potential opportunities all around us, a dualistic disregard for the whole person. On the other hand, a (usually) different group of Christians fears overly optimistic (and exhausting) utopian dreams, a loss of God-centeredness, and a diminishment of the church's urgent message of Christ crucified for hell-bound sinners.

Both are real dangers. We admit we are probably more sensitive to the second danger. And indeed one of the aims of this book is to guard the church from these errors. But we fully understand that many Christians, perhaps even the two of us, are often in danger of passing by the wounded man on the Jericho road. One of the challenges of this book—probably the biggest challenge—is that we may be seen as (or actually be!) two guys only paying lip service to good deeds. While we hope this book gives Christians a better handle on disputed texts and better categories for thinking of their service in the world, we would be disappointed to discover a year from now that our work did anything to discourage radical love and generosity for hurting people. Both of us, although far from perfect examples, have often given to hurting people and have supported organizations and individuals who work to alleviate suffering. Both our churches are involved in mercy ministry at home and abroad. All that to say, we want to be—and we want our congregants and all our readers to be—the sort of "just person" Tim Keller describes as living "a life of honesty, equity, and generosity in every aspect of his or her life."[12]

And yet this book is not about "generous justice." It is about the mission of the church. We want to help Christians articulate and live out their views on the mission of the church in ways that are more theologically faithful, exegetically careful, and personally sustainable.

---

[12]Timothy Keller, *Generous Justice: How God's Grace Makes Us Just* (New York: Dutton, 2010), 17.

A Pastoral Approach

At the beginning of a book it is often helpful to understand what kind of work you are reading. This is not a book by and for biblical or theological scholars. We will deal with a lot of texts and interact with a lot of theology (and hopefully will do so responsibly), but we are not attempting a scholarly monograph on a biblical theology of mission. We are not trying to tell mission boards what to do or to instruct missionaries on how to do their work, though we would like to think this book might be helpful to both groups. We are pastors, writing for the "average" Christian and the "ordinary" pastor trying to make sense of a whole host of missiological questions. From many conversations in print, online, and in person our sense is that this whole issue of mission (along with related issues like kingdom, social justice, shalom, cultural mandate, and caring for the poor) is the most confusing, most discussed, most energizing, and most potentially divisive issue in the evangelical church today. It is certainly a likely fault line in the so-called young, restless, and Reformed movement.

In doing research for this book we read a number of blogs and articles and a big stack of books. From time to time we'll cite these explicitly in order to interact with real people and their ideas. But we will leave a lot of our research in the background. We do this for two reasons: (1) so as not to distract the reader with gobs of footnotes, and (2) so as not to give any impression that we are trying to size up the missional church. We don't attempt to define *missional*, and we aren't trying to divide the missiological landscape into good guys and bad guys. We really don't want this to be an us-against-them kind of book. But we do want to respond to potential objections and interact with different missiological approaches. Hence, we tried to make our missions-related reading deep and wide.[13]

---

[13]Among the books we read in part or (more often) in whole are: Stott, *Christian Mission in the Modern World*; Lesslie Newbigin, *The Gospel in a Pluralist Society* (Grand Rapids: Eerdmans, 1990); Newbigin, *The Open Secret: An Introduction to the Theology of Mission* (Grand Rapids:

Back to the Question at Hand

So what is the mission of the church? We've kept you in suspense long enough. In short, we will argue that the mission of the church is summarized in the Great Commission passages[14]—the climactic marching orders Jesus issues at the ends of the Gospels and at the beginning of Acts. We believe the church is sent into the world to witness to Jesus by proclaiming the gospel and making disciples of all nations. This is our task. This is our unique and central calling.

That's the case we will seek to make in the next chapter, looking both at the Great Commission passages themselves and at several other texts that are often suggested as alternative or additional commissions for the church. The next six chapters (part 2) explore a number of larger theological concepts that are always at issue in these discussions of mission. Chapter 3 asks what the main thrust of the

---

Eerdmans, 1994); Bosch, *Transforming Mission*; P. T. O'Brien, *Gospel and Mission in the Writings of Paul: An Exegetical and Theological Analysis* (Grand Rapids: Baker, 1995); Darrell Guder, ed., *Missional Church: A Vision for the Sending of the Church in North America* (Grand Rapids: Eerdmans, 1998); Köstenberger, *The Missions of Jesus and the Disciples according to the Fourth Gospel*; James F. Engel and William A. Dyrness, *Changing the Mind of Missions* (Downers Grove, IL: InterVarsity, 2000); Andreas J. Köstenberger and Peter T. O'Brien, *Salvation to the Ends of the Earth: A Biblical Theology of Mission* (Downers Grove, IL: InterVarsity, 2001); Mark R. Gornik, *To Live in Peace: Biblical Faith and the Changing Inner City* (Grand Rapids: Eerdmans, 2002); Cornelius Plantinga, *Engaging God's World: A Christian Vision of Faith, Learning, and Living* (Grand Rapids: Eerdmans, 2002); Eckhard J. Schnabel, *Early Christian Mission*, 2 vols. (Downers Grove, IL: InterVarsity, 2004); Albert M. Wolters, *Creation Regained: Biblical Basics for a Reformational Worldview* (Grand Rapids: Eerdmans, 2005); David J. Hesselgrave, *Paradigms in Conflict: 10 Key Questions in Christian Missions Today* (Grand Rapids: Kregel, 2006); Ed Stetzer and David Putnam, *Breaking the Missional Code: Your Church Can Become a Missionary in Your Community* (Nashville: B&H, 2006); Christopher J. H. Wright, *The Mission of God: Unlocking the Bible's Grand Narrative* (Downers Grove, IL: InterVarsity, 2006); Craig Van Gelder, *The Ministry of the Missional Church: Community Led by the Spirit* (Grand Rapids: Baker, 2007); Alan Hirsch, *The Forgotten Ways: Reactivating the Missional Church* (Grand Rapids: Brazos, 2007); McNeal, *Missional Renaissance*; James Davison Hunter, *To Change the World: The Irony, Tragedy, and Possibility of Christianity in the Late Modern World* (New York: Oxford University Press, 2010); Keller, *Generous Justice*; John Piper, *Let the Nations Be Glad! The Supremacy of God in Missions*, 3rd ed. (Grand Rapids: Baker, 2010); David Platt, *Radical: Taking Back Your Faith from the American Dream* (Colorado Springs: Multnomah, 2010); M. David Sills, *Reaching and Teaching: A Call to Great Commission Obedience* (Chicago: Moody, 2010); Timothy Tennent, *Invitation to World Missions: A Trinitarian Missiology for the Twenty-first Century* (Grand Rapids: Kregel, 2010); David VanDrunen, *Natural Law and the Two Kingdoms: A Study in the Development of Reformed Social Thought* (Grand Rapids: Eerdmans, 2010); Wright, *The Mission of God's People*; Michael Horton, *The Gospel Commission: Recovering God's Strategy for Making Disciples* (Grand Rapids: Baker, 2011).

[14]Matt. 28:16–20; Mark 13:10; 14:9; Luke 24:44–49; Acts 1:8. See chapter 2 for discussion.

Bible's story line is and how that affects our understanding of the church's mission. Chapter 4 seeks to understand the structure and content of the gospel message itself and asks whether the gospel of forgiveness of sins through Jesus is "too small." Chapter 5 considers the Bible's teaching on the kingdom of God and how we relate to it. Chapters 6 and 7 form a pair, exploring the idea of "social justice" and looking carefully at several biblical texts relating to justice. In chapter 8 we think about God's intention to remake the world, and consider what that means for the church's activity in the world. Chapter 9 is our attempt to think practically about what all this means. If the mission of the church is proclamation and disciple making, then what is the theological motivation for good deeds? And how might a local church think about what it ought to be doing? Finally, chapter 10 offers a concluding perspective and an encouragement to all of us to recommit ourselves to the great work our Lord has given us.

One last word before we launch into things: We want to say again that we strongly support churches undertaking mercy ministries in their communities. Both of our churches have programs and support missionaries that aim to meet physical needs while also hoping to share the gospel whenever possible. Though we do not believe that the mission of the church is to build the kingdom or to partner with God in remaking the world, this does not mean we are against cultural engagement. Our point is simply that we must understand these endeavors in the right theological categories and embrace them without sacrificing more explicit priorities. We should not cheapen good deeds by making them only a means to some other end (evangelism), but neither do we want to exaggerate our responsibility by thinking it is our duty to build the kingdom through our good deeds. Similarly, we should not overspiritualize social action by making it equivalent to God's shalom. As the church loves the world so loved by God, we will work to relieve suffering wherever we can, but especially eternal suffering.[15]

---

[15]See D. A. Carson's editorial in *Themelios* 33, no. 2; http://thegospelcoalition.org/publications/33–2/editorial.

CHAPTER 2

What in the World Does Jesus Send Us into the World to Do?

MISSION, AS WE TRIED to demonstrate in the previous chapter, is not everything we do in Jesus's name, nor everything we do in obedience to Christ. Mission is the task we are given to fulfill. It's what Jesus sends us into the world to do. And if we want to figure out what Jesus sends disciples into the world to do, we think the best place to look is the Great Commission.

A Few Other Options First

Before we state our reasons for focusing on the Great Commission, and before we get to the Great Commission texts themselves and how they support our thesis above, it might be helpful to examine a few other passages that are sometimes pushed forward as offering a different and fuller mission identity for the church. As you'll see, our problem is not with applying these texts to our contemporary context, or even with using them to shape our missional identity. Every passage of Scripture is inspired by God and profitable for us (2 Tim. 3:16). But—and here's the rub—every passage is profitable only *if understood and applied in the right way.*

Genesis 12:1–3

We begin with Yahweh's call to Abram:

> Now the LORD said to Abram, "Go from your country and your kindred and your father's house to the land that I will show you. And I will make of you a great nation, and I will bless you and make your name great, so that you will be a blessing. I will bless those who bless you, and him who dishonors you I will curse, and in you all the families of the earth shall be blessed." (Gen. 12:1–3)

Everyone agrees that this is a pivotal text not just in Genesis but also in God's grand plan of redemptive history. After a host of curses (Gen. 3:14, 17; 4:11; 5:29; 9:25) and lots of sin run amok, Genesis 12 bursts onto the scene with the promise of universal blessing. At last, here's a spot of good news and a beautiful revelation both of God's mission and of marching orders for Abraham.

But whereas everyone recognizes Genesis 12 as a key passage in the unfolding of God's plan of salvation, others also see it "as one of the most important places in a missiological reading of the Bible."[1] What they mean is that Genesis 12 reveals the heart of God's mission *and ours*—namely, to be a blessing. Reggie McNeal argues that in this "simple but far-reaching covenant . . . the people of God are charged with the responsibility and enjoy the privilege to bless everyone."[2] Likewise, Christopher Wright maintains that "it would be entirely appropriate, and no bad

---

[1]Christopher J. H. Wright, *The Mission of God: Unlocking the Bible's Grand Narrative* (Downers Grove, IL: InterVarsity, 2006), 199.
[2]Reggie McNeal, *Missional Renaissance: Changing the Scorecard for the Church* (San Francisco: Jossey-Bass, 2009), 27.

30

thing, if we took this text as 'the Great Commission'. . . .There could be worse ways of summing up what mission is supposed to be all about than 'Go . . . and be a blessing.' "[3] Later he concludes, "The Abrahamic covenant is a moral agenda for God's people as well as a mission statement by God."[4] In missional thinking, Genesis 12 is more than a promise. It's more than a revelation of God's ultimate mission in redemptive history. It is a *command* for the children of Abraham to help the nations experience all the good gifts that God longs for them to enjoy.[5]

At first, a closer look at the grammar of Genesis 12 seems to support a "missional" understanding of the text. There are two imperative verbs: "go" in verse 1 and "be a blessing" at the end of verse 2. So, contrary to the ESV translation, it looks as though Abraham has two commands: go and bless. Wright makes much of the grammar, arguing that "both [verbs] therefore have the nature of a charge or a mission laid on Abraham. . . . 'Be a blessing' thus entails a purpose and goal that stretches into the future. It is, in short, missional."[6] But it's curious that Wright builds so much on this foundation when earlier he acknowledges that "it is a feature of Hebrew (as indeed it is in English) that when two imperatives occur together the second imperative may sometimes express either the expected result or the intended purpose of carrying out the first imperative."[7] In other words, the second grammatical imperative may not have the force of an imperative, but rather of a purpose or a result of obeying the first imperative. In fact, our English translations[8] all render the end of verse 2 "you shall be a blessing" or "so that you shall be a blessing" or something similar. There are several other places in the Old Testament where an imperative verb

---

[3]Wright, *The Mission of God*, 214. Second ellipsis in original.
[4]Ibid., 221.
[5]This language is taken from ibid. This is Wright's exposition of blessing, and it seems that he understands the command to bless to entail these things.
[6]Ibid., 211.
[7]Ibid., 201.
[8]Including the ESV, KJV, NKJV, NASB, NIV, NLT, RSV, and NRSV.

should be translated as a result clause, rather than a command. Take Genesis 42:18 for example, where Joseph says, "Do this and you will live." Both "do this" and "live" are imperative in form, but "live" is also clearly to be understood as the *result* of "doing this." It's not another command. We think this is how the second imperative in Genesis 12:1–2 should be translated—as a result clause, rather than as a command.[9] This means, to quote Eckhard Schnabel, "Abraham does not receive an assignment to carry YHWH's blessings to the nations; rather, the nations are promised divine blessing if and when they see Abraham's faith in YHWH and if and when they establish contact with his descendants."[10]

In talking about Hebrew grammar we quickly realize two things: (1) most people reading this book are ready for us to stop talking about Hebrew grammar, and (2) we are not experts in Hebrew grammar. Some (but not all) Hebrew scholars may disagree with the last paragraph. But even if the verb should be translated as a command, or even if it has that force no matter how you slice it, we still think the "missional" reading of the text says too much. Even if Abraham is told, "Go be a blessing," the entire story of the patriarchs demonstrates that God is the one doing the blessing, quite apart from any blessing strategy on the part of Abraham. True, God's blessing may be dependent (in a proximate way) on Abraham going. And true, Abraham's obedience to God results in blessings on the nations. True, Abraham and his kin are interacting with Gentiles all throughout Genesis as the chosen family is the means of blessing for some peoples

---

[9]Old Testament scholar Victor P. Hamilton explains the functions of the imperatives in Gen. 12:1–2: "Here the first imperative states the exhortation, and the second imperative touches on the results which are brought about by the implementation of the first imperative (e.g., Gen. 17:1; 1 Kings 22:6; 2 Kings 5:13; Isa. 36:16). Applied to Gen. 12:1–2, this construction means that the first imperative, *go*, is related as effect to cause to this second imperative, *be*. Abram cannot be a blessing if he stays in Haran. But if he leaves, then a blessing he will be." *The Book of Genesis*, The New International Commentary on the Old Testament (Grand Rapids: Eerdmans, 1999), 373.
[10]Eckhard Schnabel, *Early Christian Mission*, vol. 1, *Jesus and the Twelve* (Downers Grove, IL: InterVarsity, 2004), 63.

and cursing for others. But Abraham does not leave Ur intent on blessing the Canaanites. After Genesis 12, the narrative follows different individuals and nations whose plusses and minuses prove the promise of God that whoever blesses Abraham will be blessed, and whoever curses him will be cursed. God blesses Abraham's family despite themselves, and he blesses those who treat Abraham well despite Abraham's failures. This is not to suggest that Abraham's obedience is irrelevant for God's promised blessing. He has to *go* in order to be a blessing. Our point is simply that the obedient going is not going out to serve Amalekites and help them grow crops and learn to read. There is plenty of blessing to go around, but there is no evidence Abraham ever takes his call in chapter 12 as a commission to go find ways to bless the nations.

This doesn't in any way mean it's wrong for Christians to bless others, but it does mean we should not take Genesis 12:1–3 as a moral agenda or as another Great Commission. The call of Abram is not about a community blessing program. It's about God's unilateral promise to bless fumbling Abraham and bless the nations through faith in the promised Seed that will come from his family tree. Even when the blessing is connected to obedience, it is not the obedience of missional engagement but Abraham's obedience in leaving his land, in circumcising his offspring (Gen. 17:10–14), and in being willing to sacrifice his son (Gen. 22:16–18). The emphasis in Genesis is on the chosen family as recipients of God's blessing, not as the immediate purveyors of it.

Most crucially, the New Testament does not understand the call of Abram as a missional charge. Clearly, it is a glorious mission text announcing God's plans to bless the whole world. But the blessing is not something we bestow on others as we work for human flourishing. Rather the Abrahamic blessing comes to those who trust in Abraham's Offspring. This is Paul's understanding in Galatians 3:9 when, after quoting Genesis 12:3 ("In

33

you all the families of the earth shall be blessed"), he concludes, "So then, those who are of faith are blessed along with Abraham, the man of faith." If there are missiological implications from Genesis, their emphasis is not "go and bless everyone" but rather "go and call the nations to put their faith in Christ."

Exodus 19:5–6

We now turn to the well-known passage where God prepares Israel for his presence at Mount Sinai:

> Now therefore, if you will indeed obey my voice and keep my covenant, you shall be my treasured possession among all peoples, for all the earth is mine; and you shall be to me a kingdom of priests and a holy nation. These are the words that you shall speak to the people of Israel. (Ex. 19:5–6)

Some argue that the language of "kingdom of priests" indicates that we are intermediaries for the presence of God in the world. The logic usually works like this: "The Bible says we are priests. And what do priests do? They mediate God's presence. So what is our mission? We are supposed to be a kingdom of priests mediating God's blessing to the world." Reggie McNeal, commenting on Exodus 19, puts it like this: God "created a people to serve as his ongoing incarnational presence on the earth."[11] Christopher Wright puts it this way: "It is thus richly significant that God confers on Israel as a whole people the role of being his priesthood in the midst of the nations. . . . Just as it was the role of the priests to bless the Israelites, so it would be the role of Israel as a whole ultimately to be a blessing to the nations."[12]

---

[11]McNeal, *Missional Renaissance*, 30.
[12]Wright, *The Mission of God*, 331. Likewise, N. T. Wright comments on Ex. 19:4–6 saying, "The royal and priestly vocation of all human beings, it seems, consists in this: to stand at the interface between God and his creation, bringing God's wise and generous order to the world and giving articulate voice to creation's glad and grateful praise to its maker" (*After You Believe* [New York: HarperOne, 2010], 80–81). Later, N. T. Wright argues that

While it is attractive to think Israel is meant to mediate God's blessings to the nations as a kind of incarnational presence, this is not the best way to understand Exodus 19 or the phrase "kingdom of priests." Here are five reasons why:

1. The Levitical priesthood serves a mediatorial role not in terms of incarnating God's presence (his presence is in the glory cloud over the ark of the covenant) but in terms of placating his anger. The primary function of the priests in the Old Testament is to mediate between God and man by administering sacrifices. The book of Hebrews understands the priestly office of Christ in largely the same way (4:14–5:10; 7:1–28; 10:1–18).

2. "Kingdom of priests" is best understood as a designation for Israel's call to be set apart from the world and belong to God. "Kingdom of priests" is an overlapping term with (though not identical with) "holy nation." This is why the Lord tells the people at the mountain to consecrate themselves (Ex. 19:10); they are to be holy as he is holy. Likewise, when the Exodus passage is referenced in 1 Peter 2:9, the focus once again is on holiness—abstaining from the passions of the flesh (1 Pet. 2:11–12). The image of a royal priesthood in the Old Testament and in the New Testament suggests holiness and privilege, not incarnational presence.

3. If God were giving the Israelites a missionary task to bless the non-Israelites, we might expect to see this task specified and elaborated in the Mosaic Law. Yet the rules and regulations of Sinai say nothing about a mission to the Gentiles. There are commands for Israel to express care for sojourners and foreigners in its midst, but not explicit instructions for Israel to go into the world and meet the needs of the nations.

4. The Israelites conquer the surrounding nations by military force, not by any kind of incarnational mission. The nations are

---

"royal priesthood" means "carrying forward the mission of God declaring God's powerful and rescuing acts, and beginning the work of implementing the messianic rule of Jesus in all the world" (86).

more often threats to Israel's religion than they are opportunities for service, even if God's design all along is to save more than ethnic Jews (see Isa. 42:6; 49:6; 60:3). If Israel is supposed to mediate God's blessing to the nations, it has a strange way of fulfilling the task.

5. The prophets never fault Israel for neglecting its missionary or international blessing mandate. God certainly cares about how his chosen people will be an attraction or a byword among the nations. But the direction is "come and see" not "go and tell." If missional engagement were a covenant obligation, surely the Israelites would be rebuked for failing to keep this aspect of the law.[13]

Luke 4:16–21

A final popular missional text comes at the start of Jesus's public ministry:

> And he came to Nazareth, where he had been brought up. And as was his custom, he went to the synagogue on the Sabbath day, and he stood up to read. And the scroll of the prophet Isaiah was given to him. He unrolled the scroll and found the place where it was written,
>
>> "The Spirit of the Lord is upon me
>>   because he has anointed me
>>   to proclaim good news to the poor.
>> He has sent me to proclaim liberty to the captives
>>   and recovering of sight to the blind,
>>   to set at liberty those who are oppressed,
>> to proclaim the year of the Lord's favor." [Isa. 61:1–2]
>
> And he rolled up the scroll and gave it back to the attendant and sat down. And the eyes of all in the synagogue were fixed

---

[13]These last three reasons, and a few more we haven't included, can be found in Schnabel, *Early Christian Mission*, 71–72.

on him. And he began to say to them, "Today this Scripture has been fulfilled in your hearing." (Luke 4:16–21)

No doubt, this text is one of the clearest statements of Jesus's mission and the goals of his ministry. It is also one of the most misunderstood. In popular explanations, Luke 4 underscores that Jesus's mission focused on the materially destitute and the downtrodden. In this interpretation, Jesus was both Messiah *and* social liberator. He came to bring the Year of Jubilee to the oppressed. He came to transform social structures and bring God's creation back to shalom. Therefore, our mission, in keeping with Christ's mission, is at least in part—if not in its central expression—"to extend the kingdom by infiltrating all segments of society, with preference given to the poor, and allowing no dichotomy between evangelism and social transformation (Luke 4:18–19)."[14] Above all else, Luke 4 (it is argued) shows that Jesus's mission was to serve the poor. So shouldn't that be our mission too?

This common approach to Luke 4 is not entirely off base, but it misses two critical observations.

Missing the Trees for the Forest

First, this approach overlooks the actual verbs Jesus read from the Isaiah scroll. The Spirit of the Lord, resting upon Jesus as the long-awaited Messiah, would anoint him to *proclaim* good news to the poor, to *proclaim* liberty to the captives and recovery of sight to the blind, to set at liberty those who are oppressed, and to *proclaim* the year of the Lord's favor. With the exception of "to set at liberty the oppressed" (which we'll come back to in a moment), these are all words that point to speaking. While it's certainly true that Jesus healed the sick and gave sight to the blind (as pointers to his deity, signs of

---

[14]James F. Engel and William A. Dyrness, *Changing the Mind of Missions: Where Have We Gone Wrong* (Downers Grove, IL: InterVarsity, 2000), 80.

the kingdom's in-breaking, and expressions of his compassion), the messianic mission statement in Luke 4 highlights the *announcement* of good news. If Luke 4 sets the tone for the mission of the church, then the center of the church's mission should be the preaching of the gospel.

The Humble Poor

Second, the "missions as social transformation" reading of Luke 4 assumes too much about the economic aspect of "the poor" (Gk., *ptōchos*). While *ptōchos* in verse 18 is probably not without some reference to material poverty, the word has broader connotations and significance. Here are four things that lead us to that conclusion:

1. The quotation is from Isaiah 61:1–2, where the poor are lumped in with the "brokenhearted" and "all who mourn." The poor in Isaiah are not just materially poor; they are the humble poor, the mournful ones who trust in the Lord and wait for their promised "oil of gladness" and their "garment of praise" (Isa. 61:3). The Hebrew *anaoim* in verse 1 can be translated "poor" (ESV, NIV) or "meek" (KJV) or "afflicted" (NASB, ESV footnote). All are possible because clearly something more than material poverty is in mind.

2. Likewise, the Greek word *ptōchos* can speak of literal or figurative poverty. Of the ten uses of *ptōchos* in Luke, seven should be taken as literal poverty (14:13, 21; 16:20, 22; 18:22; 19:8; 21:3), while three may be figurative (4:18; 6:20; 7:22). Elsewhere in the New Testament, Revelation 3:17 is a clear instance where *ptōchos* should be taken figuratively. The church in Laodicea thought themselves rich (and they were, materially), but on a deeper spiritual level they were "wretched, pitiable, poor, blind, and naked." As in English, the Greek word for "poor" carries different shades of meaning, both literal and figurative.

3. A strictly literal understanding of "the poor" in the immediate context would not make sense. If "the poor" are

the literally financially poor, then "the captives," "the blind," and "the oppressed" should be taken literally as well. And yet there is no instance in the Gospels of Jesus setting a literal prisoner free (something that confused John the Baptist in Luke 7:18–23). Quite naturally we understand captivity and oppression to include spiritual bondage. It is not inappropriate, then, to see a fundamental spiritual aspect to "the poor" in Luke 4.

4. The slightly wider context makes the same point. In Luke 4:25–27 Jesus mentions two examples of the type of person who experienced the Lord's favor in the Old Testament. One is the widow of Zarephath. She was materially poor. But the other example is Naaman, the important Syrian general who humbled himself by dipping seven times in the Jordan River. If these are the examples of good news being proclaimed to the poor, then "the poor" has more to do with poverty of spirit than material destitution.

Summary

For all these reasons we agree with Andreas Köstenberger and Peter O'Brien that "the 'poor' to whom the good news is announced are not to be understood narrowly of the economically destitute, as most recent scholars have suggested; rather the term refers more generally to 'the dispossessed, the excluded' who were forced to depend upon God."[15] We agree with David Bosch when he concludes:

> Therefore, in Luke's gospel, the rich are tested on the ground of their wealth, whereas others are tested on loyalty toward their family, their people, their culture, and their work (Lk. 9:59–61). This means the poor are sinners like everybody else, because ultimately sinfulness is rooted in the human heart. Just as the

---

[15]Andreas J. Köstenberger and Peter T. O'Brien, *Salvation to the Ends of the Earth: A Biblical Theology of Mission* (Downers Grove, IL: InterVarsity, 2001), 117.

materially rich can be spiritually poor, the materially poor can be spiritually poor.[16]

This does not rule out an economic component to *ptōchos* in Luke 4. The poor are often the economic poor because material hardship rather than material plenty tends to be a means of cultivating spiritual sensitivity, humility, and the desperation needed to hear God's voice. There's a reason Jesus says, "Blessed are the poor," instead of, "Blessed are the rich." The poor are more apt to see their need for help than the rich. The Greek word *ptōchos*, to quote Darrell Bock, is best described as a "soteriological generalization."[17] It refers to those who are open to God, responsive to him, and who see their dependence upon him. It is to these that Jesus proclaims the year of the Lord's favor.

Therefore, Jesus's mission laid out in Luke 4 is not a mission of structural change and social transformation, but a mission to announce the good news of his saving power and merciful reign to all those brokenhearted—that is, poor—enough to believe.

What Makes the Great Commission So Great?

Having examined several common "missional" texts and come to the conclusion that these passages are often misappropriated and misunderstood, we are now in a position to turn our attention to the Great Commission, or more precisely, the Great Commission*s* (Matt. 28:16–20; Mark 13:10; 14:9; Luke 24:44–49; Acts 1:8).

---

[16]David J. Bosch, *Transforming Mission: Paradigm Shifts in Theology of Mission* (Maryknoll, NY: Orbis, 1991), 104. For ease of reading, we dropped Bosch's parenthetical citations in these two sentences. They were: Nissen 1984: 175, 176; cf. Pobee 1987: 19, 53. Many other scholars past and present, including Eckhard Schnabel, David Hesselgrave, Robert Stein, Christopher Little, I. Howard Marshall, and Darrell Bock, have come to similar conclusions. See Schnabel, *Early Christian Mission*, 225. References to many of the other authors were found in David Hesselgrave, *Paradigms in Conflict: 10 Key Questions in Christian Missions Today* (Grand Rapids: Kregel, 2005), 125–38.

[17]Darrell Bock, *Luke 1:1–9:50*, Baker Exegetical Commentary on the New Testament (Grand Rapids: Baker, 1994), 408.

Before we get to Jesus's parting words, though, we must face an honest question: Why should our theology of mission focus so intently on this cluster of postresurrection, preascension commands? After all, there's no inspired section heading that says Matthew 28:16–20 should be called "The Great Commission" (and it hasn't always been known by this illustrious title).[18] Furthermore, many Christians throughout history have believed that the apostles have already fulfilled Jesus's parting instructions and therefore they are not a direct command for the church today. More recently, missional thinkers have been reticent to ground the missionary task in specific imperatives (like we find toward the end of each Gospel). The whole Bible, they argue, is about the mission of God, not just a few isolated passages. So maybe the Great Commission isn't so great after all. Maybe John Stott was right when he said that "we give the Great Commission too prominent a place in our Christian thinking."[19]

So why should we emphasize these so-called Great Commission texts in determining the mission of the church? That's a fair question, and there are several good ways to answer it.

First, even if the entire Bible is essentially a missional book (and on one level, who would want to disagree with this assertion?), we would still do well to ground what we *must do in mission* on Scripture's explicit commands. One of the biggest missteps in much of the newer mission literature is an assumption that whatever God is doing in the world, this too is our task. So if the *missio Dei* (mission of God) is ultimately to restore shalom and renew the whole cosmos, then we, as his partners, should work to the same ends. Christopher Wright, for example, states

---

[18]For history on the title see David F. Wright's essay, "The Great Commission and the Ministry of the Word: Reflections Historical and Contemporary on Relations and Priorities (Finlayson Memorial Lecture, 2007)," *Scottish Bulletin of Evangelical Theology* 25 (2007): 132–57; http://netcommunity.rutherfordhouse.org.uk/publications/Document.Doc?id=69.

[19]John R. W. Stott, *Christian Mission in the Modern World: What the Church Should Be Doing Now* (Downers Grove, IL: InterVarsity, 1975), 29.

that "everything a Christian and a Christian church is, says and does should be missional in its conscious participation in the mission of God in God's world."[20] But what if we are not called to partner with God in all he undertakes? What if the work of salvation, restoration, and re-creation are divine gifts to which we bear witness, rather than works in which we collaborate? What if our mission is not identical with God's mission? What if we carry on Jesus's mission but not in the same way he carried it out? Isn't it better to locate our responsibility in the tasks we are given rather than in the work we see God accomplishing? In fact, there are certain things that God intends to do one day that we are to have no part in, and certainly not in this age. The slaying of the wicked comes to mind! Not only so, but there were certain elements of Jesus's mission during his first coming that were unique to him. We have no part, for example, in dying for the sins of the world. None of this is to suggest that a story or a poem or a proposition cannot carry an imperatival force, but it is to argue that it is better (surer and more straightforward) to find the church's mission in specific commands rather than in employing a hermeneutic that assumes a priori that we are partners with God in every particular of his redemptive purposes for the world.

Second, it makes sense that we would look to the New Testament more than the Old for a theology of mission. Now obviously, the Old Testament also shows God's heart for the nations. God has always been intent on blessing the whole world through his people, and the Old Testament anticipates a future ingathering of the nations. We see this plan unveiled and unfolded at numerous points in the Old Testament. But it's also obvious that the Old Testament is concerned mainly with the nation of Israel. Even in Jesus's ministry a full-fledged mission to the Gentiles lies in the future (Matt. 15:24). God's old covenant people are

---

[20]Christopher J. H. Wright, *The Mission of God's People: A Biblical Theology of the Church's Mission* (Grand Rapids: Zondervan, 2010), 26

never exhorted to engage in intentional cross-cultural mission. Their mission light shines by attraction, not by active invitation. For all these reasons the New Testament is a better place to look for a strong missionary impulse. Indeed, as Eckhard Schnabel concludes in his magisterial *Early Christian Mission,* "The missionary work of the first Christians cannot be explained with prototypes in the Old Testament or with models of an early Jewish mission."[21] Missions, in the sense of God's people being actively sent out to other peoples with a task to accomplish, is as new as the New Testament.

Third, it makes sense that we would look to Jesus for our missiological directive. As we'll see later, *the* mission in the Bible is the mission of the Father sending the Son. As the messianic king and the Lord of the church, Jesus claims the right to send the church, even as the Father had the right to send him (John 20:21). Therefore we would do well to pay close attention to what the Son explicitly tells his disciples to do in his absence.

Fourth, the placement of the Great Commissions suggests their strategic importance. They record Jesus's final words on earth, after his death and resurrection and just prior to his ascension. Common sense and biblical precedence tell us that a man's last words carry special weight,[22] especially when some form of these words is preserved in three of the Gospels (and in Mark in a slightly different form) and again at the beginning of Acts. The biblical authors and the early church understood Jesus's final words to be among the most important sentences he ever uttered, and the most significant instructions he gave for shaping their missional identity.

Fifth, the Great Commissions seem to sum up many of the major themes of the Gospels. Take Matthew, for example. More than any other Gospel, Matthew focuses on discipleship. What

---

[21]Schnabel, *Early Christian Mission,* 173.
[22]One thinks of the famous last words of several biblical characters, including Jacob, Moses, Joshua, David, Elijah, Paul (at Ephesus in Acts 20 and to Timothy in 2 Timothy), and Peter (see 2 Pet. 1:12–15).

do disciples believe about Jesus? How do they behave? What must they be willing to give up? It's no surprise, therefore, that Matthew's Great Commission stresses *discipleship*. Similarly, from the opening genealogy to his baptism in the Jordan, to his temptation in the wilderness, to the frequent references to Old Testament fulfillment, Matthew presents Jesus as a new Israel, as the Messiah to whom the Law and Prophets were pointing. So, again, it's no surprise that Jesus's closing words in Matthew emphasize his *authority*. We could go on and note the long Sermon on the Mount in Matthew, which forms the backbone of Jesus's *teaching*, or the presence of the magi in the second chapter, which hints at Jesus's *universal kingship*. These elements too find their climax in the Great Commission, with its emphasis on going to the nations and teaching them to observe all that Jesus commanded. The Great Commission, it turns out, sums up Matthew's most important themes. As Bosch puts it, "Today scholars agree that the entire gospel points to these final verses: all the threads woven into the fabric of Matthew, from chapter 1 onward, draw together here."[23]

If everything in Matthew culminates in the Great Commission, everything in Acts flows from it. Jesus tells his followers gathered in Jerusalem that they will be his witnesses in Jerusalem and in all Judea and Samaria, and to the ends of the earth (Acts 1:8). And that's exactly what the book of Acts records. First, Christ is preached in Jerusalem (Acts 2–7), then in Judea and Samaria (Acts 8), and finally, with the conversion of Paul and Peter's rooftop vision, the gospel makes headway among the Gentiles. The book even concludes with Paul under house arrest, yet "proclaiming the kingdom of God and teaching about the Lord Jesus Christ with all boldness and without hindrance" (Acts 28:31). From beginning to end, the story of Acts is of the proclamation of the gospel from Judea to Samaria to the ends of the earth, just as Jesus commanded.

---

[23]Bosch, *Transforming Mission*, 57.

The Great Commissions, therefore, whether at the close or the outset of the narrative, are more than random parting words from Jesus. They actually shape the whole story, either as the climax to which everything points or as the fountain from which everything flows.

What Do We Have Here?

With all that as necessary introduction, we can now turn to examining briefly the Great Commission texts themselves.

Matthew 28:16–20

We start with the most famous commission:

> Now the eleven disciples went to Galilee, to the mountain to which Jesus had directed them. And when they saw him they worshiped him, but some doubted. And Jesus came and said to them, "All authority in heaven and on earth has been given to me. Go therefore and make disciples of all nations, baptizing them in the name of the Father and of the Son and of the Holy Spirit, teaching them to observe all that I have commanded you. And behold, I am with you always, to the end of the age." (Matt. 28:16–20)

As if there were any doubt that this is a significant pronouncement, Matthew tells us that Jesus directed the disciples to "the mountain" (v. 16). From Sinai to the Mount of Transfiguration to the Sermon on the Mount, mountains are places where the most important instruction or revelation is given. This scene is no different. Jesus has brought his disciples together one last time for something truly significant.

Before Jesus calls the disciples to mission, he reassures them of the good news: "All authority in heaven and on earth has been given to me" (v. 18). The mission Jesus is about to give is based exclusively and entirely on his authority. There can only be a mission imperative because there is first this glorious indicative. God does not send out his church to conquer. He sends us out in the name of the One who has *already* conquered. We go only because he reigns.

Then we come to the four verbs in verses 19–20—one main verb and three supporting participles. The main verb is the imperative "make disciples." Jesus's followers are to make disciples of the nations (*ta ethnē*). As is now widely known, this is the word not for political nation-states but for people groups.[24] Jesus envisions worshipers and followers present among every cultural-linguistic group on the planet.

The remaining participles, which can have the force of imperatives, flesh out what is entailed in the disciple-making process. We *go*, we *baptize*, and we *teach*. "Going" implies being sent (see Rom. 10:15). "Baptizing" implies repentance and forgiveness as well as inclusion in God's family (Acts 2:38, 41). "Teaching" makes clear that Jesus has more in mind than initial evangelism and response. He wants obedient, mature disciples, not just immediate decisions.[25]

Finally, this discipling task is possible, Jesus reassures his audience, because "I am with you always, to the end of the age" (Matt. 28:20b). Such a far-reaching guarantee would not have been necessary if Jesus envisioned the apostles fulfilling the Great Commission. But a promise to the end of the age makes perfect

---

[24]See, for example, John Piper, *Let the Nations Be Glad! The Supremacy of God in Missions*, 3rd ed. (Grand Rapids: Baker, 2010), 155–200, and Timothy C. Tennent, *Invitation to World Missions: A Trinitarian Missiology for the Twenty-first Century* (Grand Rapids: Kregel, 2010), 138.

[25]On this general theme of discipleship versus decisions, see M. David Sills, *Reaching and Teaching: A Call to Great Commission Obedience* (Chicago: Moody, 2010). Sills has a helpful discussion of Matt. 24:14 ("And this gospel of the kingdom will be proclaimed throughout the whole world as a testimony to all nations, and then the end will come"). He explains that in context the "world" may refer to the known world of the Roman Empire and that the "end" may be the fall of Jerusalem in AD 70. Even if you don't accept this view, it is still important to note that Jesus is giving a prediction of what will happen before his return, not a formula to hasten his coming. The emphasis is on enduring persecution until the end, not on ushering in the kingdom. Matt. 24:14 highlights the centrality of proclamation, but it does not imply a "need for speed" in fulfilling the Great Commission (121–26).

sense if the work of mission also continues to the end of this age. Jesus's promise extends to the end of the age just as his commission does.

Mark 13:10; 14:9

Mark does not include a postresurrection Great Commission in his Gospel. Although Mark 16:15 has Jesus saying "Go into all the world and proclaim the gospel to the whole creation," the vast majority of modern commentators now think Mark's Gospel ends at 16:8. This explicit Great Commission then is not original to Mark, though it does represent the missionary impulse of the early church, which added this longer ending between AD 100 and 150.

Even without a traditional Great Commission, however, Mark still has two explicit references to the same missionary task.

- Mark 13:10: "And the gospel must first be proclaimed to all nations."
- Mark 14:9: "And truly, I say to you, wherever the gospel is proclaimed in the whole world, what she [the woman who anointed him with oil] has done will be told in memory of her."

We see in these texts not only a prediction that the gospel *will* be proclaimed in the whole world, but a summons that it *must*. As Jesus approaches the cross, he is already laying the groundwork for the universal proclamation of his gospel.

Luke 24:44–49

We now turn to Luke's complementary account of the Great Commission:

> Then he said to them, "These are my words that I spoke to you while I was still with you, that everything written about me in the Law of Moses and the Prophets and the Psalms must be fulfilled." Then

he opened their minds to understand the Scriptures, and said to them, "Thus it is written, that the Christ should suffer and on the third day rise from the dead, and that repentance and forgiveness of sins should be proclaimed in his name to all nations, beginning from Jerusalem. You are witnesses of these things. And behold, I am sending the promise of my Father upon you. But stay in the city until you are clothed with power from on high." (Luke 24:44–49)

Luke, like Matthew, bases the command in divine authority. But whereas the authority in Matthew 28 was Jesus's authority given to him, here the authority is rooted in the Scriptures. The disciples go forth into the world because Christ has all authority *and* because the events they will proclaim are the fulfillment of scriptural prophecy and foreshadowing. In both Matthew and Luke, the authority of the disciples comes from God.

Moreover, the command to "go and make disciples" in Matthew is stated here in terms of the disciples' own role in that task: "You are witnesses of these things" (Luke 24:48). The task set before them by their Lord is to bear witness to Jesus, that is, to proclaim the good news about him. Once again, of course, the disciples do not bear witness by their own power. The Spirit will clothe them with power from on high.

Finally, we see that Jesus makes explicit that this proclamation includes the good news concerning repentance and forgiveness of sin. All this was implied in "baptizing them" in Matthew 28:19, but now it is brought to the forefront.

In summary, the Great Commission in Luke's Gospel consists in bearing Spirit-empowered witness to the events of Christ's death and resurrection and calling all nations to repentance for the forgiveness of sins.

Acts 1:8

The same Luke who wrote the Gospel according to Luke wrote the book of Acts (see Acts 1:1). So we'll look at Jesus's last words in Acts before returning to the Gospels and looking at the Great Commission in John.

> But you will receive power when the Holy Spirit has come upon you, and you will be my witnesses in Jerusalem and in all Judea and Samaria, and to the end of the earth. (Acts 1:8)

Given the common authorship of Luke-Acts, it's no surprise that the theme of Spirit-empowered witness is as central to this Great Commission as it was in Luke. Nor is it surprising that the mission described in Acts is overwhelmingly focused on proclaiming the Word of God and bearing witness to Christ.

The book of Acts is especially important because in it we can actually see the scope and nature of the earliest Christian mission. If you are looking for a picture of the early church giving itself to creation care, plans for societal renewal, and strategies to serve the community in Jesus's name, you won't find them in Acts. But if you are looking for preaching, teaching, and the centrality of the Word, this is your book. The story of Acts is the story of the earliest Christians' efforts to carry out the commission given them in Acts 1:8.

This does not mean that the church in Acts is one big evangelistic rally or inductive Bible study. We see the church devoted to the fellowship, the breaking of bread, and prayer, as well as the apostles' teaching (Acts 2:42). We see examples of believers sharing with each other (Acts 2:44–46; 4:32–37) and hear of many signs and wonders (Acts 2:43; 5:12–16). Truly the kingdom has broken in as Jesus continues to "do" miracles through the apostles and sometimes others (Acts 1:1; Heb. 2:3–4). But there is no doubt that the book of Acts is a record first and foremost of apostolic witness expanding from Jerusalem to Judea and Samaria to the ends of the earth. As Darrell Bock puts it:

> This commission [Acts 1:8] describes the church's key assignment of what to do until the Lord returns. The priority for the

church until Jesus returns, a mission of which the community must never lose sight, is to witness to Jesus to the end of the earth. The church exists, in major part, to extend the apostolic witness to Jesus everywhere.[26]

Even a cursory overview of Acts bears this out. In Acts 1 Matthias is chosen to replace Judas, that he might become a witness to Christ's resurrection (v. 22). In Acts 2 Peter preaches at Pentecost, expounding the Scriptures, bearing witness to Christ, calling people to faith and repentance. Many received the Word, and about three thousand souls were added to the church that day (v. 41). In Acts 3 Peter heals a lame beggar in Jesus's name and then uses the occasion to bear witness to Christ and call people to repentance (see especially vv. 15, 19). As they proclaim the resurrection, many more hear the Word, and five thousand men believe (Acts 4:2, 4). In Acts 4 Peter and John testify before the council to the crucifixion, and when they are released from custody, the believers pray that they might continue to speak the Word with boldness (vv. 29, 31). While in prison again in Acts 5, an angel of the Lord sets the apostles free and commands them to "go and stand in the temple and speak to the people all the words of this Life" (v. 20). And when they heard this, Luke records, "they entered the temple at daybreak and began to teach" (v. 21).

Every chapter of Acts is like this. In Acts 6 the apostles appoint protodeacons so that they (the apostles) can stay devoted to the Word of God and prayer (v. 4). The result was that "the word of God continued to increase, and the number of the disciples multiplied greatly in Jerusalem, and a great many of the priests became obedient to the faith" (v. 7). In Acts 7 Stephen bears witness to Christ by walking through the Old Testament and refuting those who have charged him with blas-

---

[26]Darrell L. Bock, *Acts*, Baker Exegetical Commentary on the New Testament (Grand Rapids: Baker, 2007), 66.

pheming Moses. In Acts 8 Philip proclaims Christ in Samaria, Samaria receives the Word of God (v. 14), and the disciples preach the gospel to many villages of the Samaritans (v. 25). Later Philip expounds the Scriptures to the Ethiopian eunuch, after which he "preached the gospel to all the towns until he came to Caesarea" (v. 40).

Over and over Luke makes clear that the point of this book of Acts is to show the mission of Jesus being fulfilled as the Word of God increases and multiplies (Acts 12:24). Everywhere the Word goes there is opposition, but everywhere the Word goes, some believe. So Paul and Barnabas proclaim the Word in Cyprus and at Antioch in Pisidia, at Iconium and Lystra. Along the way Paul not only preaches the gospel in new frontiers, but also strengthens the disciples, encourages them in the faith, and appoints elders (Acts 14:21–23). His mission is not just evangelism, but deeper discipleship. He wins converts, plants churches, builds up existing congregations. Bearing witness to Christ and teaching the Word of God is the singular apostolic mission, but it takes on many different forms.[27]

At this point we're only halfway through the book. In the second half we see the same theme: Spirit-empowered witness—in Derbe, in Philippi, in Thessalonica, in Berea, in Athens, in Corinth, and in Ephesus, and finally in Jerusalem. Then Paul bears witness before the council, before Felix, before Festus, before Agrippa and Bernice, then on Crete and Malta, and lastly in Rome. The book ends much as it started, with the apostles (in this case Paul) "proclaiming the kingdom of God and teaching about the Lord Jesus Christ with all boldness and without hindrance" (Acts 28:31). A witness has gone out to the ends of the earth, all the way to Rome itself and from there it will ring out, we are led to believe, with great

---

[27]"Conversion to Christ meant incorporation into a Christian community" is how Köstenberger and O'Brien put it (*Salvation to the Ends of the Earth*, 268).

success. The mission Christ gave to the disciples in Acts 1:8 is well under way.

John 20:21

John's is the shortest of the postresurrection commissions, but as Schnabel notes, it "is perhaps the most striking directive from a theological point of view." It is also the most controversial.

> Jesus said to them again, "Peace be with you. As the Father has sent me, even so I am sending you." (John 20:21)

We want to highlight three significant theological points.

A Peace That Passes Understanding

First, Jesus gives the disciples his peace. Jesus's peace is the basis for their ministry and, we can imagine, shapes the content of their message. So what is this peace? Some are quick to point out that the Hebrew word for peace is *shalom* and biblical shalom entails the right ordering of all things, the way the world is supposed to be. This is no doubt true, but we must always remember (1) that biblical shalom is much deeper than societal harmony and (2) that true shalom comes only to those who have union and communion with the shalom giver. John Stott is right:

> The biblical categories of *shalom*, the new humanity and the kingdom of God are not to be identified with social renewal. . . . So according to the apostles the peace which Jesus preaches and gives is something deeper and richer, namely reconciliation and fellowship with God and with each other (e.g. Ephesians 2.13–22). Moreover, he does not bestow it on all men but on those who belong to him, to his redeemed community. So *shalom* is the blessing the Messiah brings to his people.[28]

---

[28]Stott, *Christian Mission in the Modern World*, 18–19.

We see this clearly in the way "peace" is used in John's Gospel. The peace Jesus gives is better than anything the world can offer. His peace provides the assurance that he, by his Spirit, will always be with them (John 14:26–27). This peace, Jesus says, can be found only "in me" (John 16:33). It is the peace that comes to Jesus's followers by virtue of his resurrection from the dead (John 20:19, 21, 26). In prefacing his commission with "Peace be with you" Jesus is saying nothing about the renewal of social structures and everything about the assurance and forgiveness they can have and can offer in his name (Acts 10:36; Rom. 5:1; Phil. 4:7).[29]

The Sending That Matters Most

Second, Jesus's being sent is prior to Jesus's sending. In other words, the sending of Jesus happened first and is more central. As we said earlier, Christian mission is first of all Christ's mission in the world. As we will argue shortly, our mission is not identical with Christ's earthly work. Even less do we think we must complete what the Son somehow failed to accomplish. Nevertheless, in a real way the Son is continuing to do through us what he began to say and do in his earthly ministry (Acts 1:1). The mission of Jesus is the focal point of human history. His is the fundamental, foundational, essential mission—not the mission of his disciples. But in a wonderful act of condescension, the mission of the exalted Jesus, John 20:21 tells us, will be carried out through his followers.[30]

Jesus's Mission as a Model

The third point follows from the second: Jesus's mission is in some ways a model for our mission. But this invites the ques-

---

[29]Schnabel writes, "The message of the disciples is about peace: about the restoration of peace with God through Jesus' death on the cross, about the atonement and forgiveness of sins, about the reconciliation of rebellious humankind with God" (*Early Christian Mission*, 379).

[30]See Andreas Köstenberger, *The Missions of Jesus and the Disciples according to the Fourth Gospel: With Implications for the Fourth Gospel's Purpose and the Mission of the Contemporary Church* (Grand Rapids: Eerdmans, 1998), 207, 210; Köstenberger and O'Brien, *Salvation to the Ends of the Earth*, 264–66.

tion, in what ways? How does the exalted Christ carry out his mission through us? Is it by empowering us to do what he did and to continue his incarnational presence on the earth? Or is it by empowering us to bear witness to all that he taught and accomplished?

It is very popular to assume that missions is always incarnational. And of course on one level it is. We go and live among the people. We try to emulate the humility and sacrifice of Christ (Phil. 2:5–11).[31] But incarnational*ism* in missions often means more than this.[32] It means that we model our ministry on Jesus's ministry. For Stott, and many others after him, this means the mission of the church is service. "Therefore," says Stott, "our mission, like his, is to be one of service."[33] Evangelism and social action, therefore, are full partners in Christian mission.[34] Since the most crucial form of the Great Commission is the one we see in John (argues Stott), the simplest way to sum up the missionary enterprise is this: "We are sent into the world, like Jesus, to serve."[35]

Stott's reading of John 20:31 has been very influential. There are, however, two problems.

First, it can be misleading to summarize Jesus's mission as one of service. There's no problem with this formulation if we mean "serve" in the Mark 10:45 sense of the word, that Jesus "came not to be served but to serve, and to give his life as a ransom for many." But Stott means more than this. He means that Jesus's mission was to meet human need, whether spiritual or physical.[36] Again, no one can deny, nor would we want to deny, that Jesus showed compassion to countless multitudes in extraordinary

---

[31]A moving exposition of this theme is found at the end of B. B. Warfield's sermon, "Imitating the Incarnation," in *The Savior of the World* (repr., Edinburgh: Banner of Truth, 1991), 247–70.
[32]See Hesselgrave, *Paradigms in Conflict*, 141–65, for a helpful summary of the incarnationalism versus representationalism debate. Hesselgrave argues for the latter.
[33]Stott, *Christian Mission in the Modern World*, 23, 24.
[34]Ibid., 27.
[35]Ibid., 30.
[36]Ibid., 24.

ways. Nor do we want to suggest that meeting physical needs has no place in the church's work. On the contrary, let us be zealous for good works (Titus 2:14) and walk in the good deeds prepared for us (Eph. 2:10).

But it is misleading to contend that Jesus's ministry focused on serving, and even more so to claim, as one recent book does, that "every moment of his ministry is spent with the poor, sick, helpless, and hurting."[37] Sometimes Jesus was alone and wanted to be away from people (Mark 1:35, 45). Other times he was with rich men like Zacchaeus (Luke 19:5). Often he was with the disciples, who were not destitute and were in fact supported by wealthy women (Luke 8:1–3).

We know this sounds heartless, but it's true: it simply was not Jesus's driving ambition to heal the sick and meet the needs of the poor, as much as he cared for them. He was sent into the world to save people from condemnation (John 3:17), that he might be lifted up so believers could have eternal life (3:14–15). He was sent by the Father so that whoever feeds on him might live forever (6:57–58). In his important work on the missions of Jesus and the disciples, Andreas Köstenberger concludes that John's Gospel portrays Jesus's mission as the Son sent from the Father, as the one who came into the world and returned to the Father, and as the shepherd-teacher who called others to follow him in order to help gather a final harvest.[38] If Köstenberger is right, this is a long way from saying that Jesus's fundamental mission was to meet temporal needs.

But that's John, someone may object. His Gospel is always something of an outlier. What do the other three Gospels say? Well, let's take a look at Mark as an example. No doubt, Jesus often healed the sick and cast out demons in Mark's Gospel. Teaching, healing, and exorcism were the three prongs of his

---

[37]Gabe Lyons, *The Next Christians: How a New Generation Is Restoring the Faith* (New York: Doubleday, 2010), 55.
[38]Köstenberger, *The Missions of Jesus and the Disciples*, 199.

ministry (see, for instance his quintessential first day of ministry in Capernaum in Mark 1:21–34). And yet what drove his ministry was the proclamation of the gospel, the announcement of the kingdom, and the call to repent and believe (1:15). Jesus healed and exorcised demons out of compassion for the afflicted (1:41; 9:22), but the bigger reason for the miracles was that they testified to his authority and pointed to his unique identity (e.g., 2:1–12).

Don't miss this fact: *there is not a single example of Jesus going into a town with the stated purpose of healing or casting out demons.* He never ventured out on a healing and exorcism tour. He certainly did a lot of this along the way. He was moved with pity at human need (Mark 8:2). But the reason he "came out" was "that [he] may preach" (1:38). If anything, the clamor for meeting physical needs sometimes became a distraction to Jesus. That's why he frequently commanded silence of those he helped (1:44; 7:36), and why he would not do many works in a town rife with unbelief (6:5–6).

In Mark, as in the other Gospels, there are plenty of miracles and acts of service to celebrate, but they are far from the main point. The first half of the Gospel drives toward Peter's confession in chapter 8, where Jesus's identity is revealed. The second half of the Gospel drives toward the cross, where Jesus's work is completed (three predictions of death and resurrection in chapters 9–10, and a detailed description of Holy Week in chapters 12–16). Mark's Gospel does not focus on Jesus meeting physical needs. Mark's Gospel is about who Jesus was and what he did to save sinners.

It's no wonder, then, that Jesus's first action in Mark, after preaching, is to call men to follow him and promise to make them fishers of men (1:17). Jesus's purpose statements in Mark are revealing. He came to preach (1:38). He came to call sinners (2:17). He came to give his life as a ransom for many (10:45). Or as we read elsewhere, Jesus came to seek and save the lost (Luke 19:10). The focus of his ministry is on teaching. The heart of his teaching centers on who he is. And the good news of who he is culminates in where he is going—to the cross. The mission of Jesus is not service broadly conceived, but the *proclamation* of the gospel through teaching, the *corroboration* of the gospel through signs and wonders, and the *accomplishment* of the gospel in death and resurrection.

Second, it is unwise to assume that because we are sent as Jesus was sent, we have the exact same mission he had. We must protect the absolute uniqueness of what Jesus came to do. D. A. Carson, commenting on John 17:18, concludes that when it comes to the mission of the disciples, "there is no *necessary* overtone of incarnation or of invasion from another world." Instead, we come face-to-face with "the ontological gap that forever distances the origins of Jesus' mission from the origins of the disciples' missions."[39] We cannot re-embody Christ's incarnational ministry any more than we can repeat his atonement. Our role is to *bear witness* to what Christ has already done. We are not new incarnations of Christ but his *representatives* offering life in his name, proclaiming his gospel, imploring others to be reconciled to God (2 Cor. 5:20). This is how the exalted Christ carries out his mission through us.

So how then is the Son's being sent a model for our being sent by the Son? Köstenberger explains:

The Fourth Gospel does therefore not appear to teach the kind of "incarnational model" advocated by Stott and others. Not the way in which Jesus came into the world (i.e., the incarnation), but the nature of Jesus' *relationship with his sender* (i.e., one of obedience and utter dependence), is presented in the Fourth Gospel as the model for the disciples' mission. Jesus' followers are called to imitate Jesus' selfless devotion in seeking his

---

[39]D. A. Carson, *The Gospel according to John*, The Pillar New Testament Commentary (Grand Rapids: Eerdmans, 1990), 566.

sender's glory, to submit to their sender's will, and to represent their sender accurately and know him intimately.[40]

Consequently, a focus on human service and on physical need was not, at least in John, a primary purpose of either Jesus's mission or the disciples' mission.[41] If the context of John 20:21 tells us anything, the mission of the disciples was to wield the keys of the kingdom, to open and close the door marked "Forgiveness" (20:23; see also Matt. 16:19). John wrote his Gospel so that his audience might "believe that Jesus is the Christ, the Son of God, and that by believing [they would] have life in his name" (John 20:31). This was John's mission, as he understood it. And there's every reason to think he saw this as the fulfillment of the mission he recorded from Jesus a few verses earlier. The Father sent the Son so that by believing in his name the children of God might have life (1:12). The Son sent the disciples, in the same spirit of complete surrender and obedience, so that they might go into the world to bear witness to the one who is the way, the truth, and the life (14:6).

Putting It All Together

So how should we pull all this together? Well, on the one hand, we've seen a fair amount of diversity among the Great Commissions. Matthew emphasizes discipleship, Luke-Acts stresses being witnesses, and John highlights the theological nature of our sending. The diversity, of course, is not owing to varying levels of truthfulness in the accounts, but to the unique aims of the Evangelists.

And yet the Great Commission accounts show more similarity than dissimilarity. Together they paint a complementary and fairly comprehensive picture of the mission of the first disciples. We can summarize this mission by answering seven questions:

---

[40]Köstenberger, *The Missions of Jesus and the Disciples*, 217.
[41]Ibid., 215.

- *Who?* Jesus gave this mission verbally to the first disciples, but it did not end with their deaths. As Lord of the church, he expects his followers to carry out this mission "to the end of the age." Their mission is our mission.
- *Why?* The authority for our mission comes from Christ. It is rooted in the Word of God and based on the Father's sending of the Son. We are sent because Christ was sent, and we go in his name, under his authority.
- *What?* The mission consists of preaching and teaching, announcing and testifying, making disciples and bearing witness. The mission focuses on the initial and continuing verbal declaration of the gospel, the announcement of Christ's death and resurrection and the life found in him when we repent and believe.
- *Where?* We are sent into the world. Our strategy is no longer "come and see" but "go and tell." The message of salvation is for every people group—near, far, and everywhere in between.
- *How?* We go out in the power of the Holy Spirit and in submission to the Son just as he was obedient to and dependent upon the Father.
- *When?* The mission began at Pentecost when the disciples were clothed with power from on high with the presence of the Holy Spirit. The mission will last as long as the promise of Christ's presence lasts; that is, to the end of the age.
- *To whom?* The church should make disciples of the nations. We must go to every people group, proclaiming the good news to the ends of the earth.

One More Commission

We have been looking at Jesus's postresurrection, preascension commissions. But a study of mission would seem incomplete without a glance at the missionary par excellence of the New

Testament: Paul the apostle to the Gentiles. As Jesus confronts and converts Saul (later Paul) on the Damascus Road, he also commissions him with a new mission. Paul, as Jesus's "chosen instrument" (Acts 9:15), must "go," carrying Christ's name and suffering much for his sake (vv. 15–16). In a different account of the same call Paul goes into more detail relaying precisely what Jesus sent him to do:

> I have appeared to you for this purpose, to appoint you as a servant and witness to the things in which you have seen me and to those in which I will appear to you, delivering you from your people and from the Gentiles—to whom I am sending you to open their eyes, so that they may turn from darkness to light and from the power of Satan to God, that they may receive forgiveness of sins and a place among those who are sanctified by faith in me. (Acts 26:16–18)

What did this look like in Paul's life? Obviously he knew that evangelism and disciple making were not the only worthwhile activities or the only way to help others or please God. He was a tentmaker, after all (Acts 18:3), and eager to "remember the poor" (Gal. 2:10). He also taught that love fulfilled all the horizontal requirements of the law (Rom. 13:9; Gal. 5:14). But at the same time, he did not declare "I no longer have any room for work in these regions" because he had sufficiently loved the people in those regions, but because he had founded and nurtured fledgling churches by proclaiming the gospel (Rom. 15:23).

It is sometimes argued that although Paul's ministry centered on word-based evangelism, there is little evidence he expected his congregations to pursue the same mission. In his book *Paul's Understanding of the Church's Mission*,[42] Robert

---

[42] Robert L. Plummer, *Paul's Understanding of the Church's Mission: Did the Apostle Paul Expect the Early Christian Communities to Evangelize?* (Eugene, OR: Paternoster/Wipf and Stock, 2006).

Plummer counters this claim and makes a convincing case that Paul's congregations were evangelistic communities. Consider a few examples:

- Evangelistic language is used of the Thessalonian church. The Word was at work in the believers (1 Thess. 2:13–16), the Word was running ahead (2 Thess. 3:1), and the Word was ringing and sounding forth (1 Thess. 1:8).
- Philippians 1:12–18 suggests that Paul anticipated Christ being "proclaimed in every way" by the church in Philippi.
- The gospel-armor shoes in Ephesians 6:15 should make the believers "ready to proclaim the gospel of peace" (NRSV).
- First Corinthians 4:16 exhorts the early church to imitate Paul's openness to suffer as a result of proclaiming the foolishness of the cross.
- Similarly, 1 Corinthians 11:1 calls Christians to imitate the apostle in his salvific concern for outsiders. We also see evidence that the Corinthians were to be concerned for the salvation of nonbelievers in 1 Corinthians 7:12–16 and 14:23–25.
- Besides these examples of "actively" sharing the gospel, several texts show how the early churches were to "passively" bear witness to Christ. Second Corinthians 6:3–7, 1 Thessalonians 2:5–12, and Titus 2:1–10 demonstrate that "all the various segments of the Christian community are to live praiseworthy lives—not simply for the sake of obeying God, but also because their behavior will commend or detract from the gospel."[43]

To summarize, then, we follow Paul's example of following Christ and his Great Commission. We see in Acts that

---

[43]Ibid., 104–5. These bullet points are taken from Kevin's review of Plummer's book in the 9Marks eJournal. Used by permission.

the responsibility of discipleship was given to more than the Twelve. We see the same thing in Paul's epistles and in his own ministry. The Great Commission is for the whole church, of which Paul is the most significant model. A careful study of his life and teaching shows that Paul's mission was threefold: (1) initial evangelism, (2) the nurture of existing churches by guarding them against error and grounding them in the faith, and (3) their firm establishment as healthy congregations through the full exposition of the gospel and the appointing of local leadership.[44] We believe his mission models for us what we ought to be doing in the world insofar as Paul's ambition ought to be our ambition (1 Cor. 10:33–11:1), and we should be partners in the same work he undertook (see Phil. 1:5, 14, 27, 30; 2:16).

A Preliminary Conclusion

There are still a number of theological bricks to lay in the foundation of our argument (so don't close the pages just yet), but with the ground we've covered in this chapter we're ready to offer a one-sentence answer to the question of this book. *The mission of the church is to go into the world and make disciples by declaring the gospel of Jesus Christ in the power of the Spirit and gathering these disciples into churches, that they might worship the Lord and obey his commands now and in eternity to the glory of God the Father.* We believe this is the mission Jesus gave the disciples prior to his ascension, the mission we see in the New Testament, and the mission of the church today.

This mission is a specific set of things Jesus has sent his church into the world to accomplish and is significantly narrower than "everything God commands." That's not to say that our broader obligations aren't important. They are! Jesus and the apostles command us to parent our children well, to be

---

[44]This summary owes its basic formulation to P. T. O'Brien, *Gospel and Mission in the Writings of Paul: An Exegetical and Theological Analysis* (Grand Rapids: Baker, 1993), 43, 64.

loving husbands and wives, to do good to all people, and many other things. Jesus even tells us in the Great Commission itself (as Matthew records it) to teach people "to observe *all* that I have commanded you." But that doesn't mean that everything we do in obedience to Christ should be understood as part of the church's mission. The mission Jesus gave the church is more specific than that. And that, in turn, doesn't mean that other commands Jesus gives us are unimportant. It means that the church has been given a specific mission by its Lord, and *teaching* people to obey Christ's commands is a nonnegotiable part of that mission. We go, we proclaim, we baptize, and we teach—all to the end of making lifelong, die-hard disciples of Jesus Christ who obey everything he commanded.

So here it is again: the mission of the church—as seen in the Great Commissions, the early church in Acts, and the life of the apostle Paul—is to win people to Christ and build them up in Christ. Making disciples—that's our task.

PART 2

Understanding Our Categories

CHAPTER 3

The Whole Story

Seeing the Biblical Narrative
from the Top of Golgotha

IT'S NEVER A GOOD IDEA to make a biblical case for something—especially something as monumentally important as the mission of the church—from just a few texts. The Bible isn't just a potpourri of pithy sayings from which we can pick up a nugget here and a nugget there. No, it's a grand, sweeping, world-encompassing story that traces the history of God's dealings with mankind from very beginning to very end. If we really want to understand what God is doing and what he would have us to do as his people, we need to have a good grasp of what that story is, what its main themes are, what the problem is, what God's remedy to the problem is, and what it all looks like when the story ends.

Though we started this book with a look at some specific texts, our thesis—that the mission of the church is to proclaim the gospel and make disciples—does not rest on the Great Commission texts alone. Rather, we believe that those texts are so important and have gained their nicknames precisely because the entire story line of the Bible presses forward toward them.

A Very Good Place to Start

The way to understand the Bible's story from beginning to end is actually to start at the middle, with the death and resurrection of Jesus. Have you noticed that the Gospel writers, though they tell the story of Jesus's life and teaching with different events and different perspectives, all bring their accounts to a climax with Jesus hanging on the cross, dying, and then rising from the dead? It's been said that all four of the Gospels are really passion narratives with extended introductions![1] That's probably a bit of an overstatement, but the point is well taken. The crucifixion and resurrection of Christ stand indisputably at the pinnacle of all four Gospels.

The same thing could be said of the Bible as a whole. The crucifixion-resurrection, after all, isn't just one event among many in the life of Jesus. It's *the* event to which the whole Old Testament looks forward. From God's making of animal-skin clothing for Adam and Eve, to the sacrificial system under the Mosaic Law, to the representative suffering of Israel's king, to Isaiah's prophecy of a Suffering Servant of the Lord, to Zechariah's prophecy of a Stricken Shepherd, the Old Testament longs for its fulfillment in a King who would suffer, die, and triumph.

But why? Why do the Gospels focus so squarely on the death of Jesus and his subsequent resurrection? Why do the Law and the Prophets point so relentlessly toward the death of the Messiah? And for that matter, why do the apostles say such counterintuitive

---

[1]This phrase was first coined by the nineteenth-century German theologian Martin Kähler about the Gospel of Mark in particular, but he applied it to all four Gospels. See the English translation, *The So-Called Historical Jesus and the Historic, Biblical Christ* (Philadelphia: Fortress, 1964), 80.

and dangerous things as "I decided to know nothing among you except Jesus Christ and him crucified" (1 Cor. 2:2)? The answer to that question, we think, lies in understanding one question that stands at the very heart of the Bible's story: *How can hopelessly rebellious, sinful people live in the presence of a perfectly just and righteous God?* It would be easy to answer the question, How can *righteous* people live in the presence of a righteous God? or even How can sinful people live in the presence of an *indifferent* God? But the question of how sinful people can live in the presence of a righteous God is not easy at all—especially when the Bible itself tells us that "he who justifies the wicked . . . [is] an abomination to the LORD" (Prov. 17:15; see also 24:24). In fact, we think that is the question that drives the entire biblical narrative from start to finish. It defines the original purpose of creation, it describes the problem that threatens to destroy us all, it calls out for the remedy of the gospel, and it points forward to the grand conclusion of it all, when the riddle is finally and fully solved and God's people live in his presence forever.

Now, just for clarity's sake (and for those of you who skim books instead of reading them!), let's just jump to the conclusion before we even make the case. If this understanding of the Bible's story line is correct—if it is above all the story of how God has created and is creating a redeemed people who can receive the good gift of living in his presence, both now and for all eternity—then it should not surprise us in the least that Jesus would end his earthly ministry by telling his disciples, "You will be my witnesses" (Acts 1:8). It shouldn't be surprising that he would launch them into history with the command, "Go . . . and make disciples" (Matt. 28:19). After all, that's exactly how the great riddle is solved: sinful people are brought into God's presence by becoming disciples of Jesus through faith and repentance, and they can do that only through the witness of the apostles as they proclaim the good news about who Jesus is, what he has done, and how we should respond as a result.

One Story: Four Acts

The basic structure of the Bible's narrative seems to unfold in four broad acts: creation, fall, redemption, and consummation. It starts with the creation of mankind in perfect relationship to God, continues with humanity's fall into sin, proceeds with God's plan of redemption for sinful people, and ends up at the glorious consummation (that is, the completion, the culmination, the perfection) of God's reign over his redeemed people.

Creation

The Bible begins with the unambiguous statement that "in the beginning, God created the heavens and the earth" (Gen. 1:1). Because God created everything, he rules everything (see Deut. 10:14; Job 41:11; Ps. 24:1; 115:3; etc.). That includes us as human beings, who were created as the crowning act of God's creation and designed as his image bearers (Gen. 1:26–27). We are creatures; he is the Creator; and that fact sets the stage for the entire history of humanity.

A number of authors have begun to argue that mankind is really just one part of God's vast creation, and that man in fact derives his significance from being *part* of that creation.[2] So, it's said, God loves creation, and *therefore* he loves humans. God will redeem the whole of creation, and *therefore* mankind will be redeemed. The Bible's teaching, though, seems to move in the opposite direction.[3] Priority in both curse and redemption rests on humans, not on creation. Thus God tells Adam that the

---

[2] For example, "So the earth has intrinsic value—that is to say, it is valued by God, who is the source of all value. God values the earth because he made it and owns it. It is not enough merely to say that the earth is valuable to us. On the contrary, *our own value as human beings begins from the fact that we ourselves are part of the whole creation that God already values and declares to be good.* We will have more to say about human life in a moment, but the starting point is that *we take our value from the creation of which we are part, not vice versa.*" Christopher Wright, *The Mission of God* (Downers Grove, IL: InterVarsity, 2006), 399; emphasis added.

[3] See Peter Gentry, "Kingdom through Covenant," *Southern Baptist Journal of Theology* (Spring 2008): 22–23, for several exegetical arguments that the creation of man is the crowning achievement, the high point, of the creation story.

ground is cursed "because of you" (Gen. 3:17), and Paul says in Romans that when creation is set free from its curse, it will be by means of its being caught up in "the freedom of the glory of the children of God" (Rom. 8:21).[4] The freedom *belongs* to the children of God; the creation *shares* in that freedom.

Why did God create man? Most importantly, humans were originally created to live in perfect fellowship and harmony with God. Unlike any other creature, man is made "in [God's] image and likeness," which at the very least entailed a unique relationship with him.

Besides living in fellowship with God, Adam and Eve were also to rule over and care for creation as God's vice-regents, having "dominion" over it. They were given the whole creation to rule, not of course by abusing and tyrannizing it, but instead by "work[ing] it and keep[ing] it" (Gen. 2:15).[5] The authority they had over creation, however, was not absolute. It was an authority derived from and subject to God's own rule over the creation. Yes, Adam and Eve would "have dominion" over the fish of the sea and birds of the air, but they would exercise that dominion as servants of God himself. God was the High King; they were only the stewards. Just as an ancient Near Eastern king might be said to be the "image" of his pagan god—that is, to represent the god's majesty and authority to his subjects—Adam represented God's authority to the world over which he was given dominion.

In the "very good" world that God created, therefore, human beings occupied a unique and privileged position. Not only were

---

[4]See John Piper, "The Triumph of the Gospel in the New Heavens and the New Earth"; available online at http://desiringGod.org.

[5]Peter Gentry has helpfully shown how Adam and Eve's creation "in [God's] image, in [God's] likeness" points clearly to both of these roles—fellowship and dominion. On the one hand, being created in the "likeness" of God seems to indicate Adam's special relationship of sonship to God. Just as Adam was said to have "fathered a son in his own likeness," Seth, so God is said to have created Adam "in the likeness of God" (Gen. 5:1, 3). The analogy is not exact; there's no teaching here that Adam is the *physical* son of God. But humans' creation in God's likeness does point to the unique father-like relationship that God intended to have with us. On the other hand, to be created in God's "image," Gentry argues, "indicates that Adam has a special position and status as king under God" (Gentry, "Kingdom through Covenant," 27–33).

they to rule the world under God's ultimate authority—serving as his vice-regents—but they were also to stand in a relationship with him as no other creature in all creation. They were to be as his sons, living and walking with him in perfect fellowship.

Fall

And then, of course, it all went wrong.

Genesis 3 tells the tragic story of how Adam and Eve disobeyed God, earning his wrath as well as exile from his presence. God had warned them from the very beginning that there was one tree out of all the trees in the garden that was not theirs. Their authority to rule and subdue did not extend to that tree. In fact, that tree was a stark reminder that their authority was not absolute, that there was One to whom they themselves were accountable and who had the right to command them.

That is why Adam and Eve's eating of the fruit was such a tragic sin. It was not simply that they violated some arbitrary statute that God had put in place for no good reason. Rather, by taking the fruit, Adam and Eve thought—as the Serpent said—that they could "be like God" (Gen. 3:5). They were grasping for more power and more authority than God had given them. Discontent with their exalted place in creation as his image bearers, they attempted to take what was not theirs and to challenge God's authority and rule. In essence, by eating the fruit, they fomented a rebellion against God and made a declaration of independence.

When God told Adam that he could not eat of that one tree in the middle of the garden, he explained to him in no uncertain terms: "Of the tree of the knowledge of good and evil you shall not eat, for in the day that you eat of it you shall surely die" (Gen. 2:17). It's clear from the way the story unfolds that what God meant there was not just physical death. After all, when Adam sinned, he didn't die immediately—not physically anyway. The death that Adam experienced was first and foremost a spiritual death. Because Adam failed to guard the garden (and his wife), because he allowed Satan to enter the scene and speak unchallenged, and because he failed to trust God's promises and purpose, the loving son-father relationship between Adam and God was severed.

It's important to recognize that the relationship Adam broke was not one between equals. It was the relationship of creature to Creator, of vice-regent to Ruler, steward to King. And as a result, it has not only a relational and emotional element, but also a legal and moral one. That's important to understand, because if we fail to understand the nature of the breach, we'll misunderstand the story of the entire Bible.

All this is driven home most pointedly in the last verse of Genesis 3: "[God] drove out the man, and at the east of the garden of Eden he placed the cherubim and a flaming sword that turned every way to guard the way to the tree of life" (v. 24). It was a crushing penalty for Adam. God would not take his physical life immediately. But he would immediately cast him out of Paradise and out of his presence, closing the way back to life with the flaming sword of an angel.

Summary

And so the first and second acts have ended, and the stage is set for the rest of the biblical story. Even though this is one of the most familiar parts of the biblical story line for many of us, it's important to pause and make sure we see some key things.

First, and most importantly, *the prime problem that the Bible sets up in its first three chapters is the alienation of man from God.* To be sure, there are enormous consequences that follow from man's sin and alienation from God. Relationships between human beings themselves are disrupted. God tells the woman, "Your desire will be for your husband, and he shall rule over you" (Gen. 3:16), indicating that she will sinfully desire to master her husband (cf. Gen. 4:7), and he will sinfully tend to dominate her. God also tells

Satan that there will be "enmity between [his] offspring and [the woman's]" (Gen. 3:15), the result of which will be strife not only in the family but throughout society (see Gen. 4:8, 23). Moreover, the created order itself is affected by Adam's fall (Gen. 3:17). No longer will the soil willingly yield its fruit to Adam. Now he will have to work for his food, and work "in pain," God tells him, and "by the sweat of [his] face."

In the midst of all this suffering, though, we must remember that all these tragedies—the alienation of man from his fellow man, and the alienation of man from his world—are symptoms of the underlying problem, the alienation of man from God. It was Adam's decision to rebel against God that precipitated all the rest. Twice God makes this point in the curse he pronounces over Adam:

> *Because you* have listened to the voice of your wife
>   and have eaten of the tree . . .
> cursed is the ground *because of you.* (Gen. 3:17)

The fundamental problem, the one at the root of all the others, is man's severed relationship with God.

Second, we should notice that even in the first dreadful moments after Adam's sin, *the hope of salvation is not for Adam to work to return the world to its original "very good" state, but rather for God to effect salvation through a Mediator.* In the midst of all this postfall bad news, the first hint of any "gospel," any good news, comes in Genesis 3:15. There God promises Satan that the woman's Offspring "shall bruise your head, and you shall bruise his heel." That is a poignant description of Christ's victory over the Serpent, once you know the end of the story. Satan does indeed bruise Christ's heel (a wound, but not a finally fatal one), but Christ bruises Satan's head, crushing it by his death on the cross and his resurrection. That's how God would bring about salvation.

Again, there is nothing in the early chapters of Genesis that would lead us to believe that the work of returning the world to its original "very good" state falls to Adam. God does not give him such a charge, and the reason is that Adam has already blown it. To be sure, his original mandate was to protect the garden and "cultivate" it, even to build from it a society that would perfectly glorify God. But he utterly failed at that task. When God exiles Adam from Eden, it is not with a commission to continue the work of building the world into a God-glorifying, cultivated paradise. Adam's existence in the world would not be one of continual progress toward godliness anymore; it would be one of frustration and painful work in a world that was now reluctant and even hostile toward him. No, the work of fixing the disaster fell to another, to the Offspring of the woman who would crush the Serpent's head.

Third, *these themes of alienation from God and salvation by a Mediator are central to the whole story line of the Bible.* From Genesis 3 to Revelation 21, the Bible is the story of how a gracious God who is also perfectly just and righteous acted to bring sinful human beings back into his presence and favor. It is the story of how God justly and righteously lifted the flaming sword of Genesis 3:24 and reopened for his own people the way to the tree of life. It is therefore to the act of redemption that we now turn.

Redemption

The story of how God redeemed a people for himself, making them able once again to dwell in his presence and under his kingdom, is not a short one. It begins in Genesis 3 when God promises the coming of One who will crush the Serpent's head, continues with God exiling Adam and Eve from the garden, and does not end until a redeemed humanity stands before God's throne, enjoying the great blessing of living in his presence yet again. As Revelation 22:4 puts it so gloriously, "They shall see his face!"

From Adam to Noah—The Progress of Sin

As the years pass after the fall, it becomes clear that humanity is not making its way back to faithfulness to God. The story of Genesis 4–11 is one of continual descent into greater and deeper sin. By the beginning of chapter 6, the wickedness of mankind has become rampant: "The LORD saw that the wickedness of man was great in the earth, and that every intention of the thoughts of his heart was only evil continually" (Gen. 6:5). The earth was "filled with violence" and was itself "corrupted," for "all flesh had corrupted their way on the earth" (Gen. 6:11–12). One wonders whether Adam, watching all this take place around him, recognized what his sin had done. The Bible tells us he lived 930 years, which means, fascinatingly, that he would have lived long enough to bounce Noah's father on his aged knee! Did Adam connect the growing wickedness around him to his own sin? Did he pine all his life for the joys of Eden, for the fellowship he enjoyed with God before his sin? The Bible doesn't say.

Even after the great flood, through which God rescued the one righteous man—Noah—and his family, the wickedness of man was not stamped out. Sin rears its ugly head again almost immediately with Noah's drunkenness and Ham's disrespect of his father (Gen. 9:21–22), and then comes to a head once more with men's idea that they should build a tower "with its top in the heavens" (Gen. 11:4). This is an act of enormous hubris, a bid to "make a name for ourselves" and to prove that mankind was unlimited in their reach and ability. Seeing mankind's pride, God judges them yet again, confusing their language and scattering them across the face of the earth.

Despite all this, God has not given up on saving mankind. That is clear even in his covenant with Noah after the flood, when God promises that he will never again destroy the earth with water (Gen. 9:9–17). In fact, God's intention is even greater than a simple promise not to destroy. He intends to actually *redeem* humanity and bring them back into fellowship with himself. That intention was hinted at in the promise of Genesis 3:15, and again in God's saving Noah through the judgment of the flood. The ark that God told Noah to build is a picture of God's promise that he will bring mankind—by his own saving action—through his judgment against sin.

Abraham

God's plan to bring humanity back into fellowship with him takes its next great step when God unilaterally promises to bless Abram (later Abraham) and make him a blessing to the world (Gen. 12:1–3). That promise is reiterated over and over again throughout the story of Genesis (13:14–17; 15:4–5; 17:1–14; 18:18; 22:16–18; 26:2–5; 28:13–15; 35:10–12), but the central structure of the promise is contained in chapter 12. Looking closely at that passage, we can see that God is promising Abram three things if he will obey God's calling.

First, *God promises Abraham land.* "Go . . . to the land that I will show you" (Gen. 12:1). God doesn't specify here which land, nor does he specifically say that he will *give* that land to Abram. But the idea is at least implicit, and in Genesis 13:14–17 God makes it clear that this land is to be his gift to Abraham and his descendants. Not only so, but once they are in the land, God says, he will restore fellowship with them:

> And I will establish my covenant between me and you and your offspring after you throughout their generations for an everlasting covenant, to be God to you and to your offspring after you. And I will give to you and to your offspring after you the land of your sojournings, all the land of Canaan, for an everlasting possession, and I will be their God. (Gen. 17:7–8)

That refrain, "I will be their God," shows up again and again in the story of Israel, declaring God's intention in this great work of redemption: he will bring the people into the land and cleanse them of their sin. Thus they will be his people, and he will be their God.

Second, *God promises Abraham offspring and a great name.* "I will make of you a great nation, and I will bless you and make your name great" (Gen. 12:2). Again, how exactly God will do that is left for later, but the promise is clear enough. Though Abraham is already advanced in age, and though he will take a wife who was barren, God promises that his descendants will be "as the stars of heaven and as the sand that is on the seashore" (Gen. 22:17). God also tells Abram that he will make his name great—a poignant rejection of humans' self-aggrandizing desire to "make a name for themselves" at the Tower of Babel. Abraham will not make his own name; God will make it for him.

As is so often the case in the story of the Bible, the true significance of this promise that Abraham will be the father of a great nation will be fully understood only later. The Savior of the world—the one who will finally crush the head of the Serpent—will emerge from Abraham's descendants. "Now the promises were made to Abraham and to his offspring," Paul tells us. "It does not say, 'And to offsprings,' referring to many, but referring to one, 'And to your offspring,' who is Christ" (Gal. 3:16). In other words, the ultimate point and glory of God's promise to give Abraham "offspring" is not so much that millions of "children of Abraham" will come from him, but rather the fact that the Savior himself will be one of them. As Paul says, all the promises find their fulfillment in Abraham's "Offspring," not in his "offsprings." The true greatness of the nation of Israel is that "from their race, according to the flesh, is the Christ who is God over all, blessed forever. Amen" (Rom. 9:5).

Third, *God promises that he will make Abraham a blessing.* "In you all the families of the earth shall be blessed" (Gen. 12:3; see also 12:2). As we saw earlier in this book, this is not a commission to go bless the nations, but a promise that blessing will come through Abraham's offspring (or, following Paul, Offspring).

Paul makes this point about the blessing in Galatians 3:8–9: "And the Scripture, foreseeing that God would justify the Gentiles by faith, preached the gospel beforehand to Abraham, saying, 'In you shall all the nations be blessed.' So then, those who are of faith are blessed along with Abraham, the man of faith."

Do you see how Paul understands this blessing that Abraham would bring to the nations? He ties it directly to God's intention to "justify the Gentiles by faith." The great blessing that Abraham would bring to the families of the earth was nothing other than the blessing of being justified—declared righteous—through Christ.

Moses and the Exodus

God's plan of redemption continues as he reiterates his promises to Abraham's descendants—first Isaac and then Jacob. In time, the descendants of Jacob find themselves enslaved in Egypt, and God uses Moses as the instrument of rescuing his people from their slavery to Pharaoh. That event, the exodus of the people from their slavery in Egypt, becomes crucial to Israel's own self-identity. Time and again, God reminds his people that he is the one "who brought you out of Egypt" (Ex. 20:2), "who brought you out from there with a mighty hand" (Deut. 5:15), and who "stretched out [his] right hand" against the armies of Egypt (Ex. 15:12). Not only so, but the prophets look back on the exodus as a picture of God's full and final salvation of his people.

Because of this, some have argued that the exodus from Egypt provides a paradigm by which we should understand God's entire program of redemption. Christopher Wright, for example, has argued that our understanding of redemption, of the gospel, and of the mission of the church should be "exodus-shaped." In other words, because the exodus from Egypt had political, social, and economic components, we must understand the gospel, redemption, and our mission to have political, social, and economic components as well. There's a certain compelling logic to that argument, especially since the final salvation of God's people will certainly include those aspects.

But there are also significant problems with that understanding. Perhaps the most important is that the New Testament writers simply do not treat the exodus in that fashion. In their writings as in the prophets, the exodus does function as a type (or paradigm) of redemption, but typology is not a matter of carrying *every aspect* of a type over to its antitype. Thus when the New Testament talks about the exodus as a type of salvation, what it focuses on is not *at all* its political and economic aspects, but rather the picture it provided of the *spiritual* salvation God was bringing about. In Matthew 2:15, for example, when Matthew ties Jesus explicitly to the redemption of Israel from Egypt, he doesn't draw out any political or economic implications. Rather, he has already said that Jesus's mission was to "save his people from their sins," and now he's tying the exodus itself to that aim. It's as if he is saying, "If you think the exodus was a great redemption, you haven't seen anything yet!" In Ephesians 1:7, too, Paul adopts this language of "redemption"—famously used to describe the exodus—and puts it again in terms of salvation from sin: "In him we have redemption through his blood, the forgiveness of our trespasses." Similarly in Colossians 1:13–14, the apostle evokes the exodus with the imagery of Christians being taken out of Satan's kingdom: "He has delivered us from the domain of darkness and transferred us to the kingdom of his beloved Son, in whom we have redemption, the forgiveness of sins." Again, the language and imagery of exodus are used to talk not about political and economic redemption, but about *spiritual* redemption.

So while the exodus does seem to function in Scripture as a paradigm of salvation, we have to be as careful as the apostles were in using it. We should see in the exodus God's redemption of his people from slavery, and rejoice that he has redeemed us from slavery, too—not slavery to a foreign political power, but slavery to sin. We should also recognize that on the last day, God will indeed set everything—politically, socially, and economically—to rights. And we should rejoice in that certain hope. But we would go beyond the evidence of Scripture—and beyond the practice and writings of the apostles themselves—if we appropriated the exodus in every literal respect as the pattern of our mission in the world. The Gospel writers do not use it that way, the apostles do not use it that way, and we ourselves should not use it that way, either.

Moses and the Nation of Israel

After the exodus from Egypt, God constitutes the people of Israel as a nation and gives them his Law. The central tension in the Mosaic Law, as in the rest of the story of the Bible, is how a holy and righteous God can live among a sinful, rebellious people. It's a tension that plays out at several points in the story. Even at the moment of the exodus itself, God makes it clear to his people that they are not innocent, and that in fact blood will have to be shed if they are to be redeemed. So God gives them instructions for slaughtering the Passover lamb (Exodus 12). If the people do not obey God, slaughter the lamb, and put its blood on their doorframes, they will be treated in exactly the same way as the judged Egyptians. It is not the Israelites themselves that the angel of death looks for, but rather the blood of the slain lamb.

Even after the exit from Egypt, it is clear that the people are not in a free and perfect relationship with God. They are still sinful people, and as a result they are to remain separated from him. So God tells Moses in Exodus 19:12–13 to set limits around Mount Sinai and forbid the people to go up it or even to touch the edge of it. If anyone does, God says, he will be killed. God may have chosen them and rescued them, but their sin remains and mankind's exile from Eden is still in effect.

The Law, which God hands down on Sinai and which Moses codifies in the Pentateuch, has been described facetiously as the instruction booklet to a nuclear warhead. That's an illuminating image! With the God of the universe dwelling among them, Israel is indeed living with something like a nuclear warhead in its midst, and they will have to be very careful about how they deal with him. The sons of Korah and Uzzah both learn the hard way that God is not to be trifled with.

Hence, the sacrificial system. In the Law, God gives his people instructions on how they can atone for their sin and thus not be destroyed by being in the presence of the Lord. Those sacrifices also point to the fact that sin's penalty is death, and that in order for human beings to dwell with God, that penalty will have to be paid by someone. That is the point, for example, of the scapegoat. Leviticus 16:21–22 describes the practice:

> And Aaron shall lay both his hands on the head of the live goat, and confess over it all the iniquities of the people of Israel, and all their transgressions, all their sins. And he shall put them on the head of the goat and send it away into the wilderness by the hand of a man who is in readiness. The goat shall bear all their iniquities on itself to a remote area, and he shall let the goat go free in the wilderness.

It isn't that the goat is released into the wilderness to frolic and play there, as if this were a good thing. No, to be set free in the wilderness is a sentence of death for the animal. Israel's sins are symbolically transferred to the goat, which dies in their place.

All this, of course, points forward to the sacrificial death of Jesus on the cross in his people's place. Thus the author of Hebrews writes:

> For if the blood of goats and bulls, and the sprinkling of defiled persons with the ashes of a heifer, sanctify for the purification of the flesh, how much more will the blood of Christ, who through the eternal Spirit offered himself without blemish to

God, purify our conscience from dead works to serve the living
God. (Heb. 9:13–14)

Again, in the story of Moses and the giving of the Law, the
central problem being addressed is how a sinful and rebellious
people can live in the presence of a holy God. Again and again,
Israel pushes that tension to the limit, their grumbling and com-
plaining bringing God to the point of destroying them before
Moses intercedes and makes atonement for them. This is no story,
certainly, of humanity finding its footing and working to restore
the creation to its Edenic state. On the contrary, it is the story of
even the chosen people proving that, for all their advantages, they
are still unworthy of dwelling in God's presence and of a gracious
and patient God making provision and atonement for them.

King David

The people of Israel eventually demand that God give them
a king. God does so, despite the fact that the demand represents a rejection of his direct rule over them. The first king,
Saul, turns out to be disobedient and is ultimately rejected
by God as king in favor of David, "a man after [God's] own
heart" (1 Sam. 13:14). For years, David patiently waits on God
to give him the crown, and when that finally happens, God
makes some extraordinary promises to him. He promises to
make for David a great name (2 Sam. 7:9) and to establish
David's dynasty forever (7:13, 16). Not only so, but he promises
David all the same things he has promised Abraham: There's
the promise of land in 7:10, and of offspring in 7:12. True,
there's no explicit mention of blessing to the nations here,
but the psalmists and the prophets fill that point out nicely.
Thus in Psalm 2, God says to the king,

Ask of me, and I will make the nations your heritage,
and the ends of the earth your possession. (v. 8)

83

And to the nations, the promise is clear: "Blessed are all who take refuge in him."[6]

You can see what is happening here. All the promises that God made to Abraham, which then passed down to Isaac and Jacob and then to the nation of Israel, are coming to rest in one specific person, the King of Israel. They are finding their fulfillment in and through the one who sits on the throne of Israel. In fact, as God reveals more and more of his plan to them, the prophets begin to see that all those promises will find their final fulfillment—that is, the final reconciliation of man and God will be effected—through the suffering and death of this King as the representative of his people. So in Isaiah, it becomes clear that the coming King of chapters 9 and 11 is actually *the same person* as the Suffering Servant of chapter 53. The King does not merely rule his people in a kingdom of love and compassion; he actually bears their iniquities so that they may be accounted righteous (Isa. 53:11) and brought back into a perfect and uninterrupted relationship with God.

Of course none of the kings in David's line live up to those great promises in 2 Samuel. For a time there's a golden age of peace and prosperity under David's son Solomon, but Solomon fails to usher in the salvation of God's people, and he himself falls into sin. The kingdom splits in two under David's grandson Rehoboam, and the story of the kings then descends into a parade of horribles, with notable exceptions here and there, until the throne of the northern kingdom, Israel, is lost in exile, and the last king of Judah, Zedekiah, watches as his sons are put to death, has his own eyes put out, and is dragged in chains to exile in Babylon (2 Kings 25:7). Yes, the king of Babylon treats him kindly while he's in captivity, but while there may be some foreshadowing of restoration, it is clearly pity at best, and not

---

[6]See also Isa. 2:2; 60:3–4; Jer. 3:17; Mic. 4:1–2; Zech. 2:11 and others, where the nations stream to Jerusalem to worship the Lord in the last day. See also Isa. 19:23–25, where "in that day," Egypt and Assyria are astonishingly called "my people" and "the work of my hands."

awe, that leads the Babylonian king to treat the heir of David in such a way. And that is how the story of Israel's kings ends . . . at least for a while.

Christ

From its very first pages, the New Testament makes the startling claim that the throne of David is no longer empty. The great promised King who would bring blessing to the nations and who would reconcile sinful man to a holy God has finally come—and he is none other than Jesus Christ. The first words of the New Testament, in fact, are a genealogy tracing Jesus's descendants back to King David and then further back to Abraham (Matt. 1:1–17). The point, underscored by several fascinating stylistic touches by Matthew, is that Jesus holds a legal claim to the throne of David, and that he fulfills the promises made to that great king and therefore fulfills the promises made to Abraham as well. Indeed, most commentators agree that the division of the genealogy into three sections of fourteen generations each is likely a play on the numeric value of the three letters in the Hebrew word for "David." Both implicitly and explicitly, Matthew is declaring that Jesus is the long-awaited King, or "Messiah."

Luke is perhaps even more explicit, recording the angel's announcement to Mary in no uncertain terms:

> And the angel said to her, "Do not be afraid, Mary, for you have found favor with God. And behold, you will conceive in your womb and bear a son, and you shall call his name Jesus. He will be great and will be called the Son of the Most High. And the Lord God will give to him the throne of his father David, and he will reign over the house of Jacob forever, and of his kingdom there will be no end." (Luke 1:30–33; see also 2:4)

Throughout the Gospels, the fact of Jesus's kingship is emphasized again and again, culminating with the kingly imagery surrounding his crucifixion: the purple robe, the crown of thorns, Pilate's sign with the inscription "King of the Jews"—all those details are ironic and providential testimony to what really was the case. Though it was not at all what the Jews were expecting from their Messiah, Jesus was in fact King.

It's important to see that Jesus understood that inherent to his kingship was the salvation of his people from their sin, and thus the restoration of fellowship between them and God. So the angel told Joseph regarding Mary, "She will bear a son, and you shall call his name Jesus, for he will save his people from their sins" (Matt. 1:21). Jesus himself said in Mark 10:45, "For even the Son of Man came not to be served but to serve, and to give his life as a ransom for many." And at the last supper with his disciples before his death, he told them regarding the cup, "Drink of it, all of you, for this is my blood of the covenant, which is poured out for many for the forgiveness of sins" (Matt. 26:27–28). From the very beginning of his ministry, Jesus understood that he was drawing together all the strands of the Jews' Old Testament hope. He was not just the king; he was the King who was at the same time the Suffering Servant of Isaiah, who would bear his people's iniquities and make them righteous before the Father. Only then could the perfect fellowship of Eden be restored.

That note is sounded immediately upon Jesus's death, in fact, when the curtain of the temple—the woven screen that separated the people from the Most Holy Place, where God's presence dwelt—was torn in two, from top to bottom (Matt. 27:51 and parallels). That act of God—the curtain was sixty feet high!—dramatically symbolized the end of humanity's exile from God's presence. Now, after so many millennia, they were welcome to enter again into the Most Holy Place. Moreover, the tombs around Jerusalem were opened, and those who had been dead were raised and went into the city (Matt. 27:52–53). It was another indication that the curse of death that had fallen on Adam's race was now broken.

Of course, the greatest triumph of all over death was Jesus's own resurrection on the third day. Having suffered and died as the Sin-Bearer for his people, Jesus rose from the dead and conquered death once and for all. And greatest of all, for those who are his people—for those united to him by faith—he broke the curse of Eden and restored fellowship with God. As Hebrews tells us, the risen Jesus now sits at the right hand of God the Almighty, and those who are united to him by faith, too, are even now "raised . . . up with him and seated . . . with him in the heavenly places" (Eph. 2:5–6). Moreover, there is for us who are united to Christ the glorious promise that at the last day, our physical bodies will also be raised, just like Christ's. As Paul says in Romans 8:11, "If the Spirit of him who raised Jesus from the dead dwells in you, he who raised Christ Jesus from the dead will also give life to your mortal bodies through his Spirit who dwells in you."

Consummation

After his resurrection, Jesus gave his disciples the charge to go into the world and witness to what they had seen and experienced with and about him.[7] In other words, they were to proclaim his kingship and the forgiveness of sins and salvation that were offered through him. That charge given, the Bible tells us that Jesus ascended into heaven and sat down at the right hand of his Father in heaven, his work of redemption completed (Mark 16:19; Heb. 1:3b; 10:12). Now Christ's people live in this age under his kingship, enjoying his gifts and bearing witness to him among all the nations of the world. Through their lives together in churches, they bear witness to the life of the kingdom, they encourage one another in faithfulness, and they look forward to the day when their King Jesus will return to earth, this time to fully and completely establish God's reign on a renewed and transformed earth.

---

[7] On Jesus's Great Commissions, see chapter 2.

The prophets looked forward to the end of time. Isaiah, as we've already seen, told of when the Messiah's kingdom would be established and said that it would be upheld in justice and righteousness (Isa. 9:7). He went on to tell of God's promise to create "new heavens and a new earth" (Isa. 65:17)—a place where the former things will not be remembered (65:17), where the sound of weeping is no longer heard (65:19), where infants do not die and old men do not perish (65:20), where labor will not be in vain (65:23), where the wolf will lie down with the lamb (65:25), and where no one will hurt or destroy in all the Lord's holy mountain (65:25).

What an amazing vision of the final state of God's redeemed people! A new, transformed heaven and earth where violence is no more, where sickness is no more, where death no longer reigns, and above all, where God again rejoices in his people. It's that restored relationship that represents the high-water mark of Isaiah's vision—not merely the end of violence or the end of sickness, as wonderful as those things are—but the restoration of the relationship between God and his people. No longer are they outcasts and exiles, full of shame and nakedness; now they are "a joy" and "a gladness" to God (65:18). Instead of cursing them, he "will rejoice in Jerusalem and be glad in [his] people" (65:19). Instead of casting them away from his presence, he will answer them even "before they call" (65:24). "While they are yet speaking," the Lord exults, "I will hear" (65:24). Finally that great refrain of the Old Testament is fully fulfilled, "I will be their God, and they will be my people."

The book of Revelation ends with the same vision of restored relationship, as God's redeemed people dwell in God's place under God's rule. John writes in Revelation 21:1–3:

> Then I saw a new heaven and a new earth, for the first heaven and the first earth had passed away, and the sea was no more. And I saw the holy city, new Jerusalem, coming down out of heaven from God, prepared as a bride adorned for her husband. And I

heard a loud voice from the throne saying, "Behold, the dwelling place of God is with man. He will dwell with them, and they will be his people, and God himself will be with them as their God."

Once more, the emphasis is on God dwelling again with man, the enmity between them ended, and the sin that separated man from God forgiven. John even says later that in the eternal city of God, "no longer will there be anything accursed," and, perhaps most gloriously of all, God's servants "will see his face" (Rev. 22:4). Whatever curse and division existed between God and man is now completely gone. The curtain is torn, the curse is ended, the separation is closed. Once and for all now, God's people see his face.

Conclusion

What we've seen in this short and admittedly incomplete survey of the biblical story is that the main tension of the Bible's story line seems to revolve around the question, *How can hopelessly rebellious, sinful people live in the presence of a perfectly just and righteous God?* Yes, there are other themes and emphases that we haven't even mentioned here, but that question seems to drive the story at every point. The "whole story" is not, as one author suggests, about us becoming "conduits for him to bring healing to earth and its residents." It's not about our call "to partner in a restorative work so that the torch of hope is carried until Christ returns."[8] The story is not about us working with God to make the world right again. It's about God's work to make us right so we can live with him again.

Now, understanding that story and its central features, it's not hard at all to see why Jesus would make his final commission to his disciples the charge to "be my witnesses" and declared that through them, "repentance and forgiveness of

---

[8]Gabe Lyons, *The Next Christians: How a New Generation Is Restoring the Faith* (New York: Doubleday, 2010), 55.

sins should be proclaimed in his name to all nations, beginning from Jerusalem" (Acts 1:8; Luke 24:47). After all, the way for human beings to be reconciled to God—the great burden of the Bible—is by being forgiven of sin and declared to be righteous instead of guilty. And that declaration of righteousness, that justification of the ungodly, would come only through being united to the King who suffered and died and rose triumphantly in the place of his people.

CHAPTER 4

Are We Missing the Whole Gospel?

Understanding the Good News

SOME TIME AGO, *Christianity Today* ran a series of online articles called "Is Our Gospel Too Small?" The premise of the articles was to ask the question whether an understanding of the "good news" of Christianity as the forgiveness of sins through Jesus was actually selling the biblical gospel short. Isn't it true, the articles asked, that when the Bible talks about the "good news," it is talking about something much more than, as one author indelicately put it in another place, "getting our butts into heaven when we die"? And even if the gospel *is* about the forgiveness of sins and justification before God, the authors asked, isn't it also about the remaking of the world, the end of oppression, setting captives free, the creation of a society based on righteousness and justice instead of unrighteousness and injustice? And if that's what the gospel is about, the authors asked, then isn't that what we as the church ought to be about as well?

Those questions are not easy to answer. You can't just say yes or no to them, which is why we've thought it might be helpful to write a whole book about these issues! The fact is, the question of what exactly the gospel is, and what it includes and does not include, has caused no end of controversy even among evangelicals. What we hope to do in this chapter, therefore, is look carefully at the way the New Testament talks about "the gospel" and try to come to some conclusions on this matter of whether our gospel is "too small."

Talking Past One Another

Both of us have over the past several years been immersed in the world of evangelical discussion about the gospel. We've attended the conferences, read the books, looked at the blogs, and written a few things ourselves about this most controverted and important of topics. One of the things we've concluded over the years is that in many ways evangelicals seem to be talking past one another on this question of what the gospel is.

On the one hand, some would define the gospel as the good news that God is going to remake the world, and that Jesus Christ—through his death and resurrection—is the down payment on that transformation and renewal. They look at the gospel with the widest possible lens, taking in all the promises that God has made to his people, including not only the forgiveness of sins but also the resurrection of the body, the transformation of the world, the establishment of God's kingdom, and all the rest.

On the other hand, there are those who would define the gospel as the good news that God has acted to save sinners through the death of Jesus in their place and his subsequent resurrection. They look at the gospel with a narrow lens, focusing particularly on that which lies at the foundation of salvation.

The conversation between these two camps has gotten quite tense, even heated at times, with one side accusing the other of being "reductionistic," and that side firing back with the accusation that the first side is "diluting" the gospel and losing the heart of it.

A good deal of this confusion can be untangled, we think, by making some careful observations about how this conversation often plays out. It seems to us that these two groups—those who say the gospel is the good news that God is reconciling sinners to himself through the death and resurrection of Jesus (let's call them "zoom-lens people"), and those who say that the gospel is the good news that God is going to renew and remake the world through Christ (call them "wide-angle people")—are really answering two different though highly related questions. Of course both groups *say* they are answering the question "What is the gospel?" (and they are!), but if you look closely at how they talk, it turns out there's quite a lot being assumed by both sides about that simple-sounding question.

To a zoom-lens person, the question "What is the gospel?" translates as "What is the message a person must believe in order to be saved?" And so he answers by talking about the substitutionary death of Jesus in the place of sinners and the call to repent and believe. To a wide-angle person, though, the question "What is the gospel?" translates instead to "What is the whole good news of Christianity?" And of course he answers by talking not just about forgiveness but also about all the great blessings that flow from that, including God's purpose to remake the world.

Now with that in mind, you can see where the confusion comes from. When a zoom-lens person hears a wide-angle person answer the question "What is the gospel?" by talking about the new creation, he thinks, "No! You're taking the focus off the cross and resurrection! A person doesn't need to believe that to be saved! That's diluting the gospel!" On the other hand, when a wide-angle person hears a zoom-lens person answer the same question by talking only about the forgiveness of sins through the cross, he likewise thinks, "No! The good news doesn't stop there! There's more to it than that! You're reducing the gospel to something less than it is!"

The fact is, depending on how you think about it, neither the wide-angle person nor the zoom-lens person is off base. It's true that when someone asked in the New Testament "What must I do to be saved?" the answer was to repent of sin and believe in the crucified and risen Christ. It's also true, though, that the Bible sometimes (even often!) talks about the gospel with a wide-angle lens. It includes in the whole good news of Christianity not only forgiveness of sin, but also all the other blessings that come to those who are in Christ.

Another way to put the point is that neither of these two questions is illegitimate. Neither is more biblical than the other. In fact, the Bible asks both the question "What must a person believe in order to be saved?" and the question, "What is the whole good news of Christianity?"—and it answers both in terms of the word *gospel*.

A Wide-Angle Lens and a Zoom Lens on the Gospel

As we read it, the New Testament seems to use the word *gospel* in both of these ways. Sometimes it looks at the good news of Christianity with a wide-angle lens, calling "gospel" all the great blessings that God intends to shower on his people, starting with forgiveness but cascading from there all the way to a renewed and remade creation in which they will spend eternity. Other times, though, the New Testament looks at the good news of Christianity with a very narrow focus—with a zoom lens, if you will—and is quite happy to call "gospel" the singular blessing of forgiveness of sins and restored relationship with God through the sacrificial death of Jesus.

Maybe it will be helpful if we look carefully at some wide-angle passages, some zoom-lens passages, and finally some passages where the Bible itself seems to move from zoom to wide-angle over the course of just a few words.

Wide-Angle Lens

There are more than a few passages in the Bible that seem to take a broad view of the gospel and even apply the word translated "gospel"—*euangelion*—to the entire package of blessings that Christ secures for his people. Here are a few of the most important.

Matthew 4:23

> And he went throughout all Galilee, teaching in their synagogues and proclaiming *the gospel of the kingdom* and healing every disease and every affliction among the people.

This is the first mention of the gospel in the book of Matthew, so we should expect that the evangelist would provide us with some explanation of what was included in this "gospel of the kingdom" that Jesus was preaching. And he does, back in verse 17 of the same chapter, where he records that the message Jesus preached—at least in summary form—was "Repent, for the kingdom of heaven is at hand."

We should notice several things about Matthew's use of "gospel" here. First, the burden of Matthew's entire book to this point has been to prove that Jesus is in fact the long-awaited Messiah. His opening genealogy, as we saw in the last chapter, is highly stylized to make that point, as is the story of the coming of the magi and even the way Matthew uses Old Testament texts to describe the character and mission of the Messiah (Matthew 2).

It's also significant that Jesus's declaration in Matthew 4:17 is exactly the same—word for word, in fact—as John the Baptist's declaration in Matthew 3:2—"Repent, for the kingdom of heaven is at hand." For all the similarity between their messages, however, there's an important difference between what John the Baptist preached and what Jesus preached. When John preached that the kingdom of heaven was "at hand," he meant that it was *near,* almost here but not quite yet. In fact, that understanding lay at the heart of his entire ministry. John was preparing Israel for the coming of the kingdom (Matt. 3:3).

When Jesus preached that the kingdom was "at hand," though, he meant something slightly different. He meant that the kingdom was *here,* right now. How do we know that? We know it because of the way Matthew introduces the beginning of Jesus's public ministry in Matthew 4:12–16. Noting that Jesus withdrew from Judea and moved to Capernaum in Galilee, Matthew quotes from Isaiah 9:1:

> The land of Zebulun and the land of Naphtali,
>   the way of the sea, beyond the Jordan, Galilee of the
>   Gentiles—
> the people dwelling in darkness
>   have seen a great light,
> and for those dwelling in the region and shadow of death,
>   on them a light has dawned. (Matt. 4:15–16)

There's much we could talk about here, but the important thing is that Matthew is asserting that the kingdom is no longer just near; it has dawned! On the people who had been most hammered by the Assyrian invasion, who were mocked as the backwater, mongrelized laughingstocks of the nation—on *these* people God has chosen to let the first rays of the dawning kingdom break. Thus when Jesus preached that "the kingdom of heaven is at hand," we cannot understand it any other way than in the light (!) of Matthew's quotation from Isaiah 9:1.

But what exactly has dawned? We'll consider "the kingdom of heaven" more in the next chapter, but suffice it to say for now that the Israelites' great hope was that one day, God would restore the fortunes of Israel and establish his perfect rule over the earth, vindicating his people and punishing their enemies, and he would do so through a divine King who would reign forever on David's throne. When John the Baptist and Jesus begin to preach, therefore, that the kingdom of heaven is "at hand," it is an electrifying message. It means that all the grand promises that God made to his people in the prophets are—they think—about to be fulfilled. The kingdom is about to be established (Isaiah 9), the new covenant is about to be cut (Jeremiah 33), the knowledge of the glory of the Lord is about to cover the earth (Hab. 2:14), the nations are about to stream to Jerusalem (cf. Isaiah 61), and the Lord is about to create new heavens and a new earth (Isa. 65:17). Even Matthew's quotation of Isaiah 9:1 tells us that more is in view here than the forgiveness of sins. Certainly it's not *less* than that, but Isaiah 9:1 is the introduction to Isaiah's prophecy that culminates with the Messiah sitting on David's throne and ruling "with justice and righteousness from this time forth and forevermore." What is in view here is a whole new world. That's what Jesus calls "the *gospel* of the kingdom."

One other important thing to notice is that this good news also includes a call for response—the way a person can be included in this dawning kingdom. Here in Matthew 4, Jesus preaches (as does John, for that matter), "*Repent*, for the kingdom of heaven is at hand." The gospel of the kingdom, as it's given here, is the good news that (a) the kingdom has dawned, and (b) those who repent can enter it (see also Mark 1:14–15).

Luke 4:18–19

> The Spirit of the Lord is upon me,
> because he has anointed me
> to proclaim *good news* to the poor.
> He has sent me to proclaim liberty to the captives
> and recovering of sight to the blind,
> to set at liberty those who are oppressed,
> to proclaim the year of the Lord's favor.

97

Returning to his boyhood home of Nazareth, Jesus stands to read from the prophet Isaiah to those gathered to hear him. He opens the scroll, Luke tells us, to Isaiah 61 and reads verse 1 and *part* of verse 2. When he sits down, as a synagogue teacher would have when he was about to begin teaching, Jesus simply says, "Today this Scripture has been fulfilled in your hearing" (Luke 4:21). Those words cause a stir among the people, who at first marvel and speak kind words about him (v. 22), but quickly turn into a mob that would throw Jesus off a cliff if they had the power to do so (vv. 29–30).

What has caused such a reaction is that Jesus, as he has done publicly again and again in his sermons, is proclaiming that Scripture's greatest promises are being fulfilled right now—*in him.* Not only so, but he is making a poignant statement to the people that his mission is one of grace, not judgment—at least not yet. Many of those listening to Jesus would be tracking along with his reading in their own minds, and therefore they would be surprised when he stops and closes the scroll in the middle of a sentence! The very next phrase in Isaiah's prophecy after "to proclaim the year of the LORD's favor" is "and the day of vengeance of our God." Jesus doesn't read that part—quite deliberately. This isn't the day of vengeance. Not yet. It is the year of favor, the time of good news!

The passage in Isaiah 61 has attracted a good deal of attention recently, especially from those who argue that *gospel* has a broad, world-encompassing meaning. And in this case, they are absolutely right! Isaiah 61 begins a beautiful, triumphant poem about God's final victory and the establishment of his reign through his Servant. Jerusalem would be rebuilt as a precious crown in God's hand (61:4; 62:3), God's and Israel's enemies would be destroyed by God's mighty arm (63:1–7), and former troubles would be utterly forgotten (65:16). The poem culminates, in fact, in that amazing vision we considered in the last chapter, where God creates new heavens and a new earth where the sound of weeping and distress is heard no more, where infants no longer die after living but a few days, where the wolf lies down with the lamb, and where no one, God says, will hurt or destroy anyone or anything in all his holy mountain. That's what Jesus is saying has been inaugurated with his coming. Of course, Jesus isn't suggesting all these blessings have arrived in their fullness. But the Servant of God who will eventually usher in all those great blessings, he has arrived!

Acts 13:32–33

> And we bring you *the good news* that what God promised to the fathers, this he has fulfilled to us their children by raising Jesus. . . .

These verses come at the end of a sermon Paul preaches in the synagogue of Pisidian Antioch. Having read from the Scriptures, the rulers of the synagogue ask Paul and Barnabas whether they have any exhortation for the people. (Perhaps they've had some experience with them before that day?) At any rate, Paul stands and addresses the people in a fairly lengthy rehearsal of the history of Israel. The point of the address seems to be to establish Jesus's place in Israel's story as the long-awaited Offspring of King David—even more, that he is the resurrected Messiah through whom all the promises come to fulfillment.

When Paul finishes the story of Israel down to King David, with God's promise to him of an heir, he says plainly, "Of this man's offspring God has brought to Israel a Savior, Jesus, as he promised" (Acts 13:23). Then he tells how John the Baptist also pointed to Jesus as the coming Messiah, and tells how the Jews in Jerusalem put Jesus to death, and finally how God raised him from the dead. It's here, at the culmination of the sermon, that Paul declares that he has brought to these Jews the "good news that what God promised to the fathers, this he has fulfilled to us their children by raising Jesus." By "the fathers," Paul undoubtedly means the patriarchs of Israel of whom he has just been speaking. And as we've already seen, the promises God made to those fathers—to Abraham and his sons—were enormous in scope. Land, Offspring, name, and blessing all were promised to Abraham, and all will be ours in the life, death, resurrection, and return of Jesus Christ (1 Cor. 3:21–23).

In all these passages we've seen that *gospel* can refer to the whole series of hopes and promises fulfilled in Christ. We are never told that the gospel is "God will remake the world." But, no doubt, the scope of these biblical promises is cosmic. Christ is the one we've been waiting for and all things will be made right through him. Surely, this is good news.

Zoom Lens

Though there are many passages, like the ones we've just discussed, that speak of the gospel in a very broad way, there are other passages that seem to focus "the gospel" much more narrowly on the forgiveness of sins through the substitutionary death of Jesus on the cross. Here are a few examples:

Acts 10:36–43

> As for the word that he sent to Israel, preaching *good news of peace* through Jesus Christ (he is Lord of all) . . . . To him all the prophets bear witness that everyone who believes in him receives forgiveness of sins through his name.

The sermon Peter preaches here is one he never thought he would preach. It is in the home of a Gentile, Cornelius, and happens only after God has convinced Peter in a vision that, as Peter himself puts it, "God shows no partiality." It is an important lesson for Peter to learn, for this is the moment when the gospel of Jesus penetrates into the Gentile world.

The sentence structure of verses 36–37 is a little stilted, but the message comes through clearly enough. Peter is about to explain to these Gentiles for the first time the "good news of peace through Jesus Christ," which the Lord first sent to the people of Israel. But what is this "good news of peace"? Is it the parenthetical phrase "he is Lord of all"? Probably not. For one thing, the phrase is an aside; it's not the point to which the sentence builds, and it's therefore an unlikely candidate for defining "the good news of peace." Not only so, but unless Peter expects his Gentile listeners to import huge amounts of Old Testament understanding into the way they hear that phrase, there's nothing in it that necessarily speaks of peace. It seems more likely that this is Peter's confession (again!) that Jesus is Lord not just of Jews, but "of all." It's as if Peter has to remind himself over and over that the peace Christ brings is not solely for Israel, but for the whole world.

So what's the "good news of peace"? The best understanding is that the good news of peace refers to the last phrase of the sermon: "To him all the prophets bear witness that everyone who believes in him receives forgiveness of sins through his name" (v. 43). The word "everyone" in that sentence is crucial because, again, Peter is more than a little surprised to be preaching *this* sermon to *these* people in the first place! Much to his astonishment, the good news of peace is that *everyone* who believes in Jesus—not just the Jews—receives forgiveness of sins. In other words, they are reconciled and brought to peace with God. It is the same idea, in fact, that Paul would draw upon in Ephesians 2: "But now in Christ Jesus you who once were far off have been brought near by the blood of Christ. For he himself is our peace" (vv. 13–14).

Of course there's much more Peter could have said, and perhaps would have said had the Holy Spirit not interrupted him at that crucial point! He could have talked about the coming kingdom being for Gentiles, too, or the resurrection being not just for Jews, or the new heavens and new earth being a place where Jews and Gentiles would live together. But here, at least, he does not. "The good news of peace," he's quite happy to say, is the good news of forgiveness of sins to everyone who believes.

Romans 1:16–17

> For I am not ashamed of *the gospel*, for it is the power of God for salvation to everyone who believes, to the Jew first and also to the Greek. For in it the righteousness of God is revealed from faith for faith, as it is written, "The righteous shall live by faith."

These sentences are widely understood to be the "topic sentence," the thesis, of the book of Romans. Paul declares that the gospel does not make him ashamed because it is "the power of God for salvation." The emphasis—as one would expect from Paul, the apostle to the Gentiles—is that this salvation is not just for Jews, but also for the whole world.

In verse 17, Paul gives us at least a nutshell summary of what he understands the gospel to do. "In it," he says (and he means "in the gospel"), "the righteousness of God is revealed from faith for faith." Two different phrases in that sentence tell us what Paul understands the gospel to be about. First, he says that in the gospel, "the righteousness of God" is revealed. That phrase has elicited a huge amount of discussion.[1] Does it refer to a righteousness that is *from* God in a legal sense—a righteousness that is imputed to us but is actually an alien righteousness? Or does it refer to a moral righteousness in us, or perhaps to God's own holy character? Alternatively, does it refer to the righteousness of God, defined as his wrath against human sin? What does Paul mean by saying that in the gospel is revealed the righteousness of God?

---

[1]For a brief, helpful introduction, see Thomas R. Schreiner, "What Does Paul Mean by 'the Righteousness of God'?" in *40 Questions about Biblical Law* (Grand Rapids: Kregel, 2010), 121–28.

Without doubt, the best way to get at what he means is to trace the rest of his argument through the book of Romans. Beginning with the declaration in 1:18 that "the wrath of God is revealed from heaven against all ungodliness and unrighteousness of men," Paul spends most of the first three chapters of the book indicting all of humanity with a charge of sin and rebellion against God. Chapter 1 is aimed primarily at Gentiles, chapter 2 at Jews, and then in chapter 3 he draws it all together with a devastating charge that "all, both Jews and Greeks, are under sin" and that "every mouth may be stopped, and the whole world may be held accountable to God" (vv. 10, 19). Then, having established the hopeless condition of all mankind, Paul turns to the good news: "But now," he writes, "the righteousness of God has been manifested apart from the law" (v. 21). There's that phrase again—"the righteousness of God." But what does it mean? And what does it mean that it is manifested now "apart from law"?

The answer becomes clear a few verses later, when Paul explains how Abraham came to be "counted righteous" before God (Rom. 4:3–6). That phrase helps us to understand what Paul means when he talks about "the righteousness of God." The question Paul is answering through this section of Romans is, How can a person be counted righteous before God? In other words, how can a person gain from God a final verdict of *righteous* as opposed to *guilty*? It's that final verdict of righteous that Paul is calling here "the righteousness of God."[2] It's a righteousness *from* God, a righteousness that is counted to us, or imputed to us, even though it is not our own. Paul's answer to that question, of course, is that a person will never receive a righteous verdict from God by works of the law, but only through the atoning sacrifice of Jesus Christ. Thus he says

---

[2]Note that "the righteousness of God" in Rom. 1:17 is immediately followed by discussion of a parallel term, "the wrath of God." The former stands for God's verdict of vindication; the latter, God's judgment of condemnation.

in verse 6 that that person is blessed "to whom God credits righteousness apart from works." And he uses the same idea in Philippians 3:9 to say that he hopes to be included in Christ, "not having a righteousness of my own that comes from the law, but that which comes through faith in Christ, the righteousness from God that depends on faith." Thus, the "righteousness of God" that Paul says in Romans 1:17 is revealed in the gospel is precisely this—the righteousness *from* God that comes to those who have faith in Christ.

For our purposes here, the important thing to notice is that at the beginning of this book, when Paul describes in summary what is revealed "in it [the gospel]," what he says is that the gospel reveals the glorious news that an imputed "righteousness from God" is revealed and available to sinful human beings through faith. Of course he could have talked about much more, and in fact, he does: one of the Bible's most beautiful passages about the future renewal of the creation is found in Romans 8. But here at the beginning, when Paul wants to describe in summary what the gospel reveals, he points to justification by faith in the crucified and risen Jesus.

1 Corinthians 15:1–5

> Now I would remind you, brothers, of *the gospel* I preached to you, which you received, in which you stand, and by which you are being saved, if you hold fast to the word I preached to you— unless you believed in vain.
>
> For I delivered to you as of first importance what I also received: that Christ died for our sins in accordance with the Scriptures, that he was buried, that he was raised on the third day in accordance with the Scriptures, and that he appeared to Cephas, then to the twelve.

Apparently some of the Corinthians have begun to deny a resurrection from the dead. So Paul argues here from the gospel itself—the message proclaimed by him and the other apostles—that this position cannot possibly be correct. After all, the resurrection of Jesus from the dead is at the very heart of the Christian gospel, and to argue against it is therefore to argue that Jesus is still dead, and that is to argue that the Christian faith is worthless. Paul reminds the Corinthians of the basic truths of the gospel by quoting what seems to be a well-known creedal formula. These truths, he says, are not ones that he made up himself, but are "of first importance." The Corinthians must "stand" in them. This statement of the gospel really consists of four main clauses:

(1) That Christ died for our sins according to the Scriptures

(2) and that he was buried

(3) and that he was raised on the third day according to the Scriptures

(4) and that he appeared to Cephas and the Twelve.[3]

You can easily see that this "creed" is structured around two key facts (that Christ died for our sins according to the Scriptures and that he was raised on the third day according to the Scriptures), each followed by a confirming historical fact (the burial of Christ confirming that he really died, and the appearance to Peter and the others confirming that he really rose). These two facts together with their confirmation are "the gospel I preached to you," Paul insists. They are what, at the end of it all, Christians must understand to be "of first importance."

Of course Paul goes on to trace the implications of Christ's resurrection—that those who are united to him by faith will also be raised—and we've already seen how the Bible, in other places,

---

[3]The accounts that follow, of Jesus's appearing to others including Paul, should not be understood as part of the "creed." The language is not as tight and formulaic, and it is best understood as Paul's explanation of how he came to be an apostle along with Cephas and the Twelve.

calls the whole complex of God's promises, including the resurrection of the dead, "the gospel." But at least here, in a summary form that is almost certainly an early Christian confession of faith, the "gospel" is said to be the good news that Christ died for our sins and rose from the dead—full stop.

1 Corinthians 1:17–18

> For Christ did not send me to baptize but to preach *the gospel*, and not with words of eloquent wisdom, lest the cross of Christ be emptied of its power.
> For the word of the cross is folly to those who are perishing, but to us who are being saved it is the power of God.

Not much needs to be said here for our purposes. The point is in the simple correspondence between "the gospel" and "the word of the cross." In Paul's mind, the good news is the news of the cross, the "foolish" message that through the crucified Christ, God will "save those who believe" (1 Cor. 1:21).

Pulling It All Together

Looking carefully at the New Testament, then, we can see that the early Christians seem to have used the word *gospel* in two different ways—a broad way and a narrow way. On the one hand, they often used *gospel* to refer to the whole complex of promises that God makes to those who are redeemed through Christ. We might call this broad sense "the gospel of the kingdom." On the other hand, though, there are also places where the New Testament writers were quite happy to apply the word *gospel* to the message that sinners can be forgiven through repentance and faith in the atoning death and resurrection of Jesus Christ. We might call this narrow sense "the gospel of the cross."

How, though, do we pull these two senses of *gospel* together? How do the gospel of the cross and the gospel of the kingdom relate? Are they two gospels? Are they two different things, but connected like two wings of a bird? Is the gospel of the cross *part* of the gospel of the kingdom? If so, is it central to it, or peripheral to it, or just one part among many, or something else entirely? For that matter, why are the New Testament writers content to call the one blessing of forgiveness of sin through the death of Christ "the gospel," but no other single blessing by itself ever warrants that dignity? Why do we never see Paul saying, "And that's the gospel: that the earth will be renewed"? Or why does he never preach, "The gospel is the good news that Jew and Gentile can be reconciled to one another through Jesus"? Why is the forgiveness of sins so readily called "the gospel," while no other particular blessing is?

Let's try to get at these questions by making a few things clear.

First, *there is only one gospel, not two.* I (Greg) remember speaking about these things at a conference several years ago. I went on at some length about these two senses in which the New Testament seems to use the word *gospel,* and at the end of my talk, the first questioner raised his hand and said, "So . . . you're saying there are two gospels and we can choose which one we want to preach?" No, certainly not. There is only one gospel—one message of good news—but the New Testament writers seem to have no problem zooming in and out on that one message, sometimes looking at the whole thing and calling it "gospel," and other times zooming in particularly on forgiveness through Christ and calling *that* "gospel," too.

Second, *the gospel of the kingdom* necessarily *includes the gospel of the cross.* You cannot proclaim the "full gospel" if you leave out the message of the cross, even if you talk for an hour about all the other blessings God has in store for the redeemed. To do that would be like picking up an armful of leaves and insisting that you're holding a tree. Unless those leaves are connected to the trunk, you don't have a tree; you just have an armful of dead leaves. In the same way, unless the blessings of the gospel of the kingdom are connected to the cross, you don't have a gospel at all. Take a look again at those passages from Matthew and Mark where Jesus preaches the arrival of the kingdom. If you look closely, you'll notice that Jesus never preaches simply, "The kingdom of heaven is at hand." He always preaches, "*Repent*, for the kingdom of heaven is at hand," or, "The kingdom of heaven is at hand; *therefore repent and believe the gospel*." That is a crucial thing to keep in mind; indeed it is the difference between preaching the gospel and preaching something that is not the gospel at all. To proclaim the inauguration of the kingdom and all the other blessings of God without telling people how they may become partakers of those blessings is to preach a nongospel. Indeed it is to preach an *anti*gospel—*bad news*—because you're simply explaining wonderful things that your sinful hearers will never have the opportunity to be a part of. The gospel of the kingdom—the broad sense of "gospel"—therefore, is not merely the proclamation of the kingdom. It is the proclamation of the kingdom *together with* the proclamation that people may enter it by repentance and faith in Christ. Perhaps, in fact, it would be more accurate (though clunky) to speak of the gospel of the cross and the gospel of the kingdom *through the cross*. And that leads to another point.

Third, and more specifically, *the gospel of the cross is the fountainhead of the gospel of the kingdom.* It is the gate through which all the blessings of the kingdom are to be gained. The fact repeated over and over again throughout the New Testament is that the only way a person can become a partaker of the blessings of the kingdom is by coming in faith and repentance to the crucified and risen Lord Jesus for salvation. To put it in terms of Bunyan's *Pilgrim's Progress*, a person can't simply jump the wall and partake of the blessings of the kingdom; you have to go through the Wicket Gate of faith and repentance, or the blessings of the kingdom will be closed to you.

Incidentally, that's why it makes perfect sense for the New Testament writers to call the gospel of the cross "the gospel," even as they go on calling the whole complex of good news "the gospel" as well. Because the broader blessings of the gospel are attained *only* by means of forgiveness through the cross, and because those broader blessings are attained *infallibly* by means of forgiveness through the cross, it's entirely appropriate and makes perfect sense for the New Testament writers to call forgiveness through the cross—the fountainhead of and gateway to all the rest—"the gospel." That's also why we never see the New Testament calling any *other* single promise of God to the redeemed "the gospel." For example, we never see the promise of the new creation called "the gospel." Nor do we see reconciliation between humans called "the gospel." But we do see reconciliation between man and God called "the gospel" precisely because it is the one blessing that leads to all the rest.

Zooming In, Zooming Out

Interestingly, there are a few places where the thought of the New Testament writers seems to move exactly according to this way of understanding the structure of the gospel message. The writers seem to "zoom in and out" quite readily and even within the space of a few words, from the gospel of the kingdom to the gospel of the cross, and vice versa.

Take, for instance, Paul's sermon in Acts 13:26–40. We have already seen above that Paul uses the word *gospel* in that sermon to refer to all the blessings that God gave to the fathers. But it's also instructive to see how, as the sermon progresses, he gradually "zooms in" from the whole grand panoramic of God's promises to the glorious truth that it all begins and finds its foundation in the forgiveness of sins through the death of

Christ. In fact, that's how the sermon ends: "Let it be known to you therefore, brothers, that through this man forgiveness of sins is proclaimed to you, and by him everyone who believes is freed from everything from which you could not be freed by the law of Moses" (vv. 38–39).

Similarly, in Colossians 1:15–23, Paul begins with a glorious hymn about Christ that ends with the declaration that through Jesus, God intends to "reconcile to himself all things, whether on earth or in heaven, making peace by the blood of his cross" (v. 20). But immediately Paul "zooms in" from "all things" to *"you"* (v. 21)! "And you," he says, "who once were alienated and hostile in mind, doing evil deeds, he has now reconciled in his body of flesh by his death." And that happens as they hold fast to "the gospel that [they] heard" (v. 23).[4]

In both these cases, the structure of thought is clear: "the gospel" certainly includes all the great blessings promised by God and foretold by the prophets, but the greatest promise of all—the one on which all the others depend—is the reconciliation of man to God through the forgiveness that comes through the death of Jesus.

A Few Implications

Understanding the structure of the gospel message in this way helps us to avoid a good deal of unnecessary confusion, and it also helps us make progress in answering some important questions about the mission of God's people in this age. Here are a few implications, some of which will lead us into the next chapter on the kingdom:

1. *It is wrong to say that the gospel is the declaration that the kingdom of God has come.* The gospel of the kingdom is the declaration of

---

[4]Also interesting is the thrice-repeated statement in Acts that the apostles "preached the good news about the kingdom of God and the name of Jesus Christ" (Acts 8:12; see also 28:23, 31). Is this another example of the broad good news of the kingdom and the narrow good news of the cross?

110

the kingdom of God *together with the means of entering it.* Remember, Jesus did not preach "the kingdom of God is at hand." He preached, "The kingdom of God is at hand; therefore repent and believe!"

2. *It is wrong to say that the declaration of all the blessings of the kingdom is a dilution of the true gospel.* So long as those blessings of the kingdom are connected properly and essentially to the cross, they are undoubtedly part of the whole good news of Christianity, and the Bible quite readily calls that whole message—kingdom through cross—"the gospel." In other words, so long as the question is, "What is the whole good news of Christianity?" the gospel of the kingdom through the cross is not gospel-plus; it *is* the gospel.

3. *It is wrong to say that the message of forgiveness of sins through the death and resurrection of Jesus is a reduction of the true gospel.* Because the message of forgiveness is the gateway to all the other blessings of the gospel, the Bible quite readily calls the word of the cross "the gospel." In other words, so long as the question is, "What is the message a person must believe to be saved?" the gospel of the cross is not "too small"; it *is* the gospel.[5]

4. *No one is a Christian simply because he or she is living a "kingdom life."* To be a Christian is to have come to the Christ in faith and repentance, trusting him as the only one with power and authority to forgive sins and secure a righteous verdict from God. It is never enough simply to recognize him as a good teacher or a wise rabbi, or to "follow him" as an example of moral, kingdom living. This would be to sell him short. Not only so, but it entirely misses the way into the blessings of the kingdom. If you have not come to the King in repentance and faith—recognizing him as the one who was crucified in your place and now reigns in resurrected

---

[5]Jesus himself very clearly preaches the gospel of the cross (in Mark 10:45, for instance) even if he doesn't explicitly tie the word *gospel* to it in his recorded words. On a more general note, even as we recognize the benefit of word studies, we should not tie our definition of the gospel and our identification of it in the text *too* tightly to occurrences of the word *gospel.* Otherwise, we'd have to say that John almost never talks about it, for he uses the word only once in all his New Testament writings!

life—then you are not a citizen of God's kingdom, and you are not a Christian. The New Testament could not be clearer. The only way into the kingdom is through the blood of the King.

5. *Non-Christians do* not *do "kingdom work."* The phrase "kingdom work" is confusing and nonbiblical and probably should be jettisoned, but even if we grant its use, we should at least be agreed that it cannot be applied to good things that non-Christians do. When a non-Christian does a good deed, it is most certainly good (at a certain level), and it is an instance of God's common, evil-restraining grace on all mankind. It is a singular kindness of God that human beings are not as bad as we could be. But that those good works are "good" is all we can say about them. They are not "kingdom work" because they are not done in the name of the King (see Rom. 14:23b). C. S. Lewis was wrong. You simply can't spend a lifetime serving Tash (or even yourself!) and expect Aslan to be happy about it.[6]

6. Most importantly for our purposes, *all this helps us understand why Jesus finally commissioned the church to bear witness to him and to make disciples.* If it's true that the blessings of the kingdom are finally enjoyed only by those who have come to the King in repentance and faith, then it makes perfect sense for the King to give his people as their ongoing commission the command to herald that fact. And as we've already noted, that is of course exactly what Jesus does: he commands his followers, in his last words on earth before his ascension, to tell the nations how the blessings of the kingdom can be theirs. And his followers do that! The story of the book of Acts rings with the refrain, "And the word of God increased."

That is what the early Christians took to be their mission. As we'll talk about at more length later, they were well aware that it had not been given to them to usher the kingdom of God into being themselves. God would do that without their help. Their commission, rather, was to declare that the kingdom had come,

---

[6]C. S. Lewis, *The Last Battle* (New York: HarperCollins, 2000), 188.

to call the world to enter its blessings, and to declare to them how they could do so. That's why we see, in the book of Acts, the story of the gospel's spread from Jerusalem to Judea, its crossing over to Samaria, and then its breaking the final barrier to penetrate the uttermost parts of the earth—rather than the story of Christians working for the social betterment of Jerusalem and Antioch. Those early Christians understood, as should we, that their commission from their King was to spread far and wide the good news of the kingdom and that the way into it was by coming to the King in repentance and faith. That was the only thing that would usher people into the kingdom and into a life of service to the king.

CHAPTER 5

Kings and Kingdoms

Understanding God's Redemptive Rule

NO ONE TOLD ME much about the kingdom of God when I (Greg) was growing up. The Sunday school classes and the youth group's Wednesday night "Power Hour" at the church were faithful in teaching the gospel and in encouraging Christian discipleship. But the main categories of thought were sin, grace, holiness, ethics, and obedience (all good, of course!). There was nothing much at all about "the kingdom," and when it was mentioned, it was almost always in reference to heaven.

When I went off to college and began studying Christian history, the kingdom became more of a conscious category to me. But even then it was almost exclusively the province and language of theological liberals—both past and present—and therefore it was also almost always accompanied by a certain political agenda having to do with broadened social services or a more robust welfare state.

I remember, though, the first time I realized the New Testament talks *a lot* about the kingdom of God. It's the first thing Jesus preaches (Matt. 4:17), it's a major theme of his preaching throughout his ministry (see, e.g., Matthew 13), and it's also an essential element of the apostles' preaching after Jesus's ascension and the coming of the Holy Spirit (Acts 1:3; 8:12; 19:8; 28:23, 31). That realization threw me for a bit of a loop, because I began to wonder how, in all my years of growing up and being taught in the church, I had missed this apparently enormous theme in the story of the New Testament. So I started to read. And what I read, I started to believe. After all, I didn't have much of anything to use as a foil, so when I saw someone talking about "the kingdom," I just largely swallowed what they had to say about it. The trouble, though, was that much of what I was reading and accepting as true about the kingdom simply wasn't so. In fact, it was shot through with biblical inaccuracies, bad interpretations, overgeneralizations, and overreaching implications. But never having been taught about the kingdom, I had nothing to test those errors against, and so I wound up flirting for a time with a "kingdom theology" that would have been very much at home among late nineteenth-century theological liberals.

I tell that story because more than a few other people, perhaps some reading this book, would tell the same story—an upbringing in which the kingdom of God was seldom mentioned, and only then as a synonym for heaven; a resulting "Aha!" moment when they realized that the Bible actually has a lot to say about this thing; a lingering question as to why they were never taught about it; and a resulting desire to learn more about it. That's a good desire! Over the past decades, there's been something of a renaissance in evangelical thinking about the kingdom. More scholars are turning their attention to it, and more books are being published that take the kingdom of God as their main theme. Some of those books are good resources that look carefully at the Bible's teaching about the kingdom

116

and draw solid conclusions about what the kingdom means for us, today, as Christians.[1] But there are many other books out there about the kingdom that are not so helpful, and they're the ones that most often seem to be hitting the best-seller lists and therefore doing most of the "teaching" about the kingdom of God. Sadly, that means that the kingdom-shaped hole that exists in many people's theological understanding is being filled with some really misleading material. In this chapter, we want to fill in those holes with positive, and hopefully biblical, teaching about the kingdom.

We should acknowledge from the start that both of us are convinced that the best way to understand the Bible's teaching about the kingdom of God is in terms of an "inaugurated eschatology," a position popularized several decades ago by George Eldon Ladd and others. This position holds that God's kingdom has *already* broken into this world but has *not yet* been fully realized.

The Already and Not Yet of the Last Days

Though there is much to discuss within the framework of inaugurated eschatology, evangelicals seem to have come at least to a broad consensus regarding its basic structure and outline.[2]

---

[1]Some classic twentieth-century exegetical studies include G. E. Ladd, *The Gospel of the Kingdom: Scriptural Studies in the Kingdom of God* (Grand Rapids: Eerdmans, 1959); Herman Ridderbos, *The Coming of the Kingdom* (Philadelphia: Presbyterian and Reformed, 1962); G. R. Beasley-Murray, *Jesus and the Kingdom of God* (Grand Rapids: Eerdmans, 1986).
[2]See Russell D. Moore, *The Kingdom of Christ: The New Evangelical Perspective* (Wheaton, IL: Crossway, 2004).

Of course we realize that broad consensus does not mean total consensus, and there are many evangelicals who will disagree with us entirely on this understanding of the kingdom, perhaps most notably some dispensationalists. Though we ultimately disagree with our brothers and sisters on this, we nevertheless recognize the force of many of their arguments, and we hope they will still be able to agree with and resonate with many of the finer points we make here.

What Is the Kingdom of God?

Neither "kingdom of God" nor "kingdom of heaven" is a phrase used in the Old Testament. It is a term unique to the New Testament. The uniqueness of the *term* to the New Testament, though, does not mean that the kingdom of God is a foreign *concept* to the Old Testament. On the contrary, God's kingdom pervades the entire story line of the Old Testament,[3] from God's creation of mankind to rule under him, to his giving of the Law to the nation of Israel, to his charge that Israel had "rejected [the LORD] from being king over them" by requesting a king "like all the nations" (1 Sam. 8:5, 7), to his repeated promises that the kingdom would finally belong to him alone (Obad. 1:21).

The theme of God's kingdom comes to fulfillment in the New Testament, and in a powerful way. Undoubtedly because of its prominence in Jesus's own teaching, kingdom language appears frequently in the New Testament (the word *basileia* occurs over 160 times), and often at very important points of the unfolding story. We've already seen, for example, how "kingdom" forms the major theme of Jesus's early preaching, and we should also note that it is the driving theme of Matthew's opening chapters, as well as Luke's summary of the apostles'

---

[3]Helpful introductions on this are Graeme Goldsworthy, *According to Plan: The Unfolding Revelation of God in the Bible* (Downers Grove, IL: InterVarsity, 2002), and Vaughn Roberts, *God's Big Picture: Tracing the Storyline of the Bible* (Downers Grove, IL: InterVarsity, 2003).

preaching. The final verse of the book of Acts, in fact, tells us that Paul was in Rome, "proclaiming the kingdom of God and teaching about the Lord Jesus Christ with all boldness and without hindrance" (Acts 28:31).

From all this biblical material, there are several things we can say about the nature of the kingdom of God.

The Kingdom of God Is the Redemptive Reign of God over His People

The word *kingdom* in English typically conjures images in our minds of kings and castles and knights and lands with borders that can be expanded and must be defended. Biblically, though, *kingdom* doesn't refer essentially to a piece of land, but rather to "rule" or "reign." Perhaps it's best, in fact, to think of it not in terms of *kingdom* at all, given that word's connotations, but rather as "king*ship*." In other words, kingdom is a *dynamic* or *relational* concept, not a *geographical* one.

Take a look, for example, at Psalm 145, one of the clearest declarations of God's kingdom, or kingship, in the Old Testament. Verse 11 is important in helping us to understand what David means when he talks about God's "kingdom." "All your holy ones shall bless you," David declares.

> They shall speak of the glory of your kingdom
> and tell of your power.

This line is a very good example of a common feature of Hebrew poetry—parallelism. Hebrew poets would often state a thought two or more times but in different words, looking at the same concept from several different angles, like turning a diamond so that the light refracts through it in multiple ways. The benefit of that for us, beyond its wonderful devotional promise, is that it can help us see what the poets meant when they used difficult or obscure terms. Here, the holy ones are said to both "speak of the glory of your kingdom" and "tell of your power."

But actually, those two actions are the same thing. "Kingdom" is parallel to "power."

The same thing is true in verse 13:

Your kingdom is an everlasting kingdom,
  and your dominion endures throughout all generations.

Here again, "kingdom" is parallel to "dominion." When David talks about the kingdom of God, therefore, he is not referring to a land or realm with definable borders. He's not talking finally about geography. Rather, he's talking about the "power" or "dominion" of God. It's a *dynamic* word (about power) and a *relational* word (about human beings' relationship to God their King).

That doesn't mean, of course, that geography is irrelevant to kingdom. On the contrary, God's kingship over his people throughout most of the Bible is exercised in a certain geographical locale. Before the fall, that locale was the garden of Eden. For the nation of Israel, it was Canaan, and for us in eternity it will be the new heavens and new earth. But geography isn't *essential* to kingdom. In fact, one of the most salient points about our lives as Christians in this age is that we are "strangers and exiles on the earth" (Heb. 11:13), "sojourners and exiles" (1 Pet. 2:11). We are, at least for now, a nation without a land and a kingdom without a locale.

Another important point is that the New Testament uses the term "kingdom of God" to refer to God's reign *specifically over his redeemed people*. It's true, of course, that God's rule extends over the entire universe. Nothing and no one is outside or independent from his sovereignty. And yet when Jesus and the apostles talk about the kingdom of God, they are speaking specifically of God's benevolent, redemptive reign over those he has saved. Thus Jesus can talk about those who will and will not enter the kingdom (Mark 10:14, 23–25; Luke 18:17), and even those who will be cast out of the kingdom (Matt. 8:12; Luke 13:28). Paul, too, is quite clear that there are some people who are *in* the kingdom, and others who are *out* of it: "Do you not know that the unrighteous will not inherit the kingdom of God?" (1 Cor. 6:9; see also Gal. 5:21). Paul even teaches that those who trust in Christ are transferred from one kingdom to another—from the "domain of darkness" into the "kingdom of [God's] beloved son" (Col. 1:13). Biblically speaking, therefore, not everyone is a citizen of the kingdom of God.

There are a few important ramifications that flow from understanding the kingdom of God as his redemptive rule. For one thing, understanding that *kingdom* is a dynamic, relational word rather than a geographic one keeps us from thinking that "extending the kingdom of God" is the right way to describe planting trees or delivering hot meals to the homeless. Sometimes people talk as if by renovating a city park or turning a housing slum into affordable, livable apartments, we are extending God's reign over that park or that neighborhood. We're "bringing order from chaos," someone might say, and therefore expanding the kingdom. But as we've seen, the kingdom isn't geographical. Rather, it is defined relationally and dynamically; it exists where knees and hearts bow to the King and submit to him. And therefore you cannot "expand the kingdom" by bringing peace and order and justice to a certain area of the world. Good deeds are good, but they don't broaden the borders of the kingdom. The only way the kingdom of God—the redemptive rule of God—is extended is when he brings another sinner to renounce sin and self-righteousness and bow his knee to King Jesus.

Likewise, it's important to affirm that we cannot extend the redemptive rule of God over non-Christians. Of course we can show the unbelieving world something of what the kingdom is and will be; we can testify and witness to its existence and its character. But because the kingdom is a matter of relationship between the King and his subjects, we cannot extend the kingdom of God over people who will not submit to the King's rule. It is through faith in the King that someone is transferred from the kingdom of darkness into the kingdom of the Son (Col. 1:13). Practically speaking, therefore, we should not talk about our efforts to change social structures as "extending the kingdom," even if they are successful. A non-Christian person may be living in as just and good a society as is realistically imaginable, but the Bible says that until he comes to Christ, he has no part of the kingdom of the Son. He is still captive under the kingdom of darkness—even if relatively comfortably for a while.

The Kingdom of God Is the Reign of the Messiah, Jesus

The kingdom belongs to and is ruled by King Jesus. It is "the kingdom of [God's] beloved Son" (Col. 1:13). Jesus refers to it as "my kingdom" (Luke 22:30; John 18:36; cf. Matt. 20:21; Luke 23:42). The kingdom of God is a mediated kingdom, ruled by the "one mediator between God and men, the man Christ [Messiah!] Jesus" (1 Tim. 2:5).

All this makes perfect sense when we remember the story of the Old Testament. In 2 Samuel 7, God promised the great King David that his throne would be established forever. Over time, as Israel's kings failed again and again, the Lord revealed through the prophets that there would one day come a King who would fulfill all God's promises to his people and establish an eternal kingdom where justice and righteousness would be upheld perfectly forever (Isaiah 9, 11). In Daniel 7:13–14, it even becomes clear that this Messiah would be divine. The phrase "son of man" from that passage is the one that Jesus repeatedly applied to himself, signifying that this vision of kingship being handed to "one like a Son of Man" was fulfilled in him. He is the Son of Man; he is the promised Messiah; all the authority of the kingdom of God—"all authority in heaven and on earth," in fact—has been given to him.

Of course this simple idea that Jesus alone is the promised King keeps us from a host of errors. For one thing, it keeps us from thinking that there are multiple pathways into the kingdom of God. The reality is that there is no end run around Jesus. The redemptive reign of God is exercised solely and completely by Jesus; no one comes to the Father except through him (John 14:6). That means, of course, that no one comes to the Father *directly*, either. A person cannot simply say that he is a "God-believer" or a "God-lover" and think that he is under the kingdom of God. Peter is as clear as he could be: "Let all the house of Israel therefore know for certain that God has made him both Lord and Christ, this Jesus whom you crucified" (Acts 2:36). And for that reason, "there is salvation in no one else, for there is no other name under heaven given among men by which we must be saved" (Acts 4:12). The kingdom of God is the kingdom of Jesus, and the way into the kingdom is through submission to the King.

The Kingdom of God Involves the Age to Come Breaking into the Present Age

The Bible gives us a snapshot of what awaits us at the end. It's not a very detailed picture, but it is a glorious one. Isaiah tells us that God's full and consummated reign will be one under which joy and happiness are never broken, tears are never shed, death and sickness and sin are no more, and there is perfect peace and security, God is all and all, and evil is banished forever (Isa. 65:17–25). Revelation similarly tells us of the New Jerusalem, where God and his people will dwell with one another in harmony, and where "death shall be no more, neither shall there be mourning, nor crying, nor pain anymore, for the former things have passed away." Not only so, but the gates of that city will always stand open because there are no more enemies, the tree of life will once again be available for the healing of the nations, and God's servants will worship him righteously forever (Rev. 21:1–4, 9–27; 22:1–5). All this, of course, is a picture of a reconstituted Eden. Everything is once again as it was before the fall—and even better!—for there will no longer be even the possibility of sin in the redeemed, glorified people of God.

But that, of course, is the end. We are not there yet.

And yet! And yet the New Testament's declaration about the kingdom of God is that in the person of Jesus the King, the glory of that age to come has broken into and invaded the present age. This is what we mean, in fact, by the term "inaugurated eschatology." It is the understanding that the *eschaton*—"the end"—has been *inaugurated*, or begun. We can see this truth dramatically displayed in the life and ministry of Jesus. When he heals sickness and drives out demons, those are—to be sure—signs that verify his claims to be the Son of God, but they are also the King's counteroffensive against the dominion of darkness and the effects of the fall. Even death begins to fail in its iron-fisted dominion over humanity when King Jesus speaks: "Lazarus, come out!" (John 11:43). And the dead man rises.

We see this truth also in the fact that many of the blessings that the Bible ascribes to the age to come are ours, now, in the present age. Joel 2:28–29, for example, prophesies:

> And it shall come to pass afterward,
> that I will pour out my Spirit on all flesh;
> your sons and your daughters shall prophesy,
> your old men shall dream dreams,
> and your young men shall see visions.
> Even on the male and female servants
> in those days I will pour out my Spirit.

In Joel's prophecy, that is clearly a vision of the age to come. The entire prophecy of which those verses are a part begins with the declaration that "The day of the LORD is coming; it is near." And 2:30–31 contain a common description of the day of judgment as well. When Joel says the Spirit will be poured out, he is talking about the age to come. And yet Jesus tells his followers that this blessing of the age to come is theirs now. "You will receive power when the Holy Spirit has come upon you," he says in Acts 1:8, and Peter says that the events of Pentecost are explicitly the fulfillment of Joel's prophecy. The Holy Spirit dwelling in us is a blessing of the age to come, and yet we have that blessing now.

We live in the "overlap of the ages." The present age is not yet over—"I am with you always," Jesus said, "to the end of the age" (Matt. 28:20)—and yet the age to come has begun. We are, in Christ, "new creation"! "The old has passed away; behold, the new has come" (2 Cor. 5:17)! As a result, we live with the tension of being in two "ages" at once, a tension that no Jew ever thought would exist. When the Jews read the prophecies of Isaiah and Joel and Daniel, they expected that there would be a hard break between the present age and the age to come. The one would end, and the other would begin. But in God's wisdom, the coming of the Messiah turned out to be not just one event, but two—his first coming to inaugurate the age to come in the midst of the present age, and his second coming to end, finally, the present age and consummate the age to come. Thus we enjoy the forgiveness of sin even as we struggle with it; thus we enjoy the presence of the Spirit even as we may still grieve him; thus we have been raised with Christ, seated at his right hand in the heavenly places, even as we know we will, for a time, return to dust. And thus we live in a world that is shot through with injustice and sin and oppression and evil and tears and sadness, even a world that we know *will be* shot through with such things until Jesus comes back, even as we strive to "walk as children of light" and to "shine as lights" in a "crooked and twisted generation" (Eph. 5:8; Phil. 2:15).

The Kingdom of God Is Manifested in This Present Age in the Church

There is an old hymn that begins,

I love thy kingdom Lord,
the house of thine abode,
the church our blessed Redeemer saved
with his own precious blood!

It's pretty common seminary humor to make fun of that hymn, chuckling at the naïveté of the author to equate the kingdom of God and the church like that. And of course there's some truth in that thought. Without getting into whether Timothy Dwight really *did* equate the church and the kingdom, it's important to note that biblically speaking you can't do that. The kingdom of God is indeed much more than—and different from—the church. Just try replacing "kingdom" in the New Testament with "church," or "church" with "kingdom," and you quickly realize that synonyms they are not.

However, it's also true that like your rearview mirror says, these two things—the church and the kingdom—are actually "closer than they appear," and closer than we often give them credit for.

Jesus's words in Matthew 16 are hugely important here, for it is in that chapter that he institutes his church "upon this rock" of Peter's confession of faith and then immediately says, "I will give you the keys of the kingdom of heaven, and whatever you bind on earth shall be bound in heaven, and whatever you loose on earth shall be loosed in heaven" (v. 19). "You" refers not to Peter but to the church, as becomes clear in Matthew 18. But still it's an astounding statement. The keys of the kingdom of God—the authority of that kingdom, the right to act in its name—are given in this age, by the King, to the church! It's not to the government, nor to any king or pope or any other ruler, but rather to the church—to this ragtag bunch of argumentative, self-centered, struggling-for-holiness but gloriously *forgiven* sinners—that the keys of the kingdom of God are given. To put it another way, the church acts as a sort of embassy for the government of the King. It is an outpost of the kingdom of God surrounded by the kingdom of darkness. And just as the embassy of a nation is meant, at least in part, to showcase the life of that nation to the surrounding people, so the church is meant to manifest the life of the kingdom of God to the world around it.[4]

Paul writes about this in Ephesians. After saying that in the gospel of Jesus the dividing wall of hostility between Jews and Gentiles is torn down (Eph. 2:14), he makes this extraordinary statement: God intends that "through the church the manifold wisdom of God might now be made known to the rulers and authorities in the heavenly places" (3:10). In other words, the life of reconciliation and love that exists in the church will be a manifestation of God's wisdom to the world. The life of the kingdom of God—a life of poverty of spirit, meekness, mercy, purity, and peace—will be manifested to the world *in the church*. It's not that the church is perfect, or that it showcases the life of the kingdom without flaw. But believe it or not, the church is the primary arena God has chosen to make his redemptive reign over his people visible. It is, as some have said, the initial manifestation of the kingdom of God in this age. And as the world sees and responds to that kingdom life, the church will not only *manifest* the kingdom, but also *bear witness* to it.

Summary

So the kingdom of God then, we may say, is God's redemptive reign, in the person of his Son, Jesus Messiah, which has broken into the present evil age and is now visible in the church. With that understanding, there are a few other questions we should

---

[4]See Jonathan Leeman, *Surprising Offense of the Love of God* (Wheaton, IL: Crossway, 2010).

consider about the New Testament's teaching on the kingdom of God.

The Apostles' Last Question to Jesus

Just before the apostles watched the risen Messiah ascend into heaven, they asked him, "Lord, will you at this time restore the kingdom to Israel?" (Acts 1:6). In other words, is now the time when you establish and consummate the kingdom, bringing it to completion? The answer they received from Jesus must have been most unsatisfying: "It is not for you to know times or seasons that the Father has fixed by his own authority" (v. 7). But of course they *did* know something about how and when the kingdom would be established. The Lord had taught them those things himself.

When Will the Kingdom Be Finally and Fully Established?

We've already seen that with the first coming of Jesus, the kingdom of God was inaugurated. As he preached, "The kingdom of God has come upon you" (Matt. 12:28). But it is also true that the kingdom Jesus inaugurated is not yet consummated; it has not been established in its fullness. That much is clear enough simply by comparing the Bible's snapshots of the consummation with the world around us. This is not a world of perfect justice and righteousness; far from it, in fact. Moreover, the apostles themselves knew that there was more to the kingdom than they had yet received. That was the realization behind their question in Acts 1:6. It was the realization behind the request of James and John's mother to let her boys sit at Jesus's right hand (Matt. 10:21). It was also the realization behind Paul's longing for the resurrection from the dead (1 Corinthians 15) and his declaration that the Holy Spirit is "the guarantee of our inheritance *until we acquire possession of it*" (Eph. 1:14). And it was the hope of that future that lay behind Jesus's teaching that his apostles should ask God to make his kingdom come, to make it so that his will is done as perfectly here on earth as it is in heaven (Matt. 6:10). Clearly there was something the apostles were looking forward to, even as they enjoyed the blessings of the kingdom as it had broken into the present age.

What they looked forward to was the full and final establishment of Jesus's kingdom, and that will happen *only* when King Jesus returns to do it. He told them to expect this.

> Then will appear in heaven the sign of the Son of Man, and then all the tribes of the earth will mourn, and they will see the Son of Man coming on the clouds of heaven with power and great glory. And he will send out his angels with a loud trumpet call, and they will gather his elect from the four winds, from one end of heaven to the other. (Matt. 24:30–31)

Revelation 19–20 make the same point. The final events—the defeat of the nations arrayed against the Lord and his anointed, the defeat of Satan, the creation of the new heavens and the new earth—it all happens when *and only when* King Jesus returns in glory, and not before.

That's important to remember for at least a couple of reasons. For one thing, it protects us from a wrong and ultimately discouraging optimism about just how good we should expect to be able to make this world. Paul tells us in Romans 8 that creation will one day be "set free from its bondage to corruption and obtain the freedom of the glory of the children of God" (v. 21). But he is equally clear that until that day, the creation remains "subjected to futility" and under its bondage to decay (vv. 20–21). We are afraid that many church leaders are doing their people a disservice by leading them to hope too much for the betterment of society in "this present evil age," which still languishes in bondage and futility. Mission statements like "Transform the City and the World" and "Change the City, Change the World" express a commendable desire, but simply go too far beyond what the Bible tells us we should expect to see in the world during this age, before Jesus returns. And the result, we fear, is that over the years, as cities don't become havens of virtue and justice, as poverty persists, as inadequate housing remains, as governments remain susceptible to corruption, Christians will find themselves discouraged and possibly even questioning the goodness or power of God—all because they have their hopes set too high and on the wrong things.

It seems to us that a better, more biblically realistic way to think about the world in this present age is to realize that until Jesus comes back, we will (as he told us, in fact) "always have the poor" with us (Matt. 26:11), and that our societies and civilizations will always be marked by corruption, injustice, and even oppression. Should this make us complacent? By no means! Should we strive and work against those evils? Absolutely! Is all this a reason simply to sit back, throw up our hands, and resolve not to resist evil? Absolutely not! Generosity and social concern, especially toward the poor and vulnerable, as Tim Keller reminds us, "reflects the character of God." Godly living in our world consists "of a broad range of activities, from simple fair and honest dealings with people in daily life, to regular, radically generous giving of your time and resources, to activism that seeks to end particular forms of injustice, violence, and oppression."[5] We should fight against and resist evil in the world with a square-shouldered realization that God does not expect us to be able to make the world perfect, and that those evils will persist until our King comes back to end them.

I (Greg) spent a few years ministering in Washington, DC, and one of the things I noticed there—something that surprised me, in fact—is how often college graduates would come to town

---

[5]Timothy Keller, *Generous Justice: How God's Grace Makes Us Just* (New York: Dutton, 2010), 18.

thinking they were going to change the world, only to spend three or four years banging their heads against the wall of this present evil age, and finally leave town jaded and discouraged and convinced that it was all hopeless. I think a good deal of that discouragement could have been avoided if they had just come into those jobs with a Bible-informed realism about the age we are all living in. Then they could have worked hard to accomplish good in the world, rejoiced when victories were won, and yet not been crushed when it turned out that they could not, in fact, fix the world. That would have given them both the motivation to do good *and* the flinty determination to work even through the strong and persistent opposition of the powers of this world.

Another reason it is important to remember that the kingdom will be established only when Jesus returns is that it fixes our eyes firmly on the King, rather than on what the King brings—the Giver, not just his gifts. Our great hope as Christians is, as the refrain rings out through the Bible, "We will be his people, and he will be our God." As John puts it in Revelation 22:4, "[We] will see his face" once again. That's what we look forward to—not so much the golden streets and pearl gates, or even the world emptied of injustice and oppression. Great and wonderful though these are, ultimately they are not enough. We look forward to seeing our King, face to face. As Christians, we want our eyes to be not so much on the kingdom, as on the kingdom's King.

How Will the Kingdom Be Finally and Fully Established?

If it is true that the kingdom will be fully established only *when* Jesus returns, it is equally true that it will be established *by his hand alone*. Again, the disciples' question in Acts 1:6 is instructive. They are under no illusion that it is now their task to establish the kingdom of God. It has been inaugurated without their help, and they recognize that it will be consummated without their

131

help, too. "Lord, will *you* at this time restore the kingdom to Israel?" they ask. This too they have learned from Jesus himself. Consider the passage from Matthew 24:30–31 again; the Son of Man comes on the clouds of heaven, and it is *he* who sends his angels to gather the elect. Moreover, Isaiah says that it is *God* who will "create new heavens and a new earth" (Isa. 65:17), and Revelation tells us that it is *God* again who "will wipe away every tear from their eyes" (Rev. 21:4). Not only so, but the very next two verses make it clear that it is Jesus and Jesus alone who establishes his kingdom:

> And he who was seated on the throne said, "Behold, I am making all things new." Also he said, "Write this down, for these words are trustworthy and true." And he said to me, "It is done! I am the Alpha and the Omega, the beginning and the end. To the thirsty I will give from the spring of the water of life without payment." (Rev. 21:5–6)

"*I* am making all things new," he says. And then there is the declaration of completion: "It is done!" The fact that this work is his alone redounds to his glory, for he declares in the very next sentence, "I am the Alpha and the Omega, the beginning and the end." Kingdom building is a divine, messianic act, one that is worthy of divine, messianic praise.

When you look at the Gospels and examine the verbs associated with the kingdom, you discover something surprising. Much of our language about the kingdom is a bit off. We often speak of "building the kingdom," "ushering in the kingdom," "establishing the kingdom," or "helping the kingdom grow." But is this really the way the New Testament talks about the kingdom? George Eldon Ladd, the man who put kingdom back on the map for evangelicals, didn't think so.

> The Kingdom can draw near to men (Matt. 3:2; 4:17; Mark 1:15; etc.); it can come (Matt. 6:10; Luke 17:20; etc.), arrive

132

(Matt. 12:28), appear (Luke 19:11), be active (Matt. 11:12). God can give the Kingdom to men (Matt. 21:43; Luke 12:32), but men do not give the Kingdom to one another. Further, God can take the Kingdom away from men (Matt. 21:43), but men do not take it away from one another, although they can prevent others from entering it. Men can enter the Kingdom (Matt. 5:20; 7:21; Mark 9:47; 10:23; etc.), but they are never said to erect it or to build it. Men can receive the Kingdom (Mark 10:15; Luke 18:17), inherit it (Matt. 25:34), and possess it (Matt. 5:4), but they are never said to establish it. Men can reject the Kingdom, i.e., refuse to receive it (Luke 10:11) or enter it (Matt. 23:13), but they cannot destroy it. They can look for it (Luke 23:51), pray for its coming (Matt. 6:10), and seek it (Matt. 6:33; Luke 12:31), but they cannot bring it. Men may be in the Kingdom (Matt. 5:19; 8:11; Luke 13:29; etc.), but we are not told that the Kingdom grows. Men can do things for the sake of the Kingdom (Matt. 19:12; Luke 18:29), but they are not said to act upon the Kingdom itself. Men can preach the Kingdom (Matt. 10:7; Luke 10:9), but only God can give it to men (Luke 12:32).[6]

We've quoted this section in our works. But when we've used it in the past, we've been uncomfortable with the line "we are not told that the kingdom grows." It seemed to us that the parable of the sleepy farmer (Mark 4:26–29) and the parable of the mustard seed (4:30–32) clearly teach that the kingdom grows. But as we've studied the passages more carefully, we think you can make a good case that Jesus is not teaching about the growth of the kingdom as much as he is demonstrating that the kingdom of small beginnings will, at the close of the age, be the kingdom of cosmic significance. The kingdom may look unimpressive now, with nothing but a twelve-man band of fumbling disciples, but one day all will see its glorious end.

---

[6]George Eldon Ladd, *The Presence of the Future* (Grand Rapids: Eerdmans, 1996), 193. For an exegetical explanation of this paragraph see George Eldon Ladd, *A Theology of the New Testament*, rev. ed. (Grand Rapids: Eerdmans, 1993), 89–102.

To borrow a tired cliché, the kingdom is what it is. It does not expand. It does not increase. It does not grow. But the kingdom can break in more and more. Think of it like the sun. When the clouds part on a cloudy day we don't say, "The sun has grown." We say, "The sun has broken through." Our view of the sun has changed or obstacles to the sun have been removed, but we have not changed the sun. The sun does not depend on us. We do not bring the sun or act upon it. The sun can appear. Its warmth can be felt or stifled. But the sun does not grow. (Science guys, don't get all technical, you know what we mean.) This seems a good analogy for the kingdom.

God certainly uses means and employs us in his work. But we are not makers or bringers of the kingdom. The kingdom can be received by more and more people but this does not entail *growth* of the kingdom. We herald the kingdom and live according to its rules. But we do not build it or cause it to grow because it already *is* and already has come. As Ladd put it:

> The Kingdom is the outworking of the divine will; it is the act of God himself. It is related to human beings and can work in and through them; but it never becomes subject to them. . . . The ground of the demand that they receive the Kingdom rests in the fact that in Jesus the Kingdom has come into history.[7]

The point is that, biblically speaking, we as human beings may proclaim, enter, reject, inherit, and possess the kingdom, but it is God and God alone who establishes and ushers it in. It is God who will reconcile all things to himself through Christ (Col. 1:19–20). We should not think these verses from Colossians tell us what to do in partnership with God. Rather, they speak of the cosmic scope of what God himself will accomplish through the cross. Through and through, this final consummation is God's work and for God's glory.

---

[7]Ibid., 102.

How Do You Get into the Kingdom?

If the kingdom of God is all it's cracked up to be in Scripture—God's benevolent, joy-filled, happy reign over his redeemed people—and if it's true that you can be either *in* or *out* of that kingdom, then it's hugely important to be clear about how one gets *in* it. We've already seen how the kingdom is specifically the reign of Jesus the Messiah, and that leads us to a simple answer to our question: *Inclusion in the kingdom of God is wholly conditioned on one's response to the King.*

It is not based on a life well lived, or a comparatively nonevil life next to the worst person you can think of. If you want to be included in the kingdom of God, you must respond rightly to the King of the kingdom. That is the consistent message of both Jesus and the apostles. Thus in Mark 10, when the rich young ruler asks what he must do to inherit eternal life—which Jesus later equates to "enter[ing] the kingdom of God" (v. 24)—Jesus's answer to him is, "Follow me" (v. 21). Yes, he tells him first to sell everything he owns and give to the poor, but the point is neither the selling nor the poor. The point is the man's idolatry, and Jesus calls him to renounce the idol of his possessions and cast his faith and his life on him. The same is true of the story of the sheep and the goats in Matthew 25. The dividing line between those who are welcomed into the kingdom and those who are told to depart is how they respond to Jesus and his message in the person of his "brothers," those bearing witness to him. The apostles, too, consistently teach that salvation—inclusion in the kingdom of God—is to be had by responding rightly to the King. "If you confess with your mouth that Jesus is Lord," Paul says, "and believe in your heart that God raised him from the dead, you will be saved" (Rom. 10:9). "Let it be known to you therefore, brothers, that through this man forgiveness of sins is proclaimed to you," he preaches in Acts 13:38, and Peter proclaims in Acts 2 that "God has made him both Lord and Christ" and that the way to be saved is to "repent and be baptized every one of you in the name of Jesus Christ for the forgiveness of your sins" (vv. 36, 38). Time and time again, both Jesus and the apostles make clear that forgiveness of sins, redemption, and inclusion in God's kingdom are predicated on a person coming in repentance and faith to Jesus as the only one who has both right and power to qualify anyone to share in the inheritance of the saints.

The Suffering King

The whole story of the Bible, in fact, drives toward that conclusion. Israel's prophets always understood that the Messiah they prophesied would be not only great and powerful and honored; he would also be a *representative* of God's people and *suffer* in their place. Isaiah, for example, has a wonderfully profound play on words in his description of the Servant, whom we know from several parallel passages turns out to be the promised Messiah. At first glance, it looks as if the Servant might *be* the nation of Israel. So in Isaiah 49:3, the Servant says,

> And he said to me, "You are my servant,
> Israel, in whom I will be glorified."

But then in 49:5, it's clear that the Messiah-Servant's mission is *to* the nation of Israel:

> And now the LORD says,
> he who formed me from the womb to be his servant,
> to bring Jacob back to him;
> and that Israel might be gathered to him . . .

So what's going on here? *Is* the servant Israel, or is the servant doing something *for* Israel? The answer, it seems, is both. What seems to be happening is that the Servant is at once *representing* Israel and fulfilling a mission *to* Israel.

136

Further, Isaiah goes on in chapter 53 to show how this representation reaches its height when the Servant stands in his people's place even unto death for their sins:

> Surely he has borne our griefs
>> and carried our sorrows;
> yet we esteemed him stricken,
>> smitten by God, and afflicted.
> But he was wounded for our transgressions;
>> he was crushed for our iniquities;
> upon him was the chastisement that brought us peace,
>> and with his stripes we are healed.
> All we like sheep have gone astray;
>> we have turned—every one—to his own way;
> and the LORD has laid on him
>> the iniquity of us all. (vv. 4–6)

You can see the representative suffering throughout those verses.

> He was wounded *for our transgressions*;
> he was crushed *for our iniquities*.

Indeed, to suffer and die for the people lay at the very heart of the office of the Messiah.

If that's true, then it's no wonder that the passion narratives in the Gospels are so laden with kingly imagery! We normally think of the death of Christ being connected most closely with his office as Priest, and the book of Hebrews tells us that is absolutely correct. But it's also true that his death is inherently and tightly connected to his kingship. The purple robe, the crown of thorns, the sign above his head—Jesus died *as King*, not just as Priest. What this means is that any talk about Jesus as King is wholly inadequate if it does not have at its very heart an understanding of his representative, substitutionary death in the place of his people. That, in fact, is what it *meant* to be the Messiah; it was, according to the prophets, what the Messiah would do. Yes, he would inaugurate a kingdom, and he would rule over it with wisdom and justice. But he would also bear his people's sins. The Lord would lay on him his people's iniquities, and he would be wounded for their transgressions and crushed for their rebellion. And in that way precisely, he would win forgiveness for their and make them worthy to be included in his great kingdom! Jesus is not just King; he is suffering King. Not just King Jesus the Great, but King Jesus the Crucified and Resurrected!

Understand that, and it becomes blindingly clear why inclusion in the kingdom is conditioned on one's response to the King. For it is the King alone who has—by virtue of his substitutionary death and his resurrection—the authority to forgive sins, declare righteous, and make a sinful human being worthy to share in the blessings of his kingdom. The King has come to his subjects who have rebelled against him, he has pronounced the sentence of death against them, and yet—hope of hopes!—he now holds out an offer of forgiveness, having received the sentence of death upon himself. How then could any rebel expect reprieve or acquittal to be granted any other way than through trusting in the King and accepting the offer from his hand? What foolishness for him to say, "Yes, I want your forgiveness, but not on the terms you offer!" If forgiveness and reprieve are to be had, they must be had from the King's own merciful hand.

It also becomes blindingly clear, once again, why the primary task of Christians in this age, with reference to the kingdom, is not to build it or establish it or even to build for it, but rather to be witnesses to this representing, suffering, forgiving King. You can see this logic in Matthew 28:18–20. If it's true that all authority in heaven and on earth has been given to Jesus—the authority to judge, to forgive, to bring into the kingdom, and to exclude from it—then all the nations must be told of that reality and called to come to him as King and Savior. "Tell the nations about me," Jesus seems to be saying. "All authority is mine; now tell them to follow me!"

You see, the disciples were not simply to sit and enjoy the fact that all authority now belonged to King Jesus; they were to go and proclaim that fact to a dark world that had no idea of that reality. They were to "witness"—not build, not establish, not usher in, not even build for the kingdom—but *bear witness* to it. They were to be subjects and heralds, not agents, of the kingdom.

CHAPTER 6

Making Sense of Social Justice

Exposition

A FEW YEARS AGO, I (Kevin) was a chaplain for a week at a Christian camp. This camp was like most Christian camps, replete with horses, ropes courses, a climbing wall, scores of rambunctious kids, and a troop of eager college-aged counselors. My job as chaplain was to lead a few services and try to encourage the campers and counselors. What I saw in the counselors surprised me.

I distinctly remember having a conversation with one college-aged leader and thinking, "This is the beginning of something different." Though this was a pretty conservative camp that would draw from pretty conservative churches and hire your run-of-the-mill conservative college kids, I had the sense that this student represented a shift already underway in younger evangelicals. He was reading Jim Wallis's *God's Politics*. He was sick of George W. Bush. He was passionate about social justice. This student was thoughtful, fed up with what he perceived to

141

be do-nothing Christianity, and zealous to make a difference in the world.

Since then we (Kevin and Greg) have spoken at different venues across the country, usually to youngish Christians. From our anecdotal evidence we've found no issue more debated, especially on Christian college campuses and among well-educated twenty- and thirtysomethings, than social justice. Younger evangelicals are more concerned about the poor, about digging wells, about sex trafficking, about orphans than at any other time in recent memory. Social justice is hot and is bound to stay that way for some time. One prominent scholar has gone so far as to claim that a renewed interest in social justice, or what he prefers to call a missional or holistic gospel, represents the biggest shift in evangelicalism in the last century.[1]

What Does the Bible Say about Social Justice and the Poor?

But with all the buzz and energy surrounding social justice, there have been few efforts to look at actual texts. Little time has been spent walking through the main "social justice" passages to see what they really say. Well, at the risk of being tedious, we want to do just that. This chapter will include some application along the way, but the meat will be straight-up exegesis. If you want to know what it all means, we'll get to that in the next chapter where we synthesize our findings with a series of concluding thoughts and summary statements. But right now, we're going to work our way through twelve common "social justice" texts.

You'll notice that we point out many of the same themes, same sins, and same misunderstandings in text after text. Our approach may border on being redundant, but we think it is important to go through many texts instead of few so you can see that we are not trying to be selective in our reading and so you'll get a broader view of what the Bible says about justice.

---

[1]Scot McKnight, "Jesus Creed" blog, January 29, 2010, http://blog.beliefnet.com/jesuscreed/2010/01/20th-centurys-biggest-change-i.html.

Since many of the passages we expound are whole chapters or large sections, we have not included the Scripture text to which we are referring. We strongly encourage you to work through this chapter with a Bible open.

Leviticus 19:9-18: Love Your Neighbor as Yourself

Leviticus 19 is not the most famous social justice passage, but it is representative of many similar texts. So we'll start here and spend a fair amount of time on this one.

The climax to this passage and its overarching theme is found in the last half of verse 18: "You shall love your neighbor as yourself." As most Christians know, Jesus refers to this as the second great commandment (Matt. 22:39; Mark 12:31). Paul and James also see the command as paradigmatic for the rest of the law (Rom. 13:9; Gal. 5:14; James 2:8). Love, according to the New Testament, is what we should show to the poor and to everyone else. Leviticus 19 is a terrific passage because the love here is so concrete. This passage is not flowery. It doesn't soar to the heavens. People aren't writing songs about it and playing it at weddings. It is plain and practical. We've all heard that you ought to love your neighbor as yourself. Probably 95 percent of the people in this country agree that loving our neighbor is a good idea. But what does it look like? How do we do it? Verses 9–18 show us how.

This passage applies love to five different areas of life, marked off into five sections by the concluding phrase "I am the LORD" (vv. 9–10, 11–12, 13–14, 15–16, 17–18). You might think of these verses as giving five love languages that every Christian must speak. We must love with our possessions, by our words, in our actions, by our judgments, and with our attitudes.

Loving Others with Our Possessions (vv. 9–10)

Leviticus 19:9–10 quickly summarizes the concept of gleaning—leaving some of your harvest remaining in the fields (or on the vines) so that the poor and the sojourner could gather what is left over. As many people have pointed out, the genius of gleaning is that it required not only generosity on the part of the landowner but also industry on the part of the poor. This isn't a handout (though there is a place for that too), but an opportunity to work to eat.

Still, we would be wrong to make the gleaning laws nothing but a moral lesson on personal responsibility. The main lesson to be learned is that God's people are to be generous. The principle for us is this: We must deliberately plan our financial lives so that we have extra left over to give to those in need. Don't reap to the edge of your fields. And don't spend all your money on yourself. Think of those who have less than you, and let some of your wealth slip through your fingers. In other words, don't be stingy. Don't get every last grape off the vine for yourself. Let others benefit from your harvests. As Paul puts it in the New Testament, we should work hard so that we "may have something to share with anyone in need" (Eph. 4:28).

Loving Others with Our Words (vv. 11–12)

To love is to tell the truth. We see here two contexts where honesty is paramount and sometimes in short supply: in business and in the courts. The first command here is to not steal. But the context suggests that the stealing is taking place by lying, people dealing falsely with each other, as in a business setting. By contrast, God's people love others by telling the truth in their transactions. No cheating scales, weights, or measurements (vv. 35–36).

The second scene is in the courtroom. Especially in a day without surveillance cameras or DNA testing or tape recording, everything depended on witnesses. That's why bearing false witness is such a serious crime in the Bible. Someone's life could literally be ruined by a simple lie. Love—whether for our neighbors or for our enemies—demands that we are careful with our words.

144

Loving Others by Our Actions (vv. 13–14)

Verse 13 gives the classic and most common example of oppression in the Bible: not giving the agreed-upon wage at the agreed-upon time. Oppression was not the same as inequality. Oppression occurred when day laborers were hired to work in the fields for the day, and at the end of the day the landowner stiffed them of their wages. This was a serious offense to their neighbor and before God, not least of all because the day's payment was often literally one's daily bread. People depended on this payment to survive.

It was all too easy to cheat workers out of their wages. You could say you didn't have anything to give. Or you could argue that the work was shabbily done. Or you could simply refuse to pay today, or ever. If the matter was simply one man's word against another's, there was little a worker could do to get justice, especially on *that* day, when what the worker needed was food to eat, not a legal process.

This is exactly the oppression referred to in James 5:1–6. The rich, James says, were living in self-indulgent luxury. These were not the sorts of riches that they plowed back into the company in order to hire more workers. These riches were the ill-gotten kind. The rich had kept back by fraud the wages of the laborers. The injustice James rails against was not because of a relatively low wage or because there was a disparity between rich and poor. The injustice was that the rich had hired help for the harvest, but refused to pay them (v. 4).

The broader principle in these two verses from Leviticus is that God's people must not take advantage of the weak. Don't curse the deaf, even if they can't hear you. Don't put a stumbling block before the blind, even if they won't know who did it. God knows. If others don't know the language in your country, or don't understand the system, or don't have the connections, they should elicit our compassion and generosity, not our desire to make a buck at their expense.

145

Loving Others in Our Judgments (vv. 15–16)

Leviticus 19:15 is an important verse for establishing the fact that justice in the Bible, at least as far as the courtroom is concerned (but beyond the courtroom too, we think), is a fair process, not an equal outcome. "You shall do no injustice in court. You shall not be partial to the poor or defer to the great, but in righteousness shall you judge your neighbor." Again, this does not mean we don't care when people have less than we do. This doesn't mean we should be indifferent to the disadvantages many people have in life through no fault of their own. But it means that justice strives to apply the law equally. In the context of a courtroom, judges should judge without partiality—either for the rich or for the poor.

Imagine two men from your church have a dispute. A poor man from the church has done some work at a rich man's house. The poor man says he was told he would get $10,000 for the job. The rich man claims he offered $10,000 only if the work was done by a certain date; otherwise it would be $5,000. Now the elders have to decide the case. What do you do? Should the worker get $5,000 or $10,000? What is justice here? According to verse 15, justice means rendering the just verdict. You cannot defer to the great because he will give more to the church if you side with him or because he is more influential in the community. And you can't in this instance show partiality to the poor man because he could really use the money and the rich man has more than his "fair share" anyway. Justice is always on the side of the truth, and one of the two men is not telling the truth. Charity and generosity and good stewardship are certainly called for in life. But here justice means doing what is fair, not making outcomes the way we think they should be.

Our contention is that social justice in the Bible is not an achieved result but equal treatment and a fair process. No bribes. No backroom deals. No slanderous judgments. No breaking your promises. No taking advantage of the weak. That's what the Bible means by social justice.[2] Ideally, justice is blind. That's why Lady Justice on our courthouses has her eyes covered. That's why the US Supreme Court building has inscribed on it the words "Equal Justice Under Law." Justice means there should be one standard, one law, for anyone and everyone, not different rules for different kinds of people.

Loving Others in Our Attitude (vv. 17–18)

Love is concrete, but it is also affective. "You shall not hate your brother in your heart." It's not enough to be polite on the outside and full of rage on the inside. If we are angry with our brother we should "reason frankly" with him and try to work things out. The bottom line is that you are to love as you would want to be loved (as Jesus expressed in the Golden Rule, Matt. 7:12; Luke 6:31). We are responsible not just to treat our neighbors rightly, but to take the necessary steps so that our hearts can feel rightly toward them as well.

So in the end this great commandment to love your neighbor as yourself—this commandment quoted in the New Testament more than any other—boils down to five very elementary, everyday, ordinary commands: share, tell the truth, don't take advantage of the weak, be fair, talk it out. Simpler than you might think. But still easier said than done.

Leviticus 25: The Year of Jubilee

Our next text outlines the arrangements for the famous Year of Jubilee. This is a favorite for champions of "social justice," but what the text says may be different than many imagine.

The Year of Jubilee (which probably never took place) was supposed to occur in Israel every fifty years. The celebration had two components to it: a return to the original land allotments, and freedom from servitude.

---

[2]We'll discuss the origin and meaning of this term in more depth in the next chapter.

The First Component Dealt with Land

Leviticus 25 looked forward to the time when Israel would inherit the Promised Land and receive tribal inheritances from God (see Joshua 13ff.). Over time, some people would inevitably be forced to sell some of their land. Whether that was because of death, locusts, bad weather, thieves, poor management, or laziness—no matter what precipitated selling off their land—every family would get its original allotment back during the Year of Jubilee. The poor would get relief; the rich would lose some of the land they had purchased.

Prior to the Jubilee, you could get your land back by paying the redemption price. This price of sale and the price of redemption were both calculated based on how many years remained until the next Jubilee. So in essence you could never really sell or purchase land, only lend or rent it. The original owner had the right to buy back the land at any time. So the sentence at the end of the last paragraph is not exactly accurate. The rich would not lose their land so much as the lease would run out on the land they were renting from their poorer neighbors.

There were other miscellaneous laws concerning walled cities, unwalled villages, and Levitical properties, but the basic principle for Jubilee was pretty straightforward: (1) land could be sold/leased for a price based on the number of years until the Jubilee; (2) land could be purchased back at any time according to the same principle; (3) after fifty years all land titles went back to their original holders.

The Second Component in the Jubilee Dealt with People

There's a progression going on here. If you were in financial trouble, you could sell/lease some land to your nearest relative. If that wasn't an option, you could sell/lease some land to a nonrelative. If that didn't work, or you ran out of land altogether, then you went to the next step: get an interest-free loan (i.e., a loan of subsistence, not a loan of capital), which would be forgiven every seven years. If a loan didn't fix things, you could sell yourself to another Israelite. In a worst-case scenario, you could sell yourself to a stranger or sojourner living among you. In both of these sell-yourself cases, you could be redeemed by a family member or by yourself at any time. The purchase price was calculated based on the number of years until the Jubilee. If there were more years until the Jubilee, you had to pay more for your freedom; if there were fewer years, you paid less. And if you were still a slave at the Jubilee—an Israelite slave, that is, not a foreign slave—you would automatically be released.

A Call for Caution

We've simplified things quite a bit, but this is the general outline for the Jubilee provisions. Knowing that the Year of Jubilee provided for the release of slaves and the reallocation of property, many Christians equate the Year of Jubilee with forced redistribution programs. But advocating such an approach based on Leviticus 25 runs into a lot of problems.

1. *We are not an ancient, agrarian society.* Most of us don't deal with land and farming. None of us deals with slaves or indentured servants or walled cities. More to the point, land is not our chief source of capital. Some of the richest people in the country may live in a penthouse in Manhattan and own very little land, while a farmer in South Dakota might have thousands of acres and a lower standard of living. So freeing slaves and returning land to its original owners just isn't the world most of us live in.

2. Most importantly, *our property has not been assigned directly by God.* This is the real bugaboo for trying to apply the Year of Jubilee directly. What is "year one" for landholders? Last year? 1776? 1492? The Year of Jubilee makes sense only when it is seen in the context of the Holy Land. Canaan was God's gift to Israel. He wanted his people to have it. He wanted the original tribes and

clans to keep their original inheritance. True, the Year of Jubilee was about helping the poor, but it was also about the perpetuity of the original land allotments. The whole thing holds together because God had assigned specific properties to specific tribes (and not in equal amounts either). The ownership of the land had been defined by God himself. That's why it could not truly be sold, but only leased.

3. *Our economy is not based on a fixed piece of land.* Consequently, the pie of wealth is not fixed either. In Israel (like most places in the ancient world), if someone got rich, it was probably because someone else had gotten poorer. The rich got rich because the poor got poor. Or, at the very least, the poor getting poor enabled the rich to get richer. If you squandered your money or lost it, you would have no choice but to sell your land or yourself. Bad break for you, good break for someone else. Prosperity, for the most part, was a zero-sum game.

But in a modern economy, wealth can be created. This isn't to say the rich never exploit the poor. That happens too. But in a capitalist economy, the rich can get richer while the poor also get richer. This is, in fact, what has happened in virtually every country over the last two centuries. Almost across the board, people live longer and have more, even if many people do not have anywhere near as much as people in the industrialized world enjoy.

4. *Modern nations are not under the Mosaic covenant.* We aren't promised miraculous harvests in the sixth year. The blessings and curses for the covenant people in Leviticus 26 don't make sense in our context, and don't directly apply to America or any other nation.

5. *Most of us are not Jews.* If you read the Jubilee laws carefully, you'll notice that they distinguish sharply between Israelites and foreigners. The Year of Jubilee was good news for the Israelite, but didn't do anything to help the non-Israelite. In fact, if a stranger lived among the Israelites and acquired

land, he would lose it all at the Jubilee and have no land in Israel to return to. If a foreigner was made a slave, he wasn't released. But if he had a Hebrew slave, he had to release him and his family. So if we want to make the Year of Jubilee our model for justice, how would we apply this distinction? Between legal citizens and nonlegal residents? Between people from our country and people from outside our country? Between Christians and non-Christians?

We're not saying the Year of Jubilee was unjust—only that its aim was something other than "social justice" in the way people often use the phrase today. The Year of Jubilee was about keeping the Israelites free and in the specific land allotments God gave them. Certainly an important part of Jubilee was the alleviation of poverty and God's care for his people. But if you weren't part of God's people, it didn't do much to help you.

Now What?

We mention the five points above to caution us from applying the Year of Jubilee in a feel-good way that doesn't do justice (ironically) to the text. But none of this is to say that Jubilee has no ramifications for how we look at wealth and poverty. There are several applications.

1. *We do well when we give opportunities for the poor to succeed.* Of course, we should not be ruthless to the poor. We should not take advantage of the weak. But more than that, we should look for ways to give them a fresh start.

The great thing about these Jubilee laws is that they didn't just give a lump sum of cash to poor people (though that can be called for in some situations). Jubilee did something better. It gave the poor opportunities. It gave them access to capital (i.e., land). It granted them new freedoms. It was intelligent assistance. Not everyone should be given a handout, but everyone needs the opportunities that make economic self-sufficiency

151

possible. The Year of Jubilee didn't do for people what they needed to do themselves. But it gave the poor tribes, clans, and families another opportunity, by God's grace, to make something of themselves.

2. *The Bible supports the existence of private property.* The land in Israel was owned not by the state, but by individuals, families, clans, and tribes. In fact, the property rights were guaranteed to the original landowners in perpetuity by God himself. The permanence of the landholding served as an encouragement to cultivation, development, and initiative. This was their land and they had the right to earn a living by it. There are few factors more crucial to economic prosperity than the right of personal property and a strong rule of law to protect this right.[3]

3. *The Bible relativizes private property.* The right to own property was not absolute, but derivative. The true owner of all land was God (see Lev. 25:23). "The earth is the LORD's and the fullness thereof" (Ps. 24:1). Jubilee reminded the people that they weren't going to get the big prize in this life. The Israelites had to give back newly acquired land every fifty years. We have to give everything back every seventy or eighty years (Ps. 90:10). Private property is not what we ought to be living for.

4. *Our God is the God of second chances.* A text like this might be used to support modern bankruptcy laws and prisoner rehabilitation. It would certainly support the existence of a social safety net—by the state some might argue, but certainly within the family and the covenant community. Jubilee intended to give at least some people a chance at a fresh start, and it's good to provide the same chance for the poor and disadvantaged in our day. In the New Testament, this theme gets transposed to a spiritual key, teaching us that we should be willing to

---

[3]See Hernando DeSoto, *The Mystery of Capital: Why Capitalism Triumphs in the West and Fails Everywhere Else* (New York: Basic Books, 2003), for a detailed discussion of this idea.

forgive and release others from their spiritual debts against us (Matt. 18:21–35).

5. *Jesus is Jubilee.* When Jesus read from the Isaiah scroll in Luke 4, his simple message was, in effect, "I am Jubilee." He did not lay out a plan to accomplish social reform. Instead he stated matter-of-factly, "*Today* this Scripture has been fulfilled in your hearing" (Luke 4:21). All that Jubilee pointed to and more were realized at the revealing of Jesus in Nazareth. The best news of Leviticus 25 found its fullest expression in the good news of Jesus Christ.[4]

Isaiah 1: Confronting the Sin of God's People Judah

The first chapter of Isaiah begins with the Lord's stinging rebuke of Judah and Jerusalem (v. 1). They are rebellious children (v. 2), lacking in understanding (v. 3). Judah is a "sinful nation, a people laden with iniquity" (v. 4). Because of their rebellion, God's people have been struck down, bruised, bloodied, and besieged (vv. 5–8). Of course, God offers the hope of forgiveness and cleansing (v. 10), but the dominant theme in the chapter is one of disappointment. God's people have been wicked.

How so?

Well, their failure was not for lack of religious observance. They were meeting together for worship and keeping the festivals of the Lord. But the Lord was not impressed. He could no longer endure their iniquity and solemn assembly (v. 13). He had come to hate their feasts and was burdened with their perfunctory obedience (v. 14). The Lord would not even listen to their prayers (v. 15).

Their problem was one that recurs often in prophetic literature: they were getting the details of religion right but not the heart of it. Outside of "church" the Israelites were doing evil,

---

[4]For more on Luke 4, see the discussions above in chapters 2 and 4.

not good (vv. 16–17). In particular, they were guilty of injustice toward the fatherless and the widow, the basic categories in the Bible for the helpless and vulnerable (v. 17).

What was the injustice?

> Your princes are rebels
>   and companions of thieves.
> Everyone loves a bribe
>   and runs after gifts.
> They do not bring justice to the fatherless,
>   and the widow's cause does not come to them. (v. 23)

The Lord was angry with his people because the leaders were oppressing the weak, taking bribes to side with the rich and powerful instead of treating fairly the orphan and the widow.

We'll see this in other passages, too, but Isaiah 1 is a great example of the Bible saying both more and less about social justice than we think.

On the "more" side, we see that Jerusalem is called a "whore" because of her injustice (v. 21). Oppressing the poor and the helpless is not a negligible offense. In fact, it renders all their religious obedience null and void. Until they would "seek justice" and "correct oppression," God promises that Judah would be "eaten by the sword" (vv. 17, 20).

But on the "less" side, notice that the oppression here was not a disparity between rich and poor or even that the poor in society were not taken care of. There are other biblical passages that require the covenant community to take care of the poor in their midst (which is not identical to taking care of the poor in the entire "mixed" society), but this passage is about oppression, a term not to be equated with poverty.

The injustice was not that there were poor people in society. Poverty does not inherently indicate injustice. God's people were guilty of injustice because they were defrauding the weak and helpless in order to line their own pockets. Specifically,

God was angry with the kings because "in the ancient Near East, the concerns for justice, oppression, and the helpless were the special province of the king."[5] Justice called for Judah's king (and any other pertinent officials) to stop taking bribes and start defending the just cause of the helpless instead of cheating them. The prophetic rebuke of Isaiah 1 belongs on the men and women guilty of these crimes.

Isaiah 58: God Calls His People to Righteous Responsibility More Than Religious Rituals

Isaiah 58 is the more famous cousin of Isaiah 1, but they both deal with the same theme: God is not impressed with fastidious religious observance when the daily lives of his people are filled with wickedness. God says, in effect, "Your fasting and sackcloth are meaningless to me so long as you continue in rank disobedience to more important commands."

How were the Israelites sinful? They oppressed their workers, which usually meant defrauding them of agreed-upon wages (v. 3; James 5:4). They quarreled and "hit with a wicked fist" (Isa. 58:4). They conducted business and sought their own pleasure on the Sabbath (v. 13).

What should God's people have done? They should have loosed the bonds of injustice and let the oppressed go free (v. 6). They should have shared bread with the hungry, clothed the naked, and welcomed in the homeless poor (v. 7). God promised "your light [shall] break forth like the dawn and your healing shall spring up speedily," but only when the Israelites acted righteously and poured themselves out for the hungry and the afflicted (vv. 8–10).

Clearly, caring for the poor, the hungry, the afflicted is not just a liberal thing to do. It is a *biblical thing to do*. We must allow this uncomfortable chapter to discomfort us a bit. Those of us

---

[5]John Oswalt, *The Book of Isaiah: Chapters 1–39*, The New International Commentary on the Old Testament (Grand Rapids: Eerdmans, 1986), 99.

in conservative circles can get all sorts of religious ritual right, but it counts for nothing and less than nothing if we do not love our neighbors as ourselves.

Calvin summarizes:

> Uprightness and righteousness are divided into two parts; first, that we should injure nobody; and secondly, that we should bestow our wealth and abundance on the poor and needy. And these two ought to be joined together; for it is not enough to abstain from acts of injustice, if thou refuse thy assistance to the needy; nor will it be of much avail to render thine aid to the needy, if at the same time thou rob some of that which thou bestowest on others. . . . These two parts, therefore, must be held together, provided only that we have our love of our neighbour approved and accepted by God.[6]

The implications of Isaiah 58 are straightforward: God's people should hate oppression and love to help the poor.

Jeremiah 22: Do Justice and Righteousness

The basic command of Jeremiah 22 is given in verse 3: "Do justice and righteousness." God's people (technically the kings in this verse) are commanded to do justice. We cannot obey God and ignore the divine call to justice. In fact, the Lord told the kings of Judah that judging the cause of the poor and needy (rightly) *is* to know him (vv. 15–16). It didn't matter their titles, their wealth, or their religious observance; if the kings oppressed the poor instead of treating them fairly and mercifully, they proved their own ignorance of God. And if they continued in such flagrant disobedience, the kings and their kingdom would be wiped away (vv. 24–30).

So doing justice is hugely important. But what does it mean? Thankfully, Jeremiah 22 gives us some answers.

---

[6]John Calvin, *Calvin's Commentaries*, vol. 8, *Isaiah 33–66* (Grand Rapids: Baker, 1998), 233.

Jeremiah 21 and 22 were not addressed to anyone and everyone (though the chapters apply in various ways to all). These were words directly for the kings of Judah (21:3; 22:1, 11, 18). Ancient kings had tremendous power to do good or evil. To put it anachronistically, they wielded, all by themselves, executive, legislative, and judicial authority. They tried cases, made decrees, and enforced laws, just or unjust.

Tragically, in the waning years of Judah's sovereignty, the kings acted unjustly on all three accounts. Their one overarching vice, what Phil Ryken calls "luxury by tyranny,"[7] took many forms:

- The kings did not defend the oppressed against their oppressors (22:3a).
- They wronged the weak, even to the point of murder, shedding innocent blood for dishonest gain (vv. 3b, 17).
- They built their lavish houses by unrighteousness. This was not an instance of the rich getting richer as the poor also got richer. These kings, in an effort to live like the opulent kings of the other nations, conscripted forced labor and cheated the workers of their wages (vv. 13–16). They lived in luxury on the backs of the poor. The rich got richer *because* they made the poor poorer.

Doing justice, against this backdrop of crimes, was not terribly complicated. It meant the kings would do the following: judge the poor fairly instead of exploiting them, stop cheating the poor and lining their royal pockets through oppression, and quit snuffing out the weak in order to get their land or their stuff. No king, or any Israelite for that matter, guilty of these sins could possibly know, in a covenantal sense, the God of Israel. To know God was to obey him.

---

[7]Philip Graham Ryken, *Jeremiah and Lamentations: From Sorrow to Hope* (Wheaton, IL: Crossway, 2001), 328–30.

So here's the point for us: Christians who do not cheat, swindle, rob, murder, accept bribes, defraud, and hold back agreed-upon wages are probably doing justice. Christians guilty of these things are probably not Christians at all.

Amos 5: Let Justice Roll Down Like Waters

The fifth chapter of Amos contains some of the most striking and most famous justice language in the Bible. The Lord rebukes his people for turning "justice into wormwood" (v. 7), for hating the one who speaks the truth (v. 10), for trampling on the poor (v. 11; see also 4:1), for turning aside the needy in the gate (5:12). Because of their sin, the Lord despises Israel's feasts and assemblies (v. 21) and threatens to visit the land with darkness and not light (vv. 18–20). The only hope for God's people is that they "seek good, and not evil," that they establish justice in the gate (vv. 14–15). Or, to quote the concluding exhortation made famous by Martin Luther King Jr., Israel must

> let justice roll down like waters,
> and righteousness like an ever-flowing stream. (v. 24)

Clearly, God cares about justice and the poor. Conversely, his wrath burns against those who commit injustice and trample the poor. So what are the *specific sins* condemned by Amos?

Kicking the poor when they were down instead of giving them a hand up. It seems the wealthy were selling the poor into slavery even when the poor owed as little as a pair of sandals (2:6–7). This was cruelty instead of mercy.

Doing "justice" for the highest bidder. In ancient Israel the leading men of the town would gather at the city gate to decide the cases that came to them. Instead of making fair judgment based on the truth, the men of Amos's day accepted bribes and paid no attention to the righteous plea of the poor (5:10, 12).

158

Arbitrary, excessive taxation on the poor to benefit the rich (5:11). The situation in Israel was the opposite of our current situation in America, where the very rich provide almost all the income tax revenue and the very poor pay no income tax at all and benefit from various programs and services paid for, in large part, by the taxes of the wealthy.

A smug assurance on the part of the rich who live in the lap of luxury on the backs of the poor. The wealthy in Amos's day, like many in ours, were proud of their wealth. They reveled in it (4:1; 6:4–7). They felt secure in it (6:1). To make matters worse, their getting richer had been made possible by the poor getting poorer. They had cheated, perverted justice and, according to one commentator, made their money by "outrageous seizure" and illegal "land grabbing" (cf. Isa. 5:8).[8]

Amos 5 reaffirms what we've seen in the previous Old Testament passages. God hates injustice. But injustice must be defined on the Bible's terms, not ours. Injustice implies a corrupted judicial system, an arbitrary legal code, and outright cruelty to the poor.

Micah 6:8: Do Justice, Love Kindness, and Walk Humbly with God

Micah 6:8 is the most beloved "social justice" passage of all. It is powerful, elegant, and straightforward. Micah 6 begins with a covenant lawsuit against Judah ("plead your case," v. 1). Later the question is asked, "With what shall I come before the LORD?" (v. 6). Should God's people bring a burnt offering or a thousand rams or a river of oil (vv. 6–7)? Is perfunctory ritual obedience pleasing to God? No! "He has told you, O man, what is good" (v. 8). And what is that? The Lord requires that his people

> do justice, and to love kindness,
> and to walk humbly with [their] God. (v. 8)

---

[8]William Rainey Harper, *A Critical and Exegetical Commentary of Amos and Hosea* (1905; repr., Edinburgh: T&T Clark, 1973), 49.

But what does it mean to "do justice"? That's the million-dollar question. And it must be answered exegetically. Micah unpacks his notion of justice by chastising Judah for all her injustice.

Some in Judah were coveting fields and seizing them, oppressing others through corruption and lawbreaking (2:2). Ralph Smith argues:

> The chief offenders were a relatively small group of greedy, powerful business men who spent their nights devising schemes to get possession of the land of the small farmers. The next day they carried out their schemes because they had sufficient economic, political and judicial power to accomplish their goals even when their goals deprived a man and his household of their inheritance which was a part of covenant right.[9]

In other words, these men were land-grabbers, taking what they did not own. And they had the power to get away with it. They weren't just buying more land—they were stealing it, in violation of the eighth commandment and in opposition to the stipulations about safeguarding a family inheritance.

In chapter 3, Micah inveighs against the "heads of Jacob and rulers of the house of Israel" (v. 1). This is probably a reference to the local magistrates who made judgments at the gate of the city. These men were like circuit court judges, responsible for administering blind justice that paid no attention to the status of the supplicant. Second Chronicles 19 explains how Jehoshaphat appointed judges who were to "judge not for man but for the LORD. He is with you in giving judgment. Now then, let the fear of the LORD be upon you. Be careful what you do, for there is no injustice with the LORD our God, or partiality or taking bribes" (2 Chron. 19:6–7). In this important chapter, the Chronicler gives us a

---

[9]Ralph L. Smith, *Micah–Malachi*, Word Biblical Commentary (Nashville: Nelson, 1984), 24.

clear picture of the quintessential picture of justice: judges who decide cases fairly and impartially. But tragically, the men in Micah's day did not "know justice." They hated the good and loved the evil (Mic. 3:2). They acted like cannibals toward their own people, chewing them up with their perverted power (vv. 1–3). They seem to have been especially cruel to the helpless poor (v. 5).

Shot through this corruption was a greedy love of money. The "heads" made decisions based on bribes. The priests taught for a price. And the prophets practiced divination for money (v. 11). As we've seen time after time in these "social justice" passages, *the classic form of injustice is siding with the rich against the poor because the former will pay you for it and the latter cannot do anything to stop you.* The rich, for Micah and the prophets in general, tended to be greedy bribers who took land by force, spoke lies to get their way, and oppressed the poor to increase their wealth (6:11–12). This is the sort of rich person the Lord disdains.

So what does Micah, and the Lord through him, mean by "doing justice"? He means we should not steal, bribe, or cheat. Conversely, we should, when we are in the position to do so, render fair and impartial judgments. And at all times in whatever calling, we should do good, not evil.

The Old Testament is passionate about doing justice. But Christians haven't always given much thought to what the Bible means by that phrase. Doing justice is not the same as redistribution, nor does it encompass everything a godly Israelite would do in obedience to Yahweh. Injustice refers to those who oppress, cheat, or make judicial decisions with partiality. Doing justice, then, implies fairness, decency, and honesty. Just as importantly, we see that the righteous person does more than simply refrain from evil. He positively seeks to help the weak, give to the needy, and, as he is able, addresses situations of rank injustice.

Matthew 25:31-46: The Least of These

Matthew 25 has become a favorite passage for many progressives and younger evangelicals. Even in the mainstream media it seems hardly a week goes by without someone referencing Jesus's command to welcome the stranger, feed the hungry, and clothe the naked. And few biblical phrases have gotten as much traction as "the least of these." Whole movements have emerged whose central tenet is to care for "the least of these" à la Matthew 25. The implications—whether increased government spending, increased concern for "social justice," or a general shame over not doing enough—are usually thought to be obvious from the text.

But in popular usage of the phrase, there's almost no careful examination of what Jesus actually means by "the least of these." For example, one accomplished Christian scholar (though admittedly not a biblical scholar) argues that Christ makes "our treatment of strangers" a "measure of righteousness." He then quotes from Matthew 25:34–40, followed by this conclusion: "To welcome the stranger—those outside of the community of faith—is to welcome Christ. Believer or nonbeliever, attractive or unattractive, admirable or disreputable, upstanding or vile—the stranger is marked by the image of God."[10] Now it's certainly true that we all are made in God's image. It's also true, on other grounds, that dealing kindly with strangers, even those outside the church, is a godly thing to do (Gal. 6:10). But it's difficult to conclude that this is Jesus's point in Matthew 25.

The "Least of These" in Context

So who are "the least of these" if they are not society's poor and downtrodden? *"The least of these" refers to other Christians in need,*

---

[10]James Davison Hunter, *To Change the World: The Irony, Tragedy, and Possibility of Christianity in the Late Modern World* (Oxford: Oxford University Press, 2010), 245. See also Richard Stearns, *The Hole in Our Gospel* (Nashville: Nelson, 2009), 292–93, for a similar conclusion.

in particular itinerant Christian teachers dependent on hospitality from their family of faith. Let's look at the evidence that supports this conclusion.

1. In Matthew 25:45 Jesus uses the phrase "the least of these," but in verse 40 he uses the more exact phrase "the least of these my brothers." The two phrases refer to the same group. So the more complete phrase in verse 40 should be used to explain the shorter phrase in verse 45. The reference to "my brothers" cannot be a reference to all of suffering humanity. "Brother" is not used that way in the New Testament. The word always refers to a physical-blood brother (or sister) or to the spiritual family of God. Clearly Jesus is not asking us to care only for his physical family. So he must be insisting that whatever we do for our fellow Christians in need, we do for him.

This interpretation is confirmed when we look at the last time before chapter 25 where Jesus talks about "brothers." In Matthew 23, Jesus tells the crowds and disciples (v. 1) that they are all brothers (v. 8). The group of "brothers" is narrowed in the following verses to those who have one Father, who is in heaven (v. 9), and have one instructor, Christ (v. 10). Jesus does not call all people everywhere brothers. Those who belong to him and do his will are his brothers (Mark 3:35).

2. Likewise, it makes more sense to think Jesus is comparing service to fellow believers with service to him rather than imagining him to be saying, "You should see my image in the faces of the poor." Granted, Jesus was a "man of sorrows," so to understand that sufferers may be able to identify with Jesus in a special way is wholly appropriate. But in the rest of the New Testament it's the body of Christ that represents Christ on earth, not the poor. Christ "in us" is the promise of the gospel for those who believe, not for those living in a certain economic condition. Matthew 25 equates caring for Jesus's spiritual family with caring for Jesus. The passage does

not offer the generic message, "Care for the poor and you're caring for me."

3. The word "least" is the superlative from of *mikroi* (little ones), which always refers to the disciples in Matthew's Gospel (10:42; 18:6, 10, 14; see also 11:11).

4. The similarity between Matthew 10 and Matthew 25 is not accidental. The pertinent sections in each chapter are talking about the same thing.

> Whoever receives you receives me, and whoever receives me receives him who sent me. The one who receives a prophet because he is a prophet will receive a prophet's reward, and the one who receives a righteous person because he is a righteous person will receive a righteous person's reward. And whoever gives one of these little ones even a cup of cold water because he is a disciple, truly, I say to you, he will by no means lose his reward. (Matt. 10:40–42)

Clearly, Jesus is speaking here of disciples. The context is Jesus's sending out his disciples to do itinerant ministry (10:5–15). In the face of persecution and a hostile world (10:16–39), Jesus wants to encourage his followers to care for the traveling minister no matter the cost. The disciples would be solely dependent upon the good will of others to welcome them, feed them, and support them in their traveling work. So Jesus assures his followers that to show love in this way is actually to love him.[11]

Summary

In conclusion, Matthew 25 is certainly about caring for the needy. But the needy in view are fellow Christians, especially

---

[11]One of the first postcanon documents, *The Didache*, demonstrates that caring for traveling ministers was a pressing issue in the first centuries of the church's history. *The Didache*, which has been compared to a church constitution, contains fifteen short chapters, three of which deal with the protocol for welcoming itinerant teachers, apostles, and prophets. Some so-called ministers, the document concludes, are cheats looking for a handout. But as for the true teacher, "welcome him as you would the Lord" (11:2). See also Craig Blomberg, *Matthew*, The New American Commentary (Nashville: Broadman, 1992), 378.

those dependent on our hospitality and generosity for their ministry. "The least of these" is not a blanket statement about the church's responsibility to meet the needs of all the poor (though we do not want to be indifferent to hurting people). Nor should the phrase be used as a general cover for anything and everything we want to promote under the banner of fighting poverty. What Jesus says is this: *if we are too embarrassed, too lazy, or too cowardly to support fellow Christians at our doorstep who depend on our assistance and are suffering for the sake of the gospel, we will go to hell.* We should not make this passage say anything more or anything less.

Luke 10:25–37: The Good Samaritan

The details of the story of the Good Samaritan are familiar to most Christians. A Jewish man was going down from Jerusalem to Jericho when he was attacked by robbers. As he lay beaten and bloodied on the road, three men passed by. The first two were religious leaders in Israel: first a priest, then a Levite. Both did nothing. Finally, there came a Samaritan—a "half-breed," a man from an ethnically and religiously dirty people. He alone stopped to help the man lying half dead in the street.

The point of Jesus's story is simple: "Go, and do likewise" (Luke 10:37). Jesus tells this story because a lawyer is putting him to the test (v. 25). This man wants to know how to have eternal life. After Jesus tells him to love God and love his neighbor, the lawyer, "desiring to justify himself," asks Jesus, "And who is my neighbor?" (v. 29). The lawyer is hoping to define neighbor quite narrowly, but Jesus moves in an opposite direction. The gist of the parable is: don't worry about figuring out "who is my neighbor?" but concentrate instead on *being* a good neighbor (v. 36).

What does all this mean for "social justice"? Most importantly, it means we must not limit our love to the people we like to love. The parable of the Good Samaritan is the narrative equivalent to Paul's command in Galatians 6:10 to do good to *all people* as we have opportunity. Not every need will be presented to us as dramatically and with as much "ought" as a man half dead lying all alone in the road, but where need exists, race, nationality, gender, color, and political allegiance must not stop us from being the neighbor Christ calls us to be. Bock's summary is apt: "The issue is not who we may or may not serve, but serving where need exists. We are not to seek to limit who our neighbors might be. Rather, we are to be a neighbor to those whose needs we can meet."[12]

Luke 16:19-31: The Rich Man and Lazarus

In the well-known parable of the rich man and Lazarus, a man who lived an opulent life ends up tormented in death, while a poor man who scratched a miserable existence in life is taken to Abraham's side in death. In classic Lukan style, the afterlife results in a great reversal: those on top wind up on the bottom and those on the bottom find themselves on top (16:25; cf. the Magnificat in chapter 1 and the Beatitudes in chapter 6).

It is sometimes assumed that the point of the passage is that rich people are bad for being rich, especially when there are so many poor people in the world. But this is not exactly the point. After all, why would heaven be described as "Abraham's side" if rich people (like Abraham!) are automatically excluded from heaven? No, the rich man in Luke 16 is not damned for having more than Lazarus. He is condemned because he has violated the axiom Jesus laid down earlier in the chapter: "You cannot serve God and money" (16:13). This rich man is like the rich fool of chapter 12, convinced that life consists in the abundance of one's possessions (12:15), all the while ignorant of being spiritually impoverished (12:21).

---

[12]Darrell L. Bock, *Luke 9:51–24:53*, Baker Exegetical Commentary on the New Testament (Grand Rapids: Baker, 1996), 1035.

166

Jesus is not against lavish feasting at the proper time. Just look at the parable of the prodigal son in Luke 15. Nor does he assume we are implicated by conducting business in a fallen, greedy world. See the parable of the shrewd manager in Luke 16. But Jesus is steadfastly opposed to those who love things more than God. This is why Luke records the story of the rich young ruler. Yes, wealth is a monumental danger. It can be a deadly snare (1 Tim. 6:9). It is hard for the rich to enter the kingdom. But not impossible (Luke 18:27). It's no coincidence that the story of Zacchaeus in Luke 19 follows the rich young ruler in chapter 18. Zacchaeus demonstrates how the rich can be saved. They don't have to divest themselves of everything above necessity, but they must repent of swindling, make amends for wrongdoing, and give generously from their abundance.

Moreover, the rich man in Luke 16 is damned because he ignores poor Lazarus at his gate. His sin is a sin of omission. But this omission is more than a general failure to "do more" or "do enough." His extravagant wealth makes him blind to the needs *right in front of him.* As John Schneider puts it:

> The strong obligation-generating power is in the immediate moral proximity of someone in dire need. What makes the behavior of the rich people in these parables so very hideous and damnable is not that they had wealth, or even that they enjoyed it. It is that they did so, like the rich in Amos, in spiritual obliviousness to grievous human suffering that was as near to them, in the moral sense, as it could be. It was not merely that they neglected "the poor," but that they neglected a human being in need directly in front of them.[13]

Lazarus, not the poor in abstract, was the rich man's test, and the rich man failed.

---

[13]John R. Schneider, *The Good of Affluence: Seeking God in a Culture of Wealth* (Grand Rapids: Eerdmans, 2002), 178.

2 Corinthians 8-9: Grace-Based Generosity

Paul's well-known instructions to the Corinthians on generosity can be divided into four parts: the look of generosity (8:1–7), the motivation for generosity (8:8–15), the administration of generosity (8:16–9:5), and the blessing of generosity (9:6–15). The recurring theme in both chapters is grace. Some form of the word appears ten times in these two chapters (8:1, 4, 6, 7, 9, 16, 19; 9:8, 14, 15). Paul goes to great lengths to demonstrate that the Corinthians have been given grace, they ought to be motivated by grace, their generosity will be grace to others, and it will result in more grace for them. Paul is not afraid to speak about money, but—and this is good advice for preachers—he couches the whole discussion in grace instead of shame.

One passage, 2 Corinthians 8:13–15, is particularly relevant to our examination of social justice:

> For I do not mean that others should be eased and you burdened, but that as a matter of fairness your abundance at the present time should supply their need, so that their abundance may supply your need, that there may be fairness. As it is written, "Whoever gathered much had nothing left over, and whoever gathered little had no lack."

The basic principle here is pretty easy to understand: Christians with more than enough ought to share with Christians who don't have enough. This, Paul says, is only fair. It's interesting that Paul does not use the common Greek word for justice (something from the *dik-* root), but the unusual word *isotēs*, meaning equality or fairness. Still, the concept is related to justice. Just as God provided manna for everyone in the wilderness (Ex. 16:18), so the church is to be God's manna equalizer now. If we have extra, we ought to share with our brothers and sisters who have too little so that there is some measure of *isotēs*.

168

Calvin's application is wise:

> Let us now apply the history to Paul's object. The Lord has not prescribed to us an homer, or any other measure, according to which the food of each day is to be regulated, but he has enjoined upon us frugality and temperance, and has forbidden that any one should go to excess, taking advantage of his abundance. Let those, then, that have riches, whether they have been left by inheritance or procured by industry and efforts, consider that their abundance was not intended to be laid out in intemperance or excess, but in relieving the necessities of the brethren.[14]

That's the basic principle: relieve the necessities of the brethren. But Paul is careful to guard against potential misunderstandings of this principle. For starters, the phrase "at the present time" suggests not only that the Corinthians may need help in the future, but that the present offering is a unique opportunity. The Greeks in Corinth have received spiritual blessings from the Jews; now they have an opportunity to present a material blessing to their brothers and sisters suffering from famine in Jerusalem (Rom. 15:22–29). The need of the hour is dire. Sometimes we forget that Paul's eagerness to help the poor (Gal. 2:10) is not a blanket statement about wanting to help his community flourish, but a specific goal to essentially provide disaster relief to a sister church in Jerusalem.

Further, Paul makes clear that he is not asking the rich to trade places with the poor (2 Cor. 8:13). He does not expect that everyone will have the same amount and same kind of everything. Jesus's disciples did not all have the same economic profile. Some were middle-class fishermen, one was a well-off tax collector, some women in the larger group were quite well-to-do

---

[14]John Calvin, *Calvin's Commentaries*, vol. 20, *1 Corinthians, 2 Corinthians* (Grand Rapids: Baker, 1993), 297.

(Luke 8:1–3), and others may have been quite poor. Jesus frequently warned against the dangers of money (Matt. 6:19–24), but he never insisted on a strict egalitarianism, nor did he espouse an austere utilitarianism (Matt. 26:6–13).

Just as crucially, we should note that Paul goes out of his way to explain that his appeal for generosity is neither a command (2 Cor. 8:8) nor an exaction (9:5). He has not come to tax the Corinthians, nor to impose a redistribution plan. "This is not a rigid and imposed 'equality,' as in communism," writes Paul Barnett. "The initiative to give and the dimension of the gift lie with the giver."[15] Whatever redistribution takes place is to be strictly voluntary as God moves in the hearts of the Corinthians to see the grace they have been given and seek the grace they will receive through their generosity. Acts 5 makes a similar point. The early church had all things in common (Acts 4:32–34), but it's clear this was a voluntary sharing from privately held goods. Peter rebuked Ananias and Sapphira for lying about their gift, but he also made clear that the problem was not that they owned property or that they kept some for themselves (Acts 5:4). The problem was their deception. As we give to meet the needs of our church family, then, the generosity must be honestly, cheerfully, and freely given.

James 1, 2, 5: Faith Shown through Works

The book of James is all about faith counting for something. While Paul stresses that faith alone justifies (Rom. 3:28), James emphasizes that the faith that justifies is not alone (James 2:24). "Show me your faith apart from your works," he challenges, "and I will show you my faith by my works" (2:18). James will not allow us to settle for a coasting, comfortable faith.

There are many ways for our faith to "work." Some of these relate to the poor. We should visit orphans and widows in their

---

[15]Paul Barnett, *The Second Epistle to the Corinthians*, The New International Commentary on the New Testament (Grand Rapids: Eerdmans, 1997), 415.

afflictions (1:27). We should treat the poor with dignity and not show partiality to the rich (2:1–7). We must not oppress the poor by cheating them of the payment we promised (5:1–6). The Bible condemns in the strongest terms fraud and favoritism. More than that, we are positively enjoined to show special compassion to the most helpless among us. If we truly believe the gospel of God's grace, we will be transformed to show grace to others in their time of need.

You may want to reread the previous three sentences, for they provide a good summary of the Bible's teaching on social justice: no fraud, no favoritism, help the weak, freely give as we have abundantly received.

But there is still much more that needs to be said by way of conclusion and to point the way forward on this hotly debated topic. That's what the next chapter is for.

CHAPTER 7

Making Sense of Social Justice

Application

WITH THE EXEGESIS OF twelve common social justice texts behind us, we are now in a position to offer some summary statements and suggestions. Let's put the statements and suggestions together and call them "Seven Modest Proposals on Social Justice."

Proposal #1: Don't Undersell What the Bible Says about the Poor and Social Justice

In recent years there's been so much talk about the poor and social justice that some conservative Christians, especially if that conservatism is political as well as theological, are tempted to tune out anytime a well-intentioned evangelical chastises the church for neglecting "the least of these." It's the theological equivalent of Newton's third law of motion: every passionate, radical new Christian action will produce an equal and opposite reaction. In other words, the more some Christians talk about the poor, the more other Christians will get sick of hearing about it.

But there actually is a lot in the Bible about the poor, even more if you expand the category to include wealth, money, possessions, and justice. The Old Testament Law contained numerous laws to ensure the fair treatment of the poor and to provide for their modest relief. Job's righteousness, at least in part, consisted in his compassion for the weak (see Job 29). The Psalms extol a God who promises to rescue the needy. The prophets denounce the rich oppressors and call for mercy and justice toward the helpless. Jesus warned against the accumulation of riches and found that society's outsiders generally trusted him more than the powerful insiders. The apostles, for their part, spoke against greed and the love of money and encouraged God's people in sacrificial generosity. And then there's Genesis 1, Genesis 9, and Psalm 8, where we see that every human being is made in God's image, possessing inherent worth and dignity. This alone is reason enough to care for our fellow man.

Most importantly, New Testament passages like 2 Corinthians 8–9 and Galatians 6:1–10 demonstrate the gospel motivation for mercy ministry. Because we have been given grace in Christ, we ought to extend grace to others in his name. Tim Keller is right: ministering to the poor is a crucial sign that we actually believe the gospel.[1]

If we love God and know his love, we will gladly embrace Scripture's commands that require, as the Heidelberg Catechism puts it, "that I do whatever I can for my neighbor's good, that I treat others as I would like them to treat me, and that I work faithfully so that I may share with those in need."[2]

---

[1] Tim Keller, "The Gospel and the Poor," *Themelios* 33, no. 3 (December 2008): 8–22.
[2] See the entry Lord's Day 42 in Kevin DeYoung, *The Good News We Almost Forgot* (Chicago: Moody, 2010), 198–201.

Proposal #2: Don't Oversell What the Bible Says about the Poor and Social Justice

Just as some Christians are in danger of overreacting against social justice, other Christians, in an effort to be prophetic, run the risk of making the Bible say more about the poor and social justice than it actually does. Here are a few examples of oversell.

For starters, the alleviation of poverty is simply not the main story line of Scripture. Some Christians talk like the Bible is almost entirely about the poor, as if the story from Genesis to Revelation is largely the story of God taking the side of the poor in an effort to raise the minimum wage and provide universal health care. As we tried to show earlier, the biblical narrative is chiefly concerned with how a holy God can dwell with an unholy people. Granted, one aspect of living a holy life is treating the poor with compassion and pursuing justice, but this hardly makes poverty the central theme in the Bible. If our story does not center on Jesus Christ, and the story of Jesus Christ does not center on his death and resurrection for sin, we have gotten the story all out of whack.

Likewise, we must remember that the "poor" in Scripture are usually the pious poor. They are the righteous poor, the people of God oppressed by their enemies yet still depending on him to come through on their behalf (see, e.g., Psalms 10; 69; 72; 82). This does not mean "the poor" should be evacuated of any economic component.[3] After all, the pious poor are very often the materially poor. But it does mean that the poor whom God favors are not the slothful poor (Prov. 6:6–11; 2 Thess. 3:6–12) or the disobedient poor (Prov. 30:9), but the humble poor who wait on God (Matt. 5:3; 6:33).

We should note that almost all the references to caring for the poor in the Bible are references to the poor within the covenant

---

[3]These last two sentences echo George Eldon Ladd, *A Theology of the New Testament*, rev. ed. (Grand Rapids: Eerdmans, 1993), 243.

community. As we saw in the last chapter, the "least of these" in Matthew 25 are our brothers in Christ, most likely traveling missionaries in need of hospitality. Paul was eager to help the poor (Gal. 2:10), but his concern was for the impoverished church in Jerusalem. It is simply not accurate to say, "The Bible is clear from the Old Testament through the New that God's people always had a responsibility to see that everyone in their society was cared for at a basic-needs level."[4] You can make a good case that the church has a responsibility to see that everyone in their local *church* community is cared for, but you cannot make a very good case that the church must be the social custodian for everyone in their society. Christians are enjoined to do good to all people, but the priority is "especially to those who are of the household of faith" (Gal. 6:10). When we can't do every good thing we want to do, this verse from Galatians tells us what to do first.

Justice, as a biblical category, is not synonymous with anything and everything we feel would be good for the world. We are often told that creation care is a justice issue, the gap between rich and poor is a justice issue, advocating for a "living wage" is a justice issue. But the examination of the main social justice texts has shown that justice is a much more prosaic category in the Bible. Doing justice means not showing partiality, not stealing, not swindling, not taking advantage of the weak because they are too uninformed or unconnected to stop you. We dare say that most Christians in America are not guilty of these sorts of injustices, nor should they be made to feel that they are. We are not interested in people feeling bad just to feel bad, or worse, people thinking there is moral high ground in professing most loudly how bad they feel about themselves. If we are guilty of injustice individually or collectively, let us be rebuked in the strongest terms. By the same token, if we are guilty of hoarding our resources and failing to show generosity, then let us repent, receive forgiveness, and change. But when it comes to doing good in our communities

---

[4]Richard Stearns, *The Hole in Our Gospel* (Nashville: Nelson, 2009), 123.

and in the world, let's not turn every possibility into a responsibility and every opportunity into an ought. If we want to see our brothers and sisters do more for the poor and the afflicted, we'll go farther and be on safer ground if we use grace as our motivating principle instead of guilt.

Proposal #3: Accept the Complexities of Determining a Biblical Theology of Wealth, Poverty, and Material Possessions

The biblical view of wealth, poverty, and material possessions is not simple. On the one hand, the poor seemed to be on much safer ground around Jesus than the rich. But on the other hand, we see all throughout the Bible examples of godly rich people (Job, Abraham, well-to-do women following Jesus, Joseph of Arimathea).

On the one hand, riches are a blessing from God (as seen in the patriarchs, the Mosaic covenant, Proverbs, and the accounts of the kings in Kings–Chronicles). But on the other hand, there is almost nothing that puts you in more spiritual danger than money ("It is hard for the rich to enter the kingdom of heaven" is how Jesus put it).

On the one hand, Jesus and the prophets had very little positive to say about the rich and sympathized more with the poor. On the other hand, God put the first man and woman in a paradise of plenty, and the vision of the new heavens and the new earth is a vision of opulence, feasting, and prosperity.

And then you have the famous "middle class" passage:

Remove far from me falsehood and lying;
   give me neither poverty nor riches;
   feed me with the food that is needful for me,
lest I be full and deny you
   and say, "Who is the Lord?"
or lest I be poor and steal
   and profane the name of my God. (Prov. 30:8–9)

It is impossible to give a one-sentence summary of the Bible's perspective on money.[5] Whenever we try to absolutize one strand of scriptural teaching about money we get into trouble. If you look only at the Old Testament promises of covenant blessing, you'll end up with the prosperity gospel. If you take the Magnificat and nothing else, you might end up a Marxist revolutionary. We're not suggesting the Bible teaches a little prosperity gospel and a little Marxism. What we're suggesting is that we must understand individual passages within the larger narrative.

God is a God of cosmic delight. The good life is presented in Scripture as a life of security and affluence, a life of abundance with God as the center and source of our delight. Poverty is not the ideal. Prosperity is.

And yet . . . and yet, the covenant blessings of riches are transmuted in the New Testament to a higher spiritual plane (Eph. 1:3). Our glorious inheritance awaits us in the next life (1:11–14). No doubt, this inheritance will include the material. But this new world with all its material prosperity is not close to being fully realized in this broken world. Part of the problem is that we live in the proverbial already and not yet. Heaven will be all abundance, but we're still on earth. So the enjoyments of God's good gifts must always be tempered by the call to share with those in need.

Yet on the other hand—you knew there was another hand—the call to simplicity must never silence the good news that God gives us all things richly to enjoy (1 Tim. 4:3–4). The Lord takes away, but he also gives (Job 1:21). The righteous accept both halves of the equation. We are in danger if we don't. As John Schneider puts it, "If the radical Christians and those who are sympathetic with their approach oversimplify the moral relationship in Scripture between affluence and evil, then advocates

---

[5]The previous four paragraphs come, slightly altered, from DeYoung, *The Good News We Almost Forgot*, 200–201.

of the Prosperity Gospel oversimplify the relationship between affluence and the moral good."[6] In other words, neither affluence nor austerity—abundance nor asceticism—is virtuous in its own right.

Perhaps Gilbert Meilaender, the well-respected Christian ethicist, best sums up the tension.

> Christians can, therefore, adopt and recommend no single attitude toward possessions. When they attempt to understand their lives within the world of biblical narrative, they are caught in the double movement of enjoyment and renunciation. Neither half of the movement, taken by itself, is the Christian way of life. *Trust* is the Christian way of life. In order to trust, renunciation is necessary, lest we immerse ourselves entirely in the things we possess, trying to grasp and keep what we need to be secure. In order to trust, enjoyment is necessary, lest renunciation become a principled rejection of the creation through which God draws our hearts to himself.[7]

To be a Christian, then, is to receive God's good gifts and enjoy them the most, need them the least, and give them away most freely.

Proposal #4: Be Careful with the Term "Social Justice"

We've already used "social justice" dozens of times. And yet you may have noticed that we've offered no definition of the term. That's because there really isn't one. We've used the term as it is commonly conceived, that is, as something ambiguously connected with poverty and oppression. We'd rather not use the term at all, but it is so much a part of popular parlance that we didn't feel we could do without it.

---

[6]John R. Schneider, *The Good of Affluence: Seeking God in a Culture of Wealth* (Grand Rapids: Eerdmans, 2002), 5.
[7]Gilbert Meilaender, "To Throw Oneself into the Wave: The Problem of Possessions," in *The Preferential Option for the Poor*, ed. Richard John Neuhaus (Grand Rapids: Eerdmans, 1988), 85.

But if we are going to use the term, at the very least we'd like to encourage Christians to be much more careful with it. Entire books are written without ever defining what makes justice social or what makes a society just. As Michael Novak argues:

> [Social justice] is allowed to float in the air as if everyone will recognize an instance of it when it appears. This vagueness seems indispensable. The minute one begins to define social justice, one runs into embarrassing intellectual difficulties. It becomes, most often, a term of art whose operational meaning is, "We need a law against that."[8]

For many Christians, social justice encompasses everything from hunger relief to combating sex trafficking to reducing carbon emissions. If something can be deemed a "social justice" issue, it frightens away opposition, because who in his right mind favors social injustice? But what are we actually talking about when we advocate for social justice?

As far as we know, the term was first used in 1840 by a Sicilian priest and then given prominence by another Italian thinker in 1848 and by John Stuart Mill in *Utilitarianism* a few years after that.[9] The roots of the concept go back to William Godwin's *Enquiry Concerning Political Justice* (1793), where Godwin argues that every individual in a society is entitled to share in the wealth

---

[8]Michael Novak, "Defining Social Justice," *First Things* (December 2000): 11–13; available online at http://www.firstthings.com/article/2007/01/defining-social-justice-29. John Goldingay, in his book on Old Testament ethics, also highlights this problem of definition: "The notion of social justice is a hazy one. It resembles words such as community, intimacy, and relational, warm words whose meaning may seem self-evident and which we assume are obviously biblical categories, when actually they are rather undefined and culture relative." After discussing the origin of the phrase "social justice" in nineteenth-century Roman Catholic thought, Goldingay explains how the phrase came to be used subsequently: " 'Social justice' then implies the idea of a 'just society,' one in which different individuals and groups in society get a 'fair share' of its benefits. But Christians disagree about what constitutes a just society and how we achieve it (for instance, how far by governmental intervention to effect income redistribution and how far by market forces and the encouragement of philanthropy). . . . The meaning of the phrase *social justice* has become opaque over the years as it has become a buzz expression." Goldingay, *Old Testament Theology*, vol. 3, *Israel's Life* (Downers Grove, IL: InterVarsity, 2009), 500.
[9]Ibid.

produced by the society. Hence, the rich giving of their wealth to help the poor is not a matter of charity, but one of justice.[10] In later thought, "social justice" often implies some form of command economy where the ruling class oversees an equal distribution of the society's resources. Christians of a certain bent have pursued this vision of economic equality as a matter of justice, while other believers have feared in this vision the erosion of personal responsibility and individual liberty. Social justice may sound like heaven to some, but it sounds the alarm for others.

In order to get a handle on the meaning of "social justice," one author has differentiated between what he calls the constrained and unconstrained views of justice.[11] In the unconstrained view, justice is a *result* so that wherever people don't get "their fair share" or don't have as much as others, there is injustice. Most people assume this unconstrained view when they speak of social justice. For example, the Reformed Church in America (Kevin's denomination), in one of its official study materials, includes a glossary that defines justice as "the fair, moral, and impartial treatment of all persons, especially in law. Includes concepts of right relationships and equitable distribution of resources." By this definition the inequality of opportunities, income, or outcomes is considered an injustice, a situation that in and of itself is sinful. It implicates all (or most) of us in society, and demands immediate redress. In the unconstrained vision, the society has a lump of resources, and if they are not shared roughly equally, then we do not have social justice.

In the constrained vision, by contrast, justice is a *process* in which people are treated fairly (the first half of the RCA definition). The goal is not forced redistribution, for no one distributed the resources in the first place, and no one is wise

---

[10]See Thomas Sowell, *A Conflict of Visions: Ideological Origins of Political Struggle*, rev. ed. (New York: Basic Books, 2007), 212–17.
[11]Ibid., 192–229.

enough to allocate them for the good of all. Justice, in this vision, is upheld through the rule of law, a fair court system, and equitable treatment of all persons regardless of natural diversity.

It seems to us that the constrained vision is closer to the way the Bible speaks of justice. Justice in a fallen world is not an equality of outcome, but is equal treatment under a fair law. This doesn't mean that in the constrained vision we shouldn't care for the poor, or that we simply shrug our shoulders and say, "Oh well," when we see people struggling through life with far fewer opportunities and resources than the rest of us. After all, those who "have," have (at least in part) because of favorable circumstances mostly out of their control (where they live, what family they belong to, what resources they have access to, what virtues and vices were modeled for them, etc.). It would be a mistake to think the middle class are not poor simply because they work harder and play by the rules. But as much as we may want a society of equal opportunity, no human being or human institution can make this happen. Some will always be born smarter, richer, better looking, more athletic, more connected, and so on. The door of opportunity will be opened wide for some, and others will have to beat it down.

Given this reality, the quest for cosmic justice sounds like a noble one, but we have to ask ourselves the hard questions: How do we determine what opportunities should be equalized? What is the cost of trying to fix these imbalances? Who has the power or knowledge to do so competently and benevolently? It's one thing to see that some are advantaged more than others. It's another to insist that justice demands state-sponsored attempts to ensure that opportunities are equalized.

The Christian will be generous and compassionate toward the suffering and the disadvantaged, realizing that all we have is a gift from God and that we share God's image with the poor.

But in the constrained vision, this care is a matter of love and compassion, not automatically a matter of justice.[12]

The point is that we don't all mean the same thing by "social justice," and therefore we should be careful to define what we mean if we use it. We should explain our conception of social justice and take pains to demonstrate why that conception is supported by Scripture, rather than just assuming a vague sense that "I wish things weren't this way." At the very least it would be good to recognize that using an ambiguous phrase like "social justice" to rally for our cause or defend our side without understanding what each other is really talking about is not terribly helpful.

Proposal #5: Appropriate the Concept of Moral Proximity

The principle of moral proximity is pretty straightforward, but it is often overlooked: The closer the need, the greater the moral obligation to help. Moral proximity does not refer to geography, though that can be part of the equation. Moral proximity refers to how connected we are to someone by virtue of familiarity, kinship, space, or time. Therefore, in terms of moral proximity Greg is closer to the other Southern Baptist churches in town than to First Presbyterian in Whoville. But physical distance is not the only consideration. In terms of moral proximity, too, Kevin is closer to his brother-in-law who lives in Australia than to a stranger who lives on the other side of Lansing.

You can see where this is going. The closer the moral proximity, the greater the moral obligation. That is, if a church in Whoville gets struck by lightning and burns down, Greg's church in Kentucky could help them out, but the obligation is much less

---

[12]We realize that some evangelicals have given a more expansive definition. For example, Tim Keller would say that justice, at its most basic, means fairness (*Generous Justice: How God's Grace Makes Us Just* [New York: Dutton, 2010], 3). But justice also "means to live in a way that generates a strong community where human beings can flourish" (177). In the end, we agree with Keller that a just person will live in the ways he outlines in the book, but we think it fits the evidence better to say that doing justice means treating people equitably. The kings of Israel and Judah were unjust because they were cheats, not so much because they failed to provide strong communities.

than if a church down the street in Louisville goes up in smoke. Likewise, if a man in Lansing loses his job, Kevin could send him a check, but if his brother-in-law on the other side of the world is out of work, he has more of an obligation to help. This doesn't mean we can be uncaring to everyone but our friends, close relatives, and people next door, but it means that what we *ought* to do in one situation is what we *may* do in another. Moral proximity makes obedience possible by reminding us that before Paul said "let us do good to everyone," he said, "So then, as we have opportunity" (Gal. 6:10).

The principle of moral proximity has other biblical precedence. In the Old Testament, for example, the greatest responsibility was to one's own family, then to the tribe, then to fellow Israelites, and finally to other nations. From Jubilee laws to kinsman redeemers, the ideal was for the family to help out first. They had the greatest obligation. After all, as Paul says, if you don't provide for your family, when you can, you are worse than an unbeliever (1 Tim. 5:8). If family can't help, the circle expands. Those closest to the person or situation should respond before outside persons or organizations do.[13] The reason the rich man is so despicable in Luke 16 is the same reason the priest and the Levite in Luke 10 are such an embarrassment: they have a need right in front of them, with the power to help, and they do nothing.

Obviously, this principle of moral proximity gets tricky very quickly. With modern communication and travel we have millions of needs right in front of us. So are we under an obligation to help in every instance? The answer must be no, or all of us will live under a crushing weight of guilt. The intensity of our moral obligations depends on how well we know the people, how connected they are to us, and whether those closer to the situation can and should assist first.

There are no easy answers even with the principle of moral proximity, but without it God's call to compassion seems like a

---

[13]This is sometimes called "subsidiarity," especially in Catholic social thought.

cruel joke. We can't possibly respond to everyone who asks for money. We can't give to every organization helping the poor. Some Christians make it sound like every poor person in Africa is akin to a man dying on our church's doorstep, and neglecting starving children in India is like ignoring our own child drowning right in front of us. We are told that any difference in our emotional reaction or tangible response shows just how little we care about suffering in the world. This rhetoric is manipulative and morally dubious. It doesn't work either—not in the long run. Some Christians, in response to the every-dying-child-should-be-like-my-own logic, will kick into high gear and do as much as they can, at least for a time. But just as many Christians eventually give up on ever doing much of anything because the demands are so many. Without the concept of moral proximity we end up just putting "helping the poor" in the disobedience column and start thinking about football.

We must distinguish between generosity and obligation, between a call to sacrificial love and a call to stop sinning. In 1 John 3:17 John asks, "But if anyone has the world's goods and sees his brother in need, yet closes his heart against him, how does God's love abide in him?" Clearly, the failure to give is in this case a grave sin. But in 2 Corinthians 8–9 Paul's demands are much less demanding. The difference is moral proximity. First John 3 is a reference to fellow Christians in their midst who are destitute and need relief, not just to any brother anywhere. So if a family in your church loses everything in a flood, and insurance won't replace most of it, you have an obligation to do something. If you let them starve or live out on the street, you do not have the love of God in you. But if the same thing happens to a whole bunch of families in a church three states over, it would be generous of you to help, but the obligation is not the same.

The principle of moral proximity is no excuse to ignore your neighbor in need. Neither does it preclude the appropriate urging some of us need to venture outside our safe circles of moral proximity. Almost any ethical principle can be twisted to ill effect. But the concept is important. It reminds us that we can't possibly be the same kind of good neighbor to everyone in the world, nor must we. Supporting AIDS relief in Africa is a wonderful thing to do, but a failure to do so does not automatically make a church in Cedar Rapids, Iowa, a gospel-less, selfish church. But if that same church did nothing to help their people when the river flooded in 2008, then they do not understand the love of Christ. Moral proximity should not make us more cavalier to the poor. But it should free us from unnecessary guilt and make us more caring toward those who count on us most.

Proposal #6: Connect Good Intentions with Sound Economics

If Christians are to truly help the poor, and not just help ourselves feel better, we must arm ourselves with more than good intentions. Sometimes well-meaning Christians accomplish little or even have a negative effect on the people they are trying to help because they do not understand basic economic realities. We realize that few people picked up this book hoping for a primer on economics, but let us at least point to three basic economic realities that Christians cannot afford to ignore.[14]

Rich Plus Poor Does Not Equal Zero

First, wealth in the modern world is not a zero-sum game. Most people assume that economic transactions, on either a micro or

---

[14]For a look at basic economic principles and the legitimacy of democratic capitalism from a Christian perspective, see Jay W. Richards, *Money, Greed, and God: Why Capitalism Is the Solution and Not the Problem* (New York: HarperOne, 2009); Victor V. Claar and Robin J. Klay, *Economics in Christian Perspective: Theory, Policy and Life Choices* (Downers Grove, IL: InterVarsity, 2007); and Michael Novak, *The Spirit of Democratic Capitalism* (Lanham, MD: Madison, 1991). Wayne Grudem's *Business for the Glory of God: The Bible's Teaching on the Moral Goodness of Business* (Wheaton, IL: Crossway, 2003) is a short primer on why business is compatible with Christian principles. For an eye-opening account of how tough love has proved effective on poverty and naïve good intentions disastrous, see Marvin Olasky's *The Tragedy of American Compassion* (Washington, DC: Regnery, 1992). See also the resources available from the Acton Institute, www.acton.org.

macro scale, always entail a winner and a loser. So if someone is $50,000 richer this year, someone else must be $50,000 poorer. The sum of all economic transactions together is zero. The winners are offset by the losers.

The assumption behind this myth is that there is a fixed pie of wealth that everyone must share. So if you get two pieces of pie, someone else will get none. But the economic reality is that wealth can be created. The pie gets bigger. A recession occurs when a country's economy (measured by the gross domestic product) shrinks for two consecutive quarters. Recessions are a big deal because they don't happen all that often, which tells you that the economy as a whole is usually growing. Through increased productivity, technological innovation, and smart investment, wealth is not simply transferred; it grows.

Consequently, the rich do not have to get rich at the expense of the poor. Christians often worry about the growing gap between the haves and the have-nots, but a growing gap does not necessarily mean a growing problem. In the last few decades, both in the United States and around the world, the rich have gotten richer, but the poor have gotten richer too. By one estimate, from 1970 to 2006 poverty fell by 86 percent in South Asia, 73 percent in Latin America, 39 percent in the Middle East, and 20 percent in Africa. Although there is still dire suffering, the overall global trend has been good for the past several decades. The percentage of the world population living in absolute poverty (less than $1 a day) went from 26.8 percent in 1970 to 5.4 percent in 2006.[15]

Because wealth can be created, it is misleading to always speak of wealthy countries (or individuals) "controlling" a certain percentage of wealth or "taking" a certain amount of health-care dollars, as if the rich people raided the cookie jar first and left nothing for the poor people. The biggest consumers

---

[15]Figures are from VOX Research, "Parametric Estimations of the World Distribution of Income," http://www.voxeu.org/index.php?q=node/4508.

of goods and resources are also the most productive creators of jobs and wealth.

Along the same lines, one of the geniuses of capitalism is that it discourages hoarding. This is not to suggest that people are less given to avarice now than they have always been. But whereas in the ancient world the greedy miser might store up excess grain for himself and nobody else (see Luke 12), today the wealthy invest their riches in stocks, or pour their resources into a start-up company, or at least put their money in the bank, which will in turn lend the money to others. There's little incentive to hide a billion dollars under your mattress or to do nothing with your grain except build bigger barns in which to hoard it. But there is every incentive to put that money to work back in the economy. Even when the wealthy spend their money on things that might offend middle-class sensibilities, their conspicuous consumption is nevertheless providing jobs for the yacht maker, the high-end clothing designer, and the Hummer dealership, not to mention the builder, the landscaper, and the pool maintenance man.

One other point needs to be made before moving to the second economic reality. Charity alone is not the solution to world poverty. Direct handouts work best as a form of relief, but as a means of economic development the record is mixed at best. This doesn't mean we don't give. But it means the problems of hunger, malnutrition, and grinding poverty will not be solved by rich nations giving more money, either by individuals or by whole nations. After fifty years and more than $1 trillion of aid to Africa, the results are less than inspiring.[16] This is because poverty will be overcome only when wealth is created, and wealth creation requires certain conditions.[17] The rule of law must be enforced, social capital (i.e., trust) must be increased, and

---

[16]See Dambisa Moyo, *Dead Aid: Why Aid Is Not Working and How There Is a Better Way for Africa* (New York: Farrar, Straus and Giroux, 2009); William Easterly, *White Man's Burden: Why the West's Efforts to Aid the Rest Have Done So Much Ill and So Little Good* (New York: Penguin, 2006).
[17]See David S. Landes, *The Wealth and Poverty of Nations: Why Are Some So Rich and Some So Poor* (New York: Norton, 1998).

property rights must be respected.[18] In most cases, poor nations are not poor because Westerners are rich, nor are they poor because they are less industrious or less capable than workers in the West. They are poor because they live and work in a system (often corrupt) that does not have the proper political, legal, and social structures in place to allow for the skills, brains, and ingenuity of the poor themselves to unleash the same wealth-creating process we have seen in the West. Where these measures have been put in place, nations have typically gotten richer. Such is the common grace afforded to all in a market system. As Christian economists Victor Claar and Robin Klay have remarked, "Markets are often providentially used to accomplish what no amount of Christian charity or political activism alone could achieve."[19] Or as some wag once put it, Bill Gates and Microsoft have done more to alleviate poverty in India than Mother Teresa.[20]

Thinking beyond Stage One

A second economic reality is that we must always consider the law of unintended consequences. In his classic *Economics in One Lesson* Henry Hazlitt sums up the whole economics in a single sentence: "*The art of economics consists in looking not merely at the immediate but at the longer effects of any act or public policy; it consists in tracing the consequences of that policy not merely for one group but for all groups.*"[21] Remembering this one lesson—the law of unintended consequences—can help Christians think more carefully about a whole host of issues.

---

[18]See Hernando DeSoto, *The Mystery of Capital: Why Capitalism Triumphs in the West and Fails Everywhere Else* (New York: Basic Books, 2003), for a detailed discussion of this.
[19]Claar and Klay, *Economics in Christian Perspective*, 161.
[20]We hope you read this footnote before this one sentence is all over the Internet! Of course, this statement measures only economic outcomes. It does not judge the heart. So we are not saying that Bill Gates is more virtuous or more praiseworthy than Mother Teresa—only that his actions as a businessman undoubtedly contributed more to the material well-being of India as a whole.
[21]Henry Hazlitt, *Economics in One Lesson* (1946; repr., San Francisco: Laissez Faire, 1996), 5; emphasis original.

We may not all agree on what economic policy is best (because these matters require prudential judgments on which Christians can legitimately differ), but we should at least agree that good intentions are not enough. For example, it may seem like a good idea to give away mosquito nets for free in Africa, but experience with this approach has shown that when something is free, people don't value it and won't use it. Better to charge a nominal fee. It may seem like a good idea to build buildings for the poor in other nations or to buy their medicines for them, but this can create patterns of dependency and rob them of the dignity that comes with taking care of their own problems.[22] It may seem noble to rail against "sweatshop" labor in other countries where the workers make a tiny fraction of what a similar job might yield in the West, until you realize that these may be the most desirable jobs they have, even with wages that seem unfair to us.

Closer to home, minimum wage laws may seem like a great way to help the working poor, but in reality they make employers less likely to create new entry-level positions and more likely to eliminate certain jobs entirely. Similarly, it may help the domestic sugar beet farmers to impose a harsh tariff on sugar from other countries, but it won't help those employed by the candy plant when it moves to another country to avoid the high sugar tariffs.[23] Subsidizing a failing industry may help the workers in that field, but it also delays the inevitable realignment of the workforces and props up unprofitable practices through the profits of others. Fair-trade coffee may be a good way to help Third World farmers sell their beans for a higher price, but it can also artificially distort market prices, making farmers dependent on the good will of others for their livelihood and discouraging them from making the necessary innovations and modernizations that will render them more productive and, in the long run, more profit-

---

[22]See the excellent book by Steve Corbett and Brian Fikkert, *When Helping Hurts: How to Alleviate Poverty Without Hurting the Poor and Yourself* (Chicago: Moody, 2009).
[23]See Claar and Klay, *Economics in Christian Perspective*, 38–39.

able. We could go on and on with these examples, but the point should be clear: don't just look at what you hope to accomplish for one group; look at what incentives you are creating and how, unintentionally, everyone else will be affected.

Real World Problems, Real World Solutions

Third, economics takes place in the real world, and the real world will never be utopia. This means we cannot simply ditch one system because it doesn't do everything we want. We must consider whether things would be better or worse under a different system. We may wish that wealth were more evenly distributed. And as Christians we must certainly encourage generosity. But redistribution becomes something else entirely when it is no longer voluntary. Not only is generosity robbed of its moral virtue, but we must also consider whether anyone or any group has the necessary skill and character to preside over such a redistribution. Who has the omniscient wisdom to decide what a job is worth or what the value of goods and resources should be? Who will decide whether affordable milk is more important than a better living for dairy farmers? Who will determine whether lower salaries for engineers and factory workers are a good trade-off for cheaper automobiles? Prices and wages convey invaluable information about what is needed and where. No enlightened ruler or board or administration can possibly manage millions of people with as much knowledge as the market can.

Even if such knowledge could be obtained, whom would we entrust with such power to enforce our vision of social justice? History teaches us that people who sacrifice liberty for equality end up with neither. Instead you end up with rival factions and interest groups all clamoring for favors from those handing out the money. Think K Street times a thousand. An economy based on competition and cooperation through voluntary exchange may not alleviate all the effects of the fall we would like, but it is much more effective at producing wealth and much more protective of personal dignity and freedom than a system that pursues its vision of cosmic justice through coercive force and the concentration of power.

Proposal #7: Love Your Neighbor as Yourself

In so many ways the social justice discussion would be less controversial and more profitable if we stopped talking about justice and started talking about love. Is it unjust for poverty to exist in the world alongside such wealth? Are we implicated in injustice because we live in a society with so many have-nots? Is it a moral obligation, a matter of *justice*, for a church in Spokane to do something about AIDS in Uganda? Doubtful. But should we love wildly, sacrificially, and creatively here, there, and everywhere? Absolutely.

Much of what is promoted in the name of social justice is exceedingly virtuous. More people interested in serving overseas, more people digging wells, more people giving away their money, more people adopting children, more people taking an interest in their neighborhoods—all these are encouraging signs of life in the evangelical church. The problem is that social justice has too often been sold with condemnation by implication and the heavy hand of ought. It seems much better to simply encourage churches and individual Christians to love. It's as if evangelicalism has been awakened to social concerns and now we want to smite one another's consciences while we're at it. It's too easy to wield "social justice" like a two-by-four to whack every middle-class Christian who tithes, prays, works hard, deals fairly with others, and serves faithfully in the local church but doesn't have time to give to or be involved in every cause. If we need fifty hours in every day to be obedient, we're saying more than the Bible says. It is hard to prove that most evangelical Christians are guilty of grave injustices toward the poor. Let's not stir up guilt where it doesn't belong.

On the other hand, it is not hard to prove that there is more we can do to love. Micah 6:8 and Matthew 25 may not smack the rhetorical home run we want them to, but we already have "do good to all people," be "salt and light," and "love your neighbor" to clear the bases for us. If we want every church to move into the city, drink fair-trade coffee, focus on ending world hunger, and feel like guilty oppressors when we don't do these things, we're going to have a hard time backing that up with Scripture. But if we want every church to look outside itself, exercise love beyond its doors, and give generously to those in need (especially those on its member list), we will have ample biblical support.

All that is to say, as we see the physical needs all around us, let's motivate each other by pointing out salt-and-light *opportunities* instead of going farther than the Bible warrants and shaming each other with do-this-list-or-you're-sinning *responsibilities*. We would do well to focus less on prophetic "social justice" announcements and more on boring old love. Love creatively. Love wildly. Love dangerously. Don't miss all that the Bible says about living rightly and living justly. Read through a book like Keller's *Generous Justice* and come to grips with verse after verse of God's heart for the weak, the vulnerable, and the oppressed. Don't skip these verses. Don't be suspicious of everyone who is concerned for "social justice." We really ought to love everyone, not all in the same way, but when we can, where we can, however we can.

CHAPTER 8

Seeking Shalom

Understanding the New Heavens
and the New Earth

HAVE YOU EVER WONDERED why it's become popular—in a certain subculture of evangelicalism, anyway—for people to sign off their e-mails not with "Love," or "Sincerely," or even "Blessings," but rather with the Hebrew word *shalom*? It's not as if the number of Jewish-background Christians in our normal circles has increased. In fact, most of the people wishing us "Shalom" at the end of their e-mails are as American and Gentile as we are.

Shalom is a wonderful word, packed with theological and biblical meaning. Most simply, it means "peace," and insofar as it turns Christians' minds both to the peace we now have with God through Jesus Christ *and* to the peace that awaits us in eternity—in the new heavens and new earth—it's a wonderful thing to meditate on, whether at the end of an e-mail or as one of the most encouraging themes of the Bible's story.

There's an old saying that a Christian can be "so heavenly minded he's no earthly good," and that critique can legitimately apply to some folks. But we think it's more often the case that Christians find themselves in trouble precisely *because* they don't think enough about eternity.[1] They don't meditate long and hard enough on what God intends to do for them and with them when this age is over, and their circumstances, priorities, even sufferings are not viewed through an eternal lens. It ought to be that when the world looks at a Christian's life, much of what they see simply will not make sense, and that's because the Christian's eyes are fixed on something out there in the future that the non-Christian cannot even begin to see. Eternity—the end game, the final picture, the new heavens and new earth—ought to set the trajectory of a Christian's life so profoundly that his life doesn't quite add up when the world looks at it. That's why shalom—peace—is such an important concept; it describes in a single word what Christ has wrought, and what he will finally bring about fully and forever when this age ends.

In this chapter we want to spend a bit of time thinking about shalom as it's talked about in the Bible, and ultimately about the new heavens and new earth as the place where that shalom finally reigns. There are a number of topics we need to address here:

- What is shalom?
- How should we understand the new heavens and new earth that God has promised?
- Doesn't the cultural mandate *command* us to be about the work of creating a new world?
- How much continuity will there be between the *old* earth and the *new* one?

---

[1]Note C. S. Lewis's perspective: "If you read history you will find that the Christians who did most for the present world were just those who thought most of the next." *Mere Christianity*, 3rd ed. (New York: HarperOne, 2001), 134.

All these issues bear heavily on the question, What is the mission of the church? In fact, a good number of recent books have argued from these issues to the conclusion that it is the mission of the church to provide health care, repair housing slums, plant trees, fund disease research, and clean streets—in short, to work toward the perfect, shalom-filled new heavens and new earth that God intends there to be at the end. Sometimes it's talked about as "building the kingdom," other times as "gathering the building materials of the kingdom," and other times as "bringing heaven to earth." But the upshot of all those phrases is the belief that the job of building what will be at the end is, at least in part, *ours*. Understood within a certain way of thinking, that makes perfect sense. But if you understand these issues in a different way—that God and not we will build the new heavens and new earth—well, that changes everything.

What Is Shalom Anyway?

As we've seen, *shalom* is a common Hebrew word meaning, essentially, "peace." But this peace is much more than the mere absence of hostility. *Shalom* means something more like "wholeness, completeness, soundness, well-being." At its most robust, the word points to a situation in which God's authority and rule are absolute, where his creations—including human beings—exist in right relationships with him and with each other, and where there is no separation between God and man because of sin.

Shalom, however, doesn't always have those eternal overtones. In fact, the word has a fairly broad range of meaning, and we can't simply read "eternal peace" into every instance of the word we run across in the Bible. So for example, *shalom* can refer quite simply to material prosperity, as when the psalmist says,

> I was envious of the arrogant
>   when I saw the prosperity [*shalom*] of the wicked. (Ps. 73:3)

It can also refer to physical safety, as when David reminds himself of God's goodness to him:

> In peace [*shalom*] I will both lie down and sleep;
>> for you alone, O LORD, make me dwell in safety. (Ps. 4:8)

Sometimes, the word is used similarly to the way we use the word *peace* today—referring to the absence of fighting, or perhaps even more appropriately to an alliance—as when Scripture tells us that "there was peace [*shalom*] between Hiram and Solomon, and the two of them made a treaty" (1 Kings 5:12). Sometimes the word is simply used to inquire about the health and well-being of someone, as when Joseph uses it to ask about his old father Jacob when his brothers show up in Egypt: "And he inquired about their welfare [*shalom*] and said, 'Is your father well [*shalom*], the old man of whom you spoke? Is he still alive?'" (Gen. 43:27). Sometimes the same sense of "well-being" is applied to an entire city or country (Ps. 122:6–9).

Of course in certain contexts the word takes on a much more spiritual meaning, referring to a peace or well-being between God and men. In the Pentateuch a number of sacrifices are called "*shalom* offerings," or "peace offerings." No particular occasion is specified for these, but the intent is clear. The hostility that exists between God and his people is brought to an end—or at least a temporary "cease-fire," if you will—through the shed blood of the "*shalom* offering." Look, for example, at this description from Leviticus 3:1–2:

> If his offering is a sacrifice of peace offering, if he offers an animal from the herd, male or female, he shall offer it without blemish before the LORD. And he shall lay his hand on the head of his offering and kill it at the entrance of the tent of meeting, and Aaron's sons the priests shall throw the blood against the sides of the altar.

We should notice several things here. First of all, even the need for a "peace offering" speaks to the hostility that exists between human beings and God because of sin. The author of Hebrews tells us that the priests would make these peace offerings for the sins of the people (Heb. 5:3). Also, any shalom between God and man is much more than one party or the other "forgiving and forgetting." A high cost is exacted to win that peace, one of blood and life. As the Lord explains in Leviticus 17:11, "For the life of the flesh is in the blood, and I have given it for you on the altar to make atonement for your souls, for it is the blood that makes atonement by the life." In the garden of Eden, the cost of sin had been the death of the sinner—the life and blood of the sinner. Thus it was that life, and life alone, would bring peace between God and man.

For all this, though, the people of Israel never knew true peace. The sacrifices only deferred judgment; they did not put an end to it. They did not bring full and final peace. The sacrifices never fully took away sin; the law was but a shadow of the good things to come (Heb. 10:1–4). Because of this, the Israelites began to look forward to the coming of One who *would*, in fact, bring full and final shalom to God's people. That hope was given full expression in the prophets and was realized with the coming of that child—the Prince of Peace, Jesus Christ (Isa. 9:6–7; Matt. 1:21–23). Thus Zechariah would say of his unborn son, John the Baptist, that he would "guide our feet into the way of *peace*" (Luke 1:79), and the angels would declare in joy on the night of Jesus's birth,

> Glory to God in the highest,
> and on earth *peace* among those with whom he is pleased!
> (Luke 2:14)

It's no wonder, then, that after his resurrection, the risen Lord Jesus's repeated blessing on his disciples became "Peace be with you!" (John 20:19, 21, 26; Luke 24:36).

199

The shalom that had been lacking between God and man for so long—the shalom that the sacrifices had simply patched together, the full and final shalom that the prophets had foretold—had finally been won through the death and resurrection of the Messiah, Jesus. So Paul says in Romans 5:1, "Therefore, since we have been justified by faith, we have *peace* with God through our Lord Jesus Christ." And it's surely no accident that Paul begins *every one* of his letters with some form of the blessing, "Grace to you and peace from God our Father and the Lord Jesus Christ."[2] Through God's grace to us in Jesus Christ, we now know *peace* with him.

Let's pause and see a few things here. First, any shalom between God and man—any lasting wholeness or well-being of man—is won through the death and resurrection of Jesus Christ. The shalom that the Old Testament offers comes only through the sacrificial system—which of course finds its fulfillment in the sacrificial, substitutionary death of Jesus—and the promise of a coming "Prince of Peace," which is a prophecy of the coming of Jesus, the one who would be not just Messiah, but suffering Messiah (Isaiah 9, 11, 40, 42, 53). Like all other biblical themes, shalom runs straight through the cross on Golgotha. There is no shalom between God and man apart from the cross, and we should take care not to imply otherwise.

Not only so, but it's worth remembering that shalom does not always have an ultimate, eternal meaning. Sometimes it can refer to something as simple as the health and well-being of another person. When Joseph asks about the "shalom" of his brothers and father, he doesn't want to know if they are submitted sufficiently to the authority of God and if they are enjoying the eternal blessedness of the new heavens and new earth. He wants to know, "Is he still alive?" (Gen. 43:27). He wants to know if his father is healthy and well. Similarly, the Bible surely does not mean to say

---

[2]See Rom. 1:7; 1 Cor. 1:3; 2 Cor. 1:2; Gal. 1:3; Eph. 1:2; Phil. 1:2; Col. 1:2; 1 Thess. 1:1; 2 Thess. 1:2; Philem. 3; Titus 1:4. The word "mercy" is added in 1 Tim. 1:2 and 2 Tim. 1:2.

that there was eternal blessedness between Hiram and Solomon (1 Kings 5:12); it simply means that there was a peace—at most, an alliance—contracted between them as contemporary powers.

Seeking Shalom, Sort Of

It's important to keep in mind this less-than-ultimate shalom when we come to passages like Jeremiah 29:7, where the Israelites are told to "seek the welfare [the *shalom*] of the city." If we think shalom always refers to ultimate, eternal peace, we'll misunderstand that passage and think it is telling the Israelites to seek the ultimate, eternal peace of Babylon. And that, in turn, could lead us to think that the Bible gives us, as Christians—the "Israel of God" (Gal. 6:16; cf. Rom. 9:6)—the mission of seeking the ultimate, eternal peace of Dallas and Chicago and East Lansing and Louisville and Bucksnort, Tennessee. But that doesn't seem to be the point of Jeremiah 29:7 at all. Rather, the letter that Jeremiah sent to the exiles seems to be saying something more prosaic:

- Settle in. Build houses . . . not tents (29:5).
- Grow gardens . . . with perennials (v. 5).
- Have families . . . no good putting it off (v. 6).
- Don't listen to those who give you false hope of going home. You're going to be here a while (vv. 8–10, 28).

The Lord is essentially saying to his people through Jeremiah: "You need to seek the well-being of Babylon. You're going to be here for a few generations, so your fate is tied to its fate. If things go well for Babylon, things will go well for you. If it thrives, you'll thrive. If it gets rich, you'll get rich. But if it gets invaded, you'll get invaded. If it suffers famine, you'll suffer famine. And if it dies, you'll die. So as hard as it may seem, I don't want you to work against Babylon. I'll take care of them in time, but this is the time to work *with* the city and *for* the city, not against it."

201

That's why they were to seek Babylon's shalom—not because they were to be "building for the kingdom" there, but for their own well-being. "In its welfare you will find your welfare" (Jer. 29:7). The Israelite exiles were not seeking any long-term shalom of the city, much less the ultimate, eternal kind. In fact, their ultimate hope for Babylon was that it would be not at all peaceful, but completely destroyed (Jer. 50:2, 29). Through chapters 50–51 Jeremiah prophesies the downfall of Babylon, not just as bare fact but as something the Israelite exiles are to *look forward to* and *hope for.* The whole thing ends with this:

> Jeremiah wrote in a book all the disaster that should come upon Babylon, all these words that are written concerning Babylon. And Jeremiah said to Seraiah: "When you come to Babylon, see that you read all these words, and say, 'O LORD, you have said concerning this place that you will cut it off, so that nothing shall dwell in it, neither man nor beast, and it shall be desolate forever.' When you finish reading this book, tie a stone to it and cast it into the midst of the Euphrates, and say, 'Thus shall Babylon sink, to rise no more, because of the disaster that I am bringing upon her, and they shall become exhausted.'" (Jer. 51:60–64)

Given all that, it's simply impossible to maintain the meaning of Jeremiah 29:7—"Seek the welfare of the city"—that so many modern authors want to give it: that it is an Old Testament statement of the mission of the people of God, namely, that we are to be working toward the eternal blessedness of the cities in which we live by engaging with their social structures. That reading of that particular verse entirely misses the point of what Jeremiah was commanding. The Israelites' ultimate hope was not in their efforts to "bring peace to the city"; it was rather in God who would, in fact, bring something quite *different* from peace to that city in due time. And in the meantime, they were to settle in and seek the welfare of their captors—not even primarily for Babylon's sake, but for their own sakes.

James Davison Hunter sees Jeremiah 29:7 as a good example of God's people having a "faithful presence within" a fallen culture. It wasn't that they were to work for Babylon's eternal blessedness or even temporal ascendancy; nor was it a call for a "radical and prophetic challenge to the powers that be" or a "passive acceptance of the established order." Rather, "The people of Israel were being called to enter the culture in which they were placed *as God's people*—reflecting in their daily practices their distinct identity as those chosen by God."[3] Understanding the passage in this way, we can see its relevance to us as Christians. Like the Israelites in Babylon, we are said to be "exiles in the world" and "strangers" (1 Pet. 1:1, 17; 2:11), and therefore we too should seek the good of our society. That's why Peter tells us to be "zealous for what is good" (1 Pet. 3:17), and Paul repeatedly tells us to "do good" (Gal. 6:10; 1 Thess. 5:15; 2 Thess. 3:13; 1 Tim. 6:18). Those aren't calls to seek the eternal blessedness of the city. They are simply calls to the people of God to engage the culture in which we have been placed *as God's people*, reflecting in our lives our distinct identity as believers in Christ.

How Should We Understand the New Heavens and the New Earth?

When the Bible does talk about shalom in that eternal sense, it is almost always pointing forward to the day when God will create new heavens and a new earth. It's true that we enjoy shalom with God now, being justified by faith through Jesus Christ (Rom. 5:1), but the full consummation of that peace will take place only on the last day.

There are only four biblical passages that specifically use the phrase "new heavens and new earth," though there are others that speak of the same reality without the terminology. It would

---

[3]James Davison Hunter, *To Change the World: The Irony, Tragedy, and Possibility of Christianity in the Late Modern World* (New York: Oxford University Press, 2010), 278.

be good to open your Bible and take a moment to read through those four passages—Isaiah 65:17–25; 66:22–23; 2 Peter 3:13; Revelation 21:1–22:5—so that you'll be able to follow the observations we make about them.

First, notice how the concept of shalom runs through all four of these passages. Isaiah 65:25 says that no one shall hurt or destroy in God's holy mountain, a basic invocation of the concept of peace. But even more significant is the fact that all the blessings that come to God's people in this new paradise flow from the fact that God will now "rejoice in Jerusalem" and "be glad in my people." The hostility is ended, and what now reigns is a right relationship between God and his people—shalom in the fullest sense of the word. Not only so, but in Isaiah 66:23, the Lord says that "all flesh shall come to worship before me"; in other words, they will rightly submit to him as Lord, and thus shalom will reign. Second Peter 3:13 identifies the new heavens and new earth as the place "in which righteousness dwells," that is, where all things conform to God and his standards, where everything is finally at shalom. And finally, in Revelation 21–22, God's dwelling place is again with men, nothing evil will ever enter the city, and the throne of God and of the Lamb will be there. In all these instances, then, the new heavens and new earth are tied tightly with the theological concept of shalom.

Second, it's fascinating and instructive to see how passive the people of God really are in the creation and "building" of the new heavens and new earth. In each of them, it is clear that the work of "bringing heaven to earth," so to speak, is God's, not ours. "*I* create new heavens and a new earth," he says in Isaiah 65:17. "The new heavens and the new earth that *I make* shall remain before me," he says in Isaiah 66:22. In 2 Peter 3:13, we do not build the new heavens and new earth, or even contribute to their building. We, quite simply, Peter says, "*are waiting* for new heavens and a new earth." Finally, in Revelation 21:2, the New Jerusalem comes "down out of heaven from God"; it is not built by men. And it is the one seated on the throne who is "making all things new" (Rev. 21:5–6).

Of course no one argues that we Christians are tasked with building the new heavens and the new earth from bottom to top. That would be as impossible as it is ridiculous. But there are a number of people who have argued that we as Christians at least have a hand in the creation of the new heavens and new earth—that we partner with God in his mission to restore the cosmos. As energizing as that may sound, though, it simply doesn't ring true with the way the Bible talks about the new heavens and new earth. There's the clear testimony of the passages we've just considered, but there's also the fact that the land in which God's people dwell—whether the Promised Land or the new earth—is always said to be a *gift* from God to his people.

When God's people took possession of the Promised Land, they were not earning it or building it, but *receiving* it as a gift. That truth is clear throughout the Old Testament narrative: "Then the LORD appeared to Abram and said, 'To your offspring I will *give* this land'" (Gen. 12:7; see also 13:14–15; 15:7; 15:18; and many others). Yes, they'd have to go in and *take* the land that God was giving them; it wasn't going to sprout legs on its own and move to where they were. But the point, made over and over again both in word and in example, was that even the battles they would have to fight would be fought for them and won for them by the Lord himself (Josh. 1:9–13; 6:2, 16). Take a look at this extraordinary passage in Deuteronomy 6:10–12:

> And when the LORD your God brings you into the land that he swore to your fathers, to Abraham, to Isaac, and to Jacob, to give you—with great and good cities that you did not build, and houses full of all good things that you did not fill, and cisterns that you did not dig, and vineyards and olive trees that you did not plant—and when you eat and are full, then take care lest you forget the LORD, who brought you out of the land of Egypt, out of the house of slavery.

Cities they did not build, houses they did not fill, cisterns they did not dig, and vineyards and olive trees they did not plant! The whole point is that the people of Israel did not make the land for themselves; they simply received it from the Lord's hand.

The same thing seems to hold true when we consider the new creation, which is the fulfillment of the Promised Land.[4] The new heavens and new earth are not something that we build for ourselves out of the ruins of our fallen world. They are a gift from God to his redeemed people. Christians do not build the holy city, New Jerusalem, from the ground up; it doesn't rise from the ashes of Babylon (Revelation 18–19). Rather, it *comes down* from heaven (Rev. 21:2), a gift of God to his people. It is "the city that has foundations, whose designer and builder is God" (Heb. 11:10). And thus it is the one seated on the throne who takes the glory for this new creation: "Behold," he declares, "*I am making all things new*" (Rev. 21:5).

Colossians 1:15–20 makes this point, too, saying that God was pleased "through him to reconcile to himself all things, whether on earth or in heaven, making peace by the blood of his cross" (v. 20). These are glorious verses, some of the most exalted language in the Bible about the universal and even cosmic reign of the resurrected Jesus Christ. That God intends to "reconcile to himself all things" does not point to a doctrine of universalism, but rather emphasizes the vast scope of his purposes. "Nothing less than a total new creation is envisaged."[5] Often these verses are interpreted to mean that "Christ's death

---

[4] All the blessings promised to Abraham—land, seed, and universal blessings—are said to be fulfilled in the new heavens and the new earth. See Isa. 66:22–23: *land*—"For as the new heavens and the new earth ["land"] that I make shall remain . . ."; *seed*—"so shall your offspring . . ."; *blessing*—"All flesh shall come to worship before me." It seems plain, then, that the "new land," with its security, peace, harmony, and wholeness of relationship between God and man, is the ultimate fulfillment of the promise God made to Abraham to give him "the land of [his] sojournings," which itself was a picture of the land of the garden of Eden, where that wholeness had existed in the very beginning.

[5] N. T. Wright, *Colossians and Philemon: An Introduction and Commentary*, Tyndale New Testament Commentaries (Downers Grove, IL: InterVarsity, 1986), 81.

began a process of cosmic redemption in which we are called to participate,"[6] or that "Christ's shed blood began a restorative work affecting the eternal things of heaven as well as the here and now events on earth" in which "Christians are called to partner" so that we may be "conduits for him to bring healing to earth and its residents."[7]

Statements like that are partly right, but they also take some steps that go significantly beyond what the passage actually says. They are right in pointing out God's purpose to remake the universe and to set everything in this world to rights—either by redemption or judgment. But it's important to see that it is *God* who does the reconciling. In Christ the fullness of God was pleased to dwell, Paul says, and through him God is pleased to reconcile all things through his shed blood. There's simply no call here to "partner" with God in that work, or to "participate" with him or even to become a "conduit" of that reconciling work. When Paul does say in 2 Corinthians 5 that God has given him a "ministry of reconciliation," that ministry has a specific meaning: to "persuade others" (v. 11) of the good news that "in Christ God was reconciling the world to himself, not counting their trespasses against them" (v. 19). If in Colossians 1 "reconcile" has reference to the entire cosmos, here in 2 Corinthians 5 it refers specifically to lost sinners, for it has to do with people being forgiven of their sins. *That* is the ministry of reconciliation Paul understands God to have given him—to "appeal" to lost sinners and "implore" them to "be reconciled to God" (v. 20). It is not a ministry of partnering with God in his work of renewing the cosmos by confronting social problems. The whole point of Colossians 1:19–20, in fact, is to praise God because *he alone* has done and is doing that work.

---

[6]Jonathan Merritt, "Creation Care: As Much as God Is," *Christianity Today* (June 2010); available online at http://www.christianitytoday.com/ct/2010/june/26.46.html.
[7]Gabe Lyons, *The Next Christians: How a New Generation Is Restoring the Faith* (New York: Doubleday, 2010), 55.

It would seem, therefore, to be far beyond the biblical witness to talk as if we as Christians are somehow contributing to the building of the new heavens and the new earth. It's the same idea we considered earlier, in fact, with reference to the kingdom. Just as it is God and not we who will establish his kingship over the world, so it is God and not we who will create the new earth in which that kingship is exercised. In fact, that's really the glorious thing about the gospel of Jesus. Everything we have—and everything we *will ever have*—is given to us. We will not have earned it; we will not have built it. We will simply have *received* it all. When eternity finally comes, we will live in a land that was made and created *for us*, under a kingdom that was won and established *for us* by a Savior who died and was resurrected *for us*. Put simply, the gospel is the good news of a salvation, in all its parts, that is *for us*, and not in the least *by us*.

The Cultural Mandate

But doesn't the cultural mandate, well, *mandate* that we be about the work of creating a new world? The commands that God gives to Adam in Genesis 1 and 2—namely, that he should "be fruitful and multiply," that he should "rule," and that he should "work" the garden and "keep" it—are often used to argue that since Adam was given the task of building God's world, we Christians, a new and redeemed humanity, now hold that task as our own. We, like Adam, are to be about the "working" of the world around us, the bettering and perfecting of it. Some go further and even argue that this is the very mission of the church, to be about the work of "culture making" or at least "culture renewing."

Again, that's an exciting thought. But we're not sure it stands up very well when you look carefully at the biblical story line to see how Adam's cultural mandate originally functioned, what happened to it after Adam sinned, and how it relates to us now.

Let's take a closer look at the mandate God gave to Adam in the first chapters of Genesis. That mandate really consists of two roles that Adam was to play in God's world.

The first role is given in Genesis 1:28, immediately after God creates Adam and Eve: "And God blessed them. And God said to them, 'Be fruitful and multiply and fill the earth and subdue it and have dominion over the fish of the sea and over the birds of the heavens and over every living thing that moves on the earth.' " The first role God intends Adam and Eve to fulfill is that of being his vice-regents on earth, "having dominion" or "ruling" over all the other living things on earth. Adam's dominion, though, is not complete the moment he is created. He will have to work at it. He and Eve will have to "multiply" and "fill the earth," and their goal, significantly, is to "subdue" the earth and bring it into submission to their God-given rule.

Later, in the garden of Eden, God gives Adam another role to play. In Genesis 2:15, he puts Adam in the garden "to work it and keep it." At first glance, those look like pretty straightforward commands, but there is actually something more going on. The word translated "work," *abad*, means that Adam is to be the caretaker of the garden, to cultivate it and encourage its growth in maturity and beauty. The word rendered "keep," *shamar*, means much more than just keeping the garden presentable. It means that Adam is to "guard" it and "protect" it, making sure that nothing evil or unclean ever enters it, and if anything does, to make sure that evil is judged and cast out. The most important thing to notice, however, is that these two words—*abad* ("work") and *shamar* ("keep")—are the precise job description not only of Adam, but also of the priests in Israel's temple/tabernacle. When God first tells Moses to bring near the tribe of Levi in order to give them their instructions, he says of them, "They shall *guard* [*shamar*] all the furnishings of the tent of meeting, and keep *guard* [*shamar*] over the people of Israel as they *minister* [*abad*] at the tabernacle" (Num. 3:8). Then, when the Lord describes to Aaron the duties of the Levites (Num. 18:1–7), the two words show up over and over as they are told to do the ministry (*abad*) of the tabernacle and keep guard (*shamar*) over it. This connection with the priesthood is not coincidental. The garden of Eden is, in its very essence, a perfect temple.[8] It is the dwelling place of God with man, the place where man and God meet. Like the priests who will *abad* and *shamar* the tabernacle and the temple, so Adam is to *abad* and *shamar* the temple of the garden of Eden. He is to be not only king but also priest in God's world.

Adam utterly fails at that task. He defaults in both the roles God gave him. Instead of fulfilling his duty as priestly "keeper" of God's temple—judging the Serpent and casting it out of the garden—Adam surrenders to it and allows sin to enter. Further, instead of carrying out his kingly mandate to rule the world under God, he joins the Serpent in rebellion against God and attempts to take the crown for himself.

With that tragic story in mind, how should we think about Adam's original mandate with relation to us as Christians? For one thing, it seems clear from Scripture that Adam's original mandate does not remain unaffected by the fall. Every command included in it is subjected to severe frustration by the curse God pronounces in Genesis 3. Yes, Adam and Eve will continue to be fruitful and multiply, but that reproduction will now be massively frustrated and attended by hardship (Gen. 3:16). Adam will continue to work the ground, but it will be "in pain" and "by the sweat of [his] face" (Gen. 3:17–19). As for Adam's "dominion," yes he continues to be God's image (Gen. 9:6; James 3:9), but his rule is now cruelly ironic. The earth will no longer submit to his hand; now it will only reluctantly bring forth its fruits. And

---

[8]See G. K. Beale, *The Temple and the Church's Mission: A Biblical Theology of the Dwelling Place of God*, New Studies in Biblical Theology (Downers Grove, IL: InterVarsity, 2004), and T. D. Alexander, *From Eden to the New Jerusalem: An Introduction to Biblical Theology* (Grand Rapids: Kregel, 2009).

instead of the earth being subdued before him, now Adam will be subdued before it:

> For you are dust,
> and to dust you shall return. (Gen. 3:19)

Finally, God casts Adam out of the garden he was to "keep," and God places an angel at the entrance whose flaming sword will "guard [*shamar*] the way to the tree of life" (Gen. 3:24). If the priestly vice-regent will not *shamar* the garden, then the High King will do the job himself. The upshot of all this, of course, is that the ultimate goal of Adam's mandate—the subduing of the world to man and ultimately to God—is no longer attainable by him. Yes, mankind will continue to carry out some of that original mandate's provisions, but now only with great frustration and without any hope of actually fulfilling Adam's charge to subdue the earth.

This point is only magnified when we consider God's restatement of the cultural mandate to Noah after the flood. That mandate, recorded in Genesis 9:1–7, clearly reflects the original mandate given in Genesis 1 and 2, but it's also obvious that something has gone terribly wrong, for it differs from Adam's mandate in some important respects. The mandate to "be fruitful and multiply and fill the earth" is still there, but we know already that reproduction is now to be marked by "multiplied" pain (Gen. 3:16). Moreover, Adam's "dominion" of the animals is reasserted, but this time they won't come meekly to him to receive their names. Instead, the animals will be filled with "fear" and "dread" of him. His "rule" is no longer godly "dominion," but rather a fearful domination. There is also the new and necessary institution of a sword-wielding government, one that will have the power to take human life when human blood is shed (9:6). We can see the vestiges of the original mandate here—multiplication, domination, work—but things are clearly not the same. Perhaps most significantly, the words "and subdue it" are conspicuously absent from the whole thing: the goal of the original mandate is no longer attainable. Unlike the Adamic mandate, this Noahic version is not a matter of *progression* to paradise, but rather of *preservation* in a fallen world.

It's also important to see that as the biblical story unfolds, the role of picking up Adam's failed mandate and completing it is *not* ours. That role is assumed by the last Adam, the Lord Jesus Christ (see Romans 5); in every particular, he completes what Adam failed to complete; as both King and Priest, he succeeds where Adam failed. Look at Hebrews 2:6–8, for instance. There the author of Hebrews quotes Psalm 8, which praises God for his care of mankind and speaks of his exaltation of mankind above all creation—that is, his rule. The psalm is a commentary, really, on the first two chapters of Genesis. But it's interesting to see to whom the dominion of Adam is said ultimately to fall. It's Jesus whom we see "crowned with glory and honor" (Heb. 2:9). Interpreted by the author of Hebrews, the mandate given to Adam to rule the earth is fulfilled not ultimately by us, but by the last Adam, Jesus. Where Adam failed as king, Jesus succeeds. The same is true of Adam's priestly role. Where Adam failed to protect the garden and condemn the Serpent, Jesus does so. That was the promise of Genesis 3:15, and it is fulfilled by him who "binds the strong man" (Matt. 12:29; Mark 3:27), who defeats the beast (Rev. 19:20) and commands that "the dragon, that ancient serpent, who is the devil and Satan" be locked into the bottomless pit (Rev. 20:1–3), and who ultimately crushes his head by throwing him in the lake of fire, where he "will be tormented day and night forever and ever" (Rev. 20:7–10).

Thus Jesus, the last Adam, does what the first Adam failed so miserably to do: he reigns as King, bringing all things into submission to himself (Eph. 1:22; Heb. 2:8) and ultimately to God (1 Cor. 15:24), and he completes his work as Priest by destroying the Serpent once and for all.

All this means, to put it simply, that we are not little Adams striving to accomplish Adam's original work. No, that work has been picked up and completed by our Lord Jesus. We simply share in the fruits of his victory and even in his reign (Eph. 2:6). But it's also crucial to recognize that our reign with Christ hasn't been consummated yet. Yes, we reign with him now, but we will reign with him in fullness only then. The throne is ours in Christ *now*, but we will not fully exercise its authority until the last day (Matt. 19:28; 2 Tim. 2:11–12). Until then, we continue to live in a world where the curse yet remains; we still live in the age of the Noahic version of the cultural mandate. Childbirth still involves pain, work still involves sweat, the animals still run from us in fear, and the creation is still subjected to frustration.

How Much Continuity Will There Be between the Old Earth and the New One?

Another question influencing one's response to these issues has to do with how we should understand the relationship of this world to the new one that God will create. Are they completely distinct, meaning that this present world will be destroyed and replaced? Or are they more continuous, meaning that we can be relatively sure that our cultural works in the present will be "carried over" into the age to come?

We've heard those questions answered with great confidence by people on both sides of the issue. The fact is, both sides are making legitimate points, since the Bible contains passages that teach both substantial continuity and radical discontinuity. There's simply no way to read the entire Bible and come away thinking that there is no continuity between this world and the next, and there's no way to read it and think that it will be seamlessly continuous, either.

Let's consider some of the passages that are important in this discussion.

Radical Discontinuity

First, there is in Scripture a strong note sounded of a radical discontinuity between this world and the next. Isaiah says the heavens will vanish like smoke, and the earth will wear out like a garment (Isa. 51:6). Psalm 102 says the foundations of the earth will perish, and the created order will be changed like a robe (vv. 25–26; see also Heb. 1:10–12). And Jesus himself tells us that "heaven and earth will pass away, but my words will not pass away" (Matt. 24:35; Mark 13:31; Luke 21:33).

There is also the famous passage in 2 Peter 3:10, where the apostle Peter writes, "But the day of the Lord will come like a thief, and then the heavens will pass away with a roar, and the heavenly bodies will be burned up and dissolved, and the earth and the works that are done on it will be exposed." There is some debate over the meaning of the word "exposed" (Gk., *heurethēsetai*) at the end. Some translations use the words "will be burned up" (KJV, NASB) because some Greek manuscripts have the word *katakaēsetai*. But "will be exposed" (ESV), "will be laid bare" (NIV), or "will be disclosed" (HCSB) is probably the better rendering. Thus instead of teaching that the earth and the works that are done on it "will be burned up" into nothing, the passage probably teaches that when the last day dawns, nothing will remain hidden. All will be uncovered before him who judges.

Nevertheless, the passage still contains a strong note of radical discontinuity. Even if Peter says "exposed" and not "burned up," he still says that the heavens will "be burned up and dissolved" and that "the *stoicheia* [the stuff, or elements, of which the universe is made[9]] will melt as they burn" (2 Pet. 3:12). Perhaps most significantly, he also joins Jesus, the Psalms, and other apostles (Matt. 24:35; Mark 13:31; 1 Cor. 7:31; 1 John 2:17) in saying that the world will "pass away," a phrase that must mean something like

---

[9]So Thomas R. Schreiner, *1, 2 Peter, Jude*, The New American Commentary (Nashville: B&H, 2003), 384; Douglas J. Moo, *2 Peter, Jude*, The NIV Application Commentary (Grand Rapids: Zondervan, 1997), 190.

disappear (Job 6:15–17), *cease* (1 Cor. 13:8), *go away* (Amos 6:7), *die* (Job 34:20), *perish* (Ps. 102:26).

Whatever else we understand about the new heavens and the new earth, therefore, we must not think that there is a full, one-to-one continuity between this world and the new one that God will create. This world will pass away, and there will be a radical discontinuity between this world and the next.

Genuine Continuity

For all that, though, there are other passages of Scripture that teach that there will indeed be some kind of continuity between this world and the next. Romans 8:18–25 is probably the most important passage to consider here. Paul says without ambiguity that during this age, the creation is "subjected to futility," but in the certain hope that on the last day, "the creation itself will be set free from its bondage to corruption and obtain the freedom of the glory of the children of God." To say that the creation will be "set free from its bondage to decay" and that it will "obtain the freedom of the glory of the children of God" is a glorious image, one that speaks of God's refusal to let man's default on his obligations be the last word.

In thinking about this very idea, Charles Spurgeon envisions the creation as a vast orchestra, poised with their bows drawn, their mallets raised, their fingers on the cello and violin strings, their mouths open as if ready to sing—and yet totally still, covered with cobwebs, and unable to accomplish the task for which they were gathered. The problem? The conductor has defaulted; he, like mankind, has failed to step to the dais to direct the symphony of creation, and so now creation waits, both in frustration and in eager expectation, for the conductor to arrive and begin the music. That's an arresting and even beautiful image for exactly what Paul is talking about in Romans 8. On the last day, when the sons of God are revealed and receive "the freedom of their glory," they will finally follow their Lord to the dais. The bows will move, the mallets will fall, the voices will rise, and the music will begin. The creation will be released from its bondage and restored to its original purpose—the unfettered and unfrustrated praise of God.

Of course, the image of creation *restored, freed,* and *released from bondage* is quite a different image from that of it "passing away." And yet they are both taught in the Bible, and therefore they are both true. But how? How can the world both "pass away" and at the same time be "set free from its bondage to decay"? It's important that we don't lean so far in one direction that we undercut the other. We should not so emphasize continuity that we wind up denying that there will be a cataclysmic end to this age and even to the present heavens and earth. The transition to eternity will not be a smooth one. On the other hand, we also should not so emphasize *dis*continuity that we wind up saying that this world does not matter. Scripture tells us that there is in fact continuity of some kind between this world and the next; the cataclysm is not absolute.

But how do we draw these two ideas together? Perhaps the best way to think about it is that creation will experience a kind of death and resurrection that is more or less analogous to the death and resurrection that we ourselves will experience. There is most certainly a continuity between my body now and the resurrection body I will one day have. In 1 Corinthians 15 Paul compares that relationship to the continuity between a seed and the full-grown wheat (v. 37). But there also will be a radical discontinuity between my body now and the resurrection body I will have. It will be something crucially different. As Paul says, "So is it with the resurrection of the dead. What is sown is perishable; what is raised is imperishable. It is sown in dishonor; it is raised in glory. It is sown in weakness; it is raised in power. It is sown a natural body; it is raised a spiritual body" (vv. 42–44). Perhaps then we should understand that the creation itself will experience something similar. Perhaps it will "pass away" in a

216

kind of death but then be "released from its bondage to decay" in a kind of resurrection. Death and resurrection. Discontinuity *and* continuity.[10]

Implications of Continuity and Discontinuity in the World to Come

All this should lead to a great deal of humility in our claims about what we are really accomplishing with our cultural achieve-ments. Of course we can point to some kinds of continuity with a great deal of confidence. For example, even though Jesus rose from the dead in a glorified body, he was still Jesus. So, too, we will be the same people in eternity that we are now. Greg will be Greg, Kevin will be Kevin, and you will be you. Also, we've already seen that there will be some continuity between our present body and our resurrection body, and it also seems that the world itself will be continuous in its physical substance. The world isn't destined to be annihilated and remade from scratch; rather, as we've seen, it is destined to be "released from its bond-age to decay."[11] The comparison to the flood in 2 Peter 3:5–7 is a helpful analogy here. The earth is said to have "perished" in the flood (v. 6). But we know the earth was not obliterated. In the same way, perhaps, everything will be burned up at the end of history. The earth will be destroyed, but the planet will still be here, still the same earth ready like a phoenix to rise from the ashes. The present form of the world will pass away

---

[10]In a very helpful section, Herman Bavinck draws the analogy with the person who is now "new creation" in Christ: "Just as anyone in Christ is a new creation in whom the old has passed away and everything has become new (2 Cor. 5:17), so also this world passes away in its present form as well, in order out of its womb, at God's word of power, to give birth and being to a new world. Just as in the case of an individual human being, so at the end of time a rebirth of the world will take place as well (Matt. 19:28)." Herman Bavinck, *Reformed Dogmatics*, vol. 4, *Holy Spirit, Church, and New Creation* (Grand Rapids, Baker, 2008), 717.

[11]As Bavinck argues strongly, "The passages that are assumed to teach [the destruction of the world's substance] do indeed describe in very graphic terms the change that will set in after the day of the Lord, but they do not imply the destruction of the substance of the world. . . . God's honor consists precisely in the fact that he redeems and renews the same humanity, the same world, the same heaven, and the same earth that have been corrupted and polluted by sin" (ibid., 716–17).

(1 Cor. 7:31), but that doesn't mean the whole universe will be annihilated. We will spend eternity here, on the earth. It won't be this same world, but it won't be a completely different world either. It will be a new world, a cleansed world, a reborn world. Not only so, but Revelation 7 seems to indicate that there will be some continuation of our ethnolinguistic identity. When John turns to see the great multitude standing before the throne, he realizes immediately that they are "from every nation, from all tribes and peoples and languages" (Rev. 7:9).

But what about our cultural achievements and artifacts? Is it possible that cultural works will "make it" into eternity? Well, maybe. But we have nothing in Scripture that promises that to us, and so we should not talk as if we do. To be sure, there are some images in Scripture that seem to indicate that certain aspects of human culture will "make it" into eternity. Isaiah 60, for example, says that at the last day, "the wealth of the nations" will be brought to Jerusalem, and even that "ships" will make their way into the ports. But then again, we're dealing there with poetic imagery—and besides, doesn't Revelation say there will be no more sea (or is that just apocalyptic imagery, too)?

You can see the point. If we want to use such language, we should frame it in terms of a possible implication, not as a definitive certainty, being careful not to go beyond what is written. Can we really say, "We already have biblical assurance that the ships of Tarshish will be there; perhaps they will share a harbor with an America's Cup yacht and a lovingly carved birch bark canoe"?[12] At the end of the day, we simply can't know with any certainty, and therefore we should not be so bold as to insist that our efforts at cultural renewal will have an impact on the renewed earth. That would be like insisting that when I lift weights with this present body I am somehow guaranteeing bigger biceps on my resurrection body! We wouldn't say such a thing about the resurrection; why would we think we can so confidently say it about the renewal of the earth?

---

[12]Andy Crouch, *Culture Making* (Downers Grove, IL, InterVarsity: 2008), 170.

No, our task, as it has always been for the people of God, is to live in this passing age with simple faithfulness. We are to strive for a "faithful presence" in a fallen world. That is a more chastened posture toward the world—and far more biblical, we think—than a claim that we are somehow building culture for eternity, that we somehow expect our cultural and social works to "make it" through the judgment. The fact is, the Bible simply doesn't give us enough information to know. What we know is that there will be cataclysmic judgment (Rev. 11:19; 16:17–21)—this world and its desires will "pass away"—and we also know that on the other side of that judgment the creation will be released from its bondage to decay. But we fool ourselves if we think we can figure out the details of what happens in between.

Conclusion

This is an area of biblical theology that could use some scholarly attention. Too often the discussion just bounces back and forth between strong assertions of extremes—Continuity! Discontinuity!—without a sober acknowledgment that the Bible in fact teaches both. This chapter has offered an initial, cautious proposal for how we might draw those two emphases together, but there are many other questions that could be asked, answered, and applied to important issues in our life and doctrine as Christians.

Of course, we should also note again that, once we step back from the technical aspects of this discussion, we find ourselves right back at the main point we have been laboring to make in this book all along. The most important thing we can say about shalom and about the new heavens and new earth is that they are only to be obtained by those who have been redeemed through the blood of the resurrected Lord Jesus. Therefore, even if we *could* wrap an entire city in shalom and push it over the threshold of eternity, the citizens of that city would not go with it unless they had heard from our lips and believed the gospel of the Lord Jesus.

219

PART 3

*Understanding What We Do
and Why We Do It*

CHAPTER 9

Zealous for Good Works

Why and How We Do Good, both as Individuals and as Churches

WHEN PEOPLE HEAR or read arguments like the ones we have presented here, they have often responded with something like, "But I think good deeds *are* important. We *are* supposed to be doing good things for the people around us, even the non-Christians around us."

Please underline, circle, or put a star beside this: We agree! Fully, wholeheartedly, unreservedly, and without the slightest contrary shiver in the liver, we agree! We are of the strong opinion that the Bible teaches that we Christians are to be a people of both declaration and demonstration, and that our churches are to be communities of both declaration and demonstration. God has redeemed us from all lawlessness and made us a people for his own possession who are zealous for good works (Titus 2:14). Our hope in this book, in fact, has not been in any way to discourage good works, but rather to *encourage* them in the long run by being crystal clear about where and how good works fit into Christian theology and into the Christian life.

So why do we do good? If "building for the kingdom," "proclaiming the gospel without words," and "joining God in his work of making all things new" are not the correct motivations for good works, what are? Why should we do good works at all if those motivations are not biblically sustainable? Actually, the Bible gives us plenty of reasons to do good works, and they are not small ones, either. We don't want to leave anyone with the sinking feeling that we've pulled the rug out from under the Christian's duty and desire to "not grow weary of doing good" (Gal. 6:9), so here are just a few of the motivations that Scripture *does* give us for living a life that is filled with good works.

We Do Good Works to Obey God, Whom We Love

Of course there's more to say, but the foundation of it all is obeying God out of love. At the end of the day, God commands us in his Word to do good works and to live good lives. "This is the love of God, that we keep his commandments. And his commandments are not burdensome" (1 John 5:3). After all, "we love because he first loved us" (1 John 4:19).

We Do Good Works Because We Love Our Neighbors

Jesus said that the greatest commandment of all is this: "You shall love the Lord your God with all your heart and with all your soul and with all your mind." And the second, he said, is like it: "You shall love your neighbor as yourself" (Matt. 22:36–40). Not only so, but he also blew the walls out of the narrow strictures the Pharisees had placed on the definition of a "neighbor."

> You have heard that it was said, "You shall love your neighbor and hate your enemy." But I say to you, Love your enemies and pray for those who persecute you, so that you may be sons of

your Father who is in heaven. For he makes his sun rise on the evil and on the good, and sends rain on the just and on the unjust. (Matt. 5:43–45)

If the definition of "loving our neighbors" includes praying even for our *enemies*, then it includes everyone! Part of the reason is that each of us, from the least to the greatest, is a person created in the image of God (Gen. 1:27). Therefore, in loving our neighbors we are showing that we value the fact that they, too, are works of our God and fellow creatures. So we Christians are to be a people characterized and marked by love—not just for those who are like us, or those who are in our churches, or those who are in our particular social groups, but for everyone.

We've argued elsewhere in this book that precisely *how* that love is expressed is a matter that requires much wisdom and a sensitivity to the fact that we can't do everything. We are finite creatures, and therefore it's important for us not to flog ourselves with undue guilt because we cannot show full, unbounded, active, suffering-relieving love to all seven billion people on the planet. But neither can we use our finitude to build walls around ourselves and excuse a lack of love toward those who are in a close "moral proximity" to us. We as Christians should be marked by a posture of love and generosity toward our neighbors, and that includes everyone, according to Jesus, from our best friends to our worst enemies.

We Do Good Works to Show the World God's Character and God's Work

Jesus told his followers, "Let your light shine before others, so that they may see your good works and give glory to your Father who is in heaven" (Matt. 5:16). When we approach the world with a posture of love and generosity, our good works provide a powerful confirmation of our declaration that "God is love." They show the world that we really mean what we say, and they make it just that much more plausible that God really is there and that his influence in our lives is real, powerful, and different from anything else in the world.

That is at least part of what Jesus was saying when he told his followers, "You are the salt of the earth" (Matt. 5:13). Salt was known for doing many things. It preserved, it cleaned, and it enhanced taste. But figuring out what exactly salt did is not the point—probably all those things are evoked by Jesus's words. The point is that the salt does all those things precisely because there is something about it that makes it *different* from the thing onto which it is sprinkled. If you sprinkle broccoli bits on broccoli, you haven't accomplished much. Salt is useful, Jesus was saying, exactly because it is salty, and if it loses its saltiness—if it becomes no different from what it is sprinkled on—then it's of no use at all. The same is true of light; its use comes in the fact that it is not darkness. It is different, and if you take away its "lightness" by hiding it under a basket, it's no good for anything.

Do you see the point here? We Christians are to be conspicuous in our following of our King Jesus. We are to do good works as a testimony that God has made us into something different from what we once were, and from the unredeemed world around us. As people of the kingdom, we are to be salt and light in a fallen world. That is, we are to be *different*, and by those good deeds together with our true words, we are to testify to God's character.

We Do Good Works Because They Are the Fruit of the Spirit's Work in Us

Simply put, apples grow on apple trees, oranges grow on orange trees, and good works grow on Christians. It's just the way the world works. Jesus is as clear about this as he can be:

> You will recognize them by their fruits. Are grapes gathered from thornbushes, or figs from thistles? So, every healthy tree bears good fruit, but the diseased tree bears bad fruit. A healthy tree cannot bear bad fruit, nor can a diseased tree bear good fruit. Every tree that does not bear good fruit is

cut down and thrown into the fire. Thus you will recognize them by their fruits. (Matt. 7:16–20)

It's not that good works are in the *root* of the tree; they're not the thing that makes the tree what it is. They're not the ground or the basis of our standing with God. But if we truly are redeemed through the blood of Christ, if the Holy Spirit truly dwells in us, then we will be people who bear fruit in good works. Our lives will be marked by what Paul calls "the fruit of the Spirit: love, joy, peace, patience, kindness, goodness, faithfulness, gentleness, self-control" (Gal. 5:22–23). And if those fruits are not present in us, Jesus says, we have reason to question whether the tree was ever really healthy at all.

James is perhaps evoking this image of a tree bearing fruit when he says that "faith apart from works is dead" (James 2:26). What he means is that a living faith, one that has the sap of the Spirit's life running through it, will inevitably bear fruit. It will produce a life that is marked by good works. Abraham's faith was that kind of living faith: it issued in the good fruit of obedience to God, even when God's command was that he should kill his own son. Rahab's faith, too, was a living one: it issued in obedience to God through her protection of the Israelite spies, even when the cost of her obedience could have been her very life (James 2:21–25).

"Every healthy tree bears good fruit," Jesus says (Matt. 7:17). If we claim to be Christians, then we are claiming to be "healthy trees," and therefore we should be bearing "good fruit." For we are his workmanship, created in Christ Jesus for good works (Eph. 2:10).

We Do Good Works to Win a Hearing for the Gospel

Sometimes the argument is made that when Christians do good things for other people and then share the gospel with them, they've pulled a bait-and-switch trick. That could be the case, especially if the Christian is thinking of his evangelism as a way to put notches in his religious belt. Then neither his good works nor his evangelism would be founded on care for the other person. His good works would be grounded on a desire to get to the evangelism, and the evangelism would be grounded in a desire to make himself look good. Love doesn't figure in there at all.

But that's really a terrible way to think about evangelism. Evangelism is the act of telling other people about the plight they are in and how they can be saved from it. Sharing the good news of Jesus Christ is an act of deep love and compassion for that person. So the argument that one act of love and compassion (evangelism) can't legitimately be accompanied by other, less important, acts of love and compassion doesn't hold water. Christians, as we've seen, are to love the whole person, and therefore it makes perfect sense to love someone by giving him food and at the same time to love him in a different, higher way by giving him the gospel. There's no bait-and-switch there; that's simply holistic compassion—compassion for the whole person, not just part of him.[1]

Understanding that, we can also see an opposite danger for those who buy the bait-and-switch argument. It's that they will compassionately meet physical and even emotional needs, but out of fear of falling into a bait-and-switch scenario, they'll neglect to compassionately meet the other person's spiritual needs by sharing the gospel with them. In other words, they'll show compassion to people only at the basest levels—and one could legitimately question whether that is real compassion at

---

[1] If this were a different kind of book, this would be a good place to talk about the dilemmas many missionaries face relative to helping the poor. For example, they don't want the people they serve to become "rice Christians," those who profess Christ because they know they'll get food if they do or they feel obligated to profess Christ after having been fed. There are also the dynamics of creating dependencies with our Western money that need to be considered. See Steve Corbett and Brian Fikkert, *When Helping Hurts: How to Alleviate Poverty Without Hurting the Poor and Yourself* (Chicago: Moody, 2009), especially 161–218, for practical suggestions on how to help without hurting.

all. The reality is that people who make that mistake see evangelism as no more an act of compassion than the person who sees it as a way to put a notch in his belt; it's just that they see the gospel as something they are trying to sell, and therefore they don't want to "corrupt" their compassion by moving into the sales pitch.

If we understand evangelism itself, though, as a deep and profound act of love for another person, we will do it *more often* (because we won't have the awkward feeling that we're just giving a sales pitch), and we'll do it with the *right motives*, too (love for people, instead of regard for ourselves). In fact, if we are Christians whose love and compassion is aroused not just by physical and emotional needs, but also by spiritual needs, then sharing the gospel will always be in the forefronts of our minds. We will naturally and readily move toward it as we are loving other people.

Does this, by the way, mean that good deeds that aren't followed by the sharing of the gospel are somehow illegitimate or not worth doing? Of course not! They are worth doing! You can give a donation to Toys for Tots, or pick up a piece of litter in the street, or plant a tree when no one's watching, or buy someone a sandwich when you're already late to work and not say a word to them. And when you do, you will be doing a good thing, something that is motivated by your status both as a human being and, more particularly, as a Christian bearing fruit under the loving rule of Jesus Christ. But when you do those things, you also need to know and admit that you are *not* fulfilling part of the church's mission, you are not "expanding the borders of the kingdom," and you are not "sharing the gospel without words." You are simply doing things that redeemed human beings do. You are living as a human being who has been saved and regenerated by the grace of God. And who knows? Maybe the next time you buy the guy a sandwich, you'll have time to explain why you're doing it in the first place!

A New Category between Unimportant and Ultimately Important

Our generation tends to think about motivation in two speeds and two speeds only—there are things that are of the utmost importance, and things that are of no importance. There's no in-between. That's one of the reasons this whole conversation about the mission of the church is so difficult. The minute you start arguing that good works are not of *the utmost importance*, people accuse you of saying that they are of no importance at all. The thinking seems to be that good works have to be motivated by the highest imaginable reasons—We're building for the kingdom! We're *doing* the gospel! We're joining God in his mission! We're spreading shalom!—or else people will think they're not important at all.

We need another speed. We need a speed that's somewhere between *of the utmost importance* and *of no importance*. Something like *really, really important* might do the trick. The fact is, we as Christians have a lot of things on our plate. There are many things that the Lord calls us to do that are not of the utmost importance, in the sense that they are earth-shattering, kingdom-building, eternity-making things. And yet they are really, really important, and we are called to be faithful in doing them. If we're honest with ourselves, we already have this speed, and we use it all the time. Think about our marriages, for example. Our marriages are not going to make it into eternity; they're not *of the utmost importance* (Matt. 22:30). And yet they are really, really important, and we give much of our lives and our love and our energy to them. We don't default to saying that because they're not of the utmost importance, they must be of no importance at all.

So why must those be our only two options when it comes to good works and social ministry and culture building and our occupations and all the rest? Why can't we be content with saying simply that we do those things, and we do them well, out of love for people and obedience and love to God? It seems to us that such an understanding, such a set of motivations, would not only be more faithful to Scripture, but also be better at motivating good works for the long haul because we won't be discouraged from doing them even when our cities don't change over a decade or two. We will be sufficiently motivated by loving God, loving people, and being "faithfully present" as we wait on the Lord Jesus to return.

And What about the Church?

We've been arguing in this book that the mission of the church is best defined not by a charge to engage the world's social structures in an effort to build the kingdom or join God in his work of remaking the world, but rather by the Great Commission that Jesus gave to his followers just before his ascension—that is, verbal witness to him and the making of disciples. But while we've argued that tasks like disciple making, proclamation, church planting, and church establishment constitute the mission of the church, we've tried to walk a fine line so as not to insinuate that any other kind of work—say, humanitarian work or justice work or love work—is somehow un-Christian. Please, please, *please* know that is not what we are saying. Any book that comes across as suggesting that loving our neighbors is somehow sub-Christian is a very poor book indeed.

In order to walk this tightrope, we've described the disciple-making mission of the church with words like *central, priority, focus,* and *emphasis.* As Tim Keller has argued, even if "more broadly conceived, it is the work of Christians in the world to minister in word and deed and to gather together to do justice," it is still "best to speak of the 'mission of the church,' strictly conceived, as being the proclamation of the Word."[2] But, you

---

[2]Timothy Keller, *Generous Justice: How God's Grace Makes Us Just* (New York: Dutton, 2010), 216n128. Likewise, Keller states (approvingly it seems): "In the end, Strange ["Evangelical Public Theology"], Carson [*Christ and Culture Revisited*], and Hunter [*To Change the World*] all recommend a chastened approach that engages culture but without the triumphalism of transformationism. All of them also insist that the priority of the institutional church must be to preach the Word, rather than to 'change culture'" (223n153).

may ask, what does this really mean? If blessing nonbelievers in our communities by meeting physical needs is not a bad thing, and indeed a good thing, what difference does it make that the Great Commission is the church's mission or focus or priority or whatever you want to call it?

Is There a Difference between a Church and a Bunch of Christians?

For starters, it means we need to bear in mind that there is a difference between the church considered as a bunch of individual Christians and the church understood as an institution—as an organization of Christians that can and indeed *must* do some things that individual Christians cannot and indeed *should* not do. Perhaps we can talk about these two different entities as "the church organic" and "the church institutional."

When a group of Christians decides to become a church, they covenant together to take on certain responsibilities. They take on the responsibility, for example, to make sure the Word is preached regularly among them, to make sure the ordinances—baptism and the Lord's Supper—are regularly practiced, and to make sure that discipline is practiced among them, even to the point of delivering one of their number over to Satan by excommunicating them (1 Cor. 5:5).

Not only so, but you can see the difference between the church and an individual Christian just by looking at the way Scripture talks to each—that is, by looking at the commands it gives. Think about it. There are some commands given to the local church that an individual Christian just should not undertake to obey on his own. An individual Christian, for example, can't excommunicate another Christian; but the local church is commanded to do so in certain situations. Nor should an individual Christian take the Lord's Supper on his own; that's an activity the local church is to do "when you come together" (1 Cor. 11:17–18, 20, 33–34). In the same way, there are commands given to individual Christians that are clearly not meant for the local church as an organized group. A Christian man is commanded to "give to his wife her conjugal rights," but the church institutional better not try that! (Roll your eyes—but it makes the point!) There is a difference between the individual Christian and the local church, and therefore we can't just say that whatever we see commanded of the individual Christian is also commanded of the local church.

To put perhaps a finer point on it: If I am commanded to do justice, does that mean *ipso facto* that it is the church's mission to do justice? By the same token, if I am commanded to love my wife as my own body, does that mean it is the church's mission to love my wife as it loves its own body? What sense would that even make? Our point is simply to say that defining the mission of the church institutional is just not as simple as identifying all the Bible's commands to individual Christians and saying, "There, *that's* the church's mission." The mission of the church, as we've been arguing throughout this book, seems to be something narrower than the set of all commands given to individual Christians—it's proclamation, witness, and disciple making (which includes teaching everything that Jesus commanded). This is simply another way of saying that bearing witness to Christ is the church's unique responsibility in a way that film making or auto repair or tree planting is not, though all of these may be examples of ways in which an individual Christian follows Jesus.

So What Should We Do, as Churches?

If that's true, what do we say about the church institutional when it comes to things like justice ministries and social action? It seems to us that there are two questions to think through: *Can* the church institutional spend its time and resources doing those things? And *must* the church institutional spend its time and resources doing those things?

Let's take the second question first. *Should* the church institutional do social ministries? *Must* it do so? Really, the answer to that question comes down to how you understand the church's mission, doesn't it? If you think the church's mission is to build a better, more just world, then of course the church *must* be involved, in some way or another, in increasing the social, economic, and political well-being of its city's citizens (and also of its nation's citizens and the world's inhabitants). If that's what you believe, then you're actually defaulting on the mission if you're not doing things that work toward that goal. But if you understand (as we've argued) that the church's mission is actually the proclamation of the gospel and making disciples, then bettering the city's and the world's social condition becomes, at best, a less direct way of furthering that mission, and therefore it falls somewhat short of being a universal *obligation* for the local church.

But that brings us back to the first question: *Can* the local church do such things? Might it not be *good* for the local church to do such things? Of course this question is moot for those who understand the mission of the church to be the social transformation of the world. For those Christians, the answer is that of course the church *can*, precisely because it *must*. But for those who understand the church's mission to be proclamation and disciple making, this is a real question. Is it *illegitimate* for the church to do anything other than evangelism? We don't think so.

Imagine a company whose mission is to make and sell widgets. Would it be *illegitimate* for that company to spend some of its resources holding a company picnic for its employees? No. Actually, the company's leaders may well decide that a picnic will further the company's mission of selling widgets by raising corporate morale, fostering teamwork, and so on. Of course the picnic furthers that mission more *indirectly* than buying airtime for a widget commercial, but it still furthers the mission. In the same way, we believe that a local church could very well decide that adopting a local school and spending time and resources improving that school is actually a good way—though an indirect one—of furthering their mission of bearing witness to Jesus and making disciples. Maybe it raises the profile of the church or wins a hearing for the gospel among the people of the town. Another local church could decide to support a local soup kitchen, even one that doesn't present the gospel at every meal, for the same reasons. It's a display of love that may help to break down misconceptions of the church, circumvent people's defense mechanisms against Christians, and open the way for the gospel to be heard. Yet another local church may decide that it can support and further the mission by giving money to and taking trips with a group that digs clean wells in impoverished countries—not because they necessarily think they're bringing in the kingdom or building for the kingdom or participating in God's work of remaking the world, but rather because, over time, they are making friends and breaking down barriers to the good news of Jesus being heard and accepted.

To put this in terms of a principle, generally speaking we would suggest that a local church should tend toward doing those activities and spending its resources on those projects that *more directly*, rather than *less directly*, further its central mission. Again, that doesn't mean that the church will only ever do activities that are a *direct* fulfillment of its mission. (Think again about the widget company and its picnic.) The point is simply that there is in fact a mission given to the church by its Lord that is narrower than "everything we could do," and therefore church leaders have to be thinking in these categories all the time: What is our mission, and what will further that mission?

Even more, church leaders have to be asking, What will *best* further our mission? That's because our resources are not unlimited. We don't have an infinite amount of money and time and energy to spend on all the good things we could think of, so we have to make decisions about which ideas will *best* further the church's mission. One of the troubles with this whole discussion about what the church can and must do is that it far too often stays in the abstract. The questions run along the lines of, *Would it be wrong* for a church to do this or that? Or *could* a church do this or that? And in the abstract, the answer to those questions is usually going to be "of course a church can do those things!" But any church leader with more than a budget cycle of experience is not going to want to answer those questions in the abstract; he's going to be thinking about the fact that the church can't do everything. Decisions have to be made; trade-offs have to be done. You have to decide not just if something will further the mission, but also *how directly* it will do so, and therefore whether it is worth doing that thing when there are five other good ideas on the table.

Of course there's no way we could ever tell you, in a book like this, what decisions you should and shouldn't make as a church. We don't pretend to have a formula for what keeps disciple making properly in focus. Nor can we give you an ironclad set of priorities, as if supporting a missionary is always a better decision than improving a school. What we can say, though, is that *in general* we think the best way for church leaders to think through these things is to lean toward supporting those things that *more* directly support the mission of the church that the Lord Jesus has given it, over those things that *less* directly support it.

How that works out in any particular church will depend on the wisdom of the leadership of the local church. Some churches may decide to support only those missionaries and ministries who explicitly focus on Great Commission kinds of activities. Other churches may support medical or agricultural missions with an aim toward evangelism and disciple making wherever possible. Other churches may commit some resources to disaster relief simply because it shows the love of Christ. But even here it is often best to partner with local churches in the area that can follow up with the contacts we make through serving. The point, though, is that when discipleship is central, we'll always be asking how the good deeds we undertake can give us an opportunity to bear witness to Jesus Christ.

Conclusion: Keeping the Main Thing the Main Thing

Perhaps the most important point we want to make is that we should not be, as one new missional book puts it, "changing the scorecard for the church."[3] That book closes with a final example of "missional renaissance in full flower." The author's example is the "Souper Bowl of Caring," a charity that raises money to fight local poverty and hunger. "All [necessary missional] elements are present," he says. "You have a movement that involves cross-domain collaboration for tackling a huge social issue. Not only do the efforts of the participants benefit others, but the participants themselves also grow by fulfilling their own fundamental needs as human beings to serve others." Moreover, the event is led by "a true kingdom-oriented leader who raises his own support."[4] This, then, is a model for the missional church. It's this sort of work that counts on the missional scorecard.

Again, who is against fighting poverty and hunger? Nobody. But this model is not just a statement of kudos for fighting hunger. It is supposed to be one of the best examples of being the missional *church*. Yet there's no mention in the example of making disciples, no mention of sin or the gospel, no talk even of Christ. To be fair, we know this author wants these things too, but this is the climactic example he chooses. If "missional renaissance in full flower" doesn't have to include discipleship or proclamation or gospel categories, then this is not the right kind of plant. Neglect or tamper with the root issues—the cross

---

[3]See Reggie McNeal, *Missional Renaissance: Changing the Scorecard for the Church* (San Francisco: Jossey-Bass, 2009).
[4]Ibid., 178.

of Christ, justification of sinners, the holiness of God, the sinfulness of man, the need for repentance—and the fruits will surely wither.

The image of a scorecard, however, is a good one. If you are playing football, good blocking on offense is important, playing your gaps on defense is important, getting the snap down on special teams is important—but if you do all these things well and don't get the ball in the end zone or through the uprights, you won't win any games. The scorecard reminds the team what matters most. The analogy is appropriate for the church too. If we improve our schools, get people off welfare, clean up the park, and plant trees in the neighborhood, but aren't seeking to make disciples, we may "bless" our communities, but we're not accomplishing the church's mission.

Ultimately, if the church does not preach Christ and him crucified, if the church does not plant, nurture, and establish more churches, if the church does not teach the nations to obey Christ, no one else and nothing else will. And yet, many others *will* meet physical needs. As Christopher Little writes in his provocative article "What Makes Mission Christian?," "There is nothing particularly Christian about humanitarian work in the first place. For example, Bill Gates, Oprah Winfrey, the United Nations, USAID, Oxfam, the Red Cross and Red Crescent, etc., are all striving to alleviate the ailments of humanity for basically philanthropic reasons."[5]

In today's cultural climate, where the accolades come quickly to those with humanitarian strategies and the opprobrium falls fast on those with evangelistic concerns, it is even more imperative that we keep the main thing the main thing. The danger is real. If we do not share the gospel—with words!—the story will not be told. Just as bad, if our priorities mirror the Millennium Development goals, we will be

---

[5] *International Journal of Frontier Missions* 25, no. 2 (2008): 68. See also, in the same issue, "Responses to Christopher Little's 'What Makes Mission Christian?,'" 75–85.

redundant. Gilbert Meilaender puts it well: "The church risks irrelevance, in fact, when it makes central in its vocation God's preference for the poor and not his universal favor toward the poor in spirit."[6] Our scorecard is still the same as it ever was. The One who has been given all authority in heaven and on earth calls us to make disciples of all nations.

---

[6]Gilbert Meilaender, "To Throw Oneself into the Wave: The Problem of Possessions," in *The Preferential Option for the Poor*, ed. Richard John Neuhaus (Grand Rapids: Eerdmans, 1988), 74.

CHAPTER 10

The Great Commission Mission

What It Means and Why It Matters

THIS BOOK HAS BEEN BUILT around a single question: What is the mission of the church? We've argued, to put it succinctly, that the Great Commission is the mission of the church. Or a bit longer: *the mission of the church is to go into the world and make disciples by declaring the gospel of Jesus Christ in the power of the Spirit and gathering these disciples into churches, that they might worship and obey Jesus Christ now and in eternity to the glory of God the Father.* In contrast to recent trends, we've tried to demonstrate that mission is not everything God is doing in the world, nor the social transformation of the world or our societies, nor everything we do in obedience to Christ.

This may sound like mere semantics, but it's not. In a world of finite resources and limited time the church cannot do everything. We will not be effective in our mission if everything is mission. Likewise, we will not deliver on our mission if we are not sure what it is. If our mission is discipleship, this will set us on a different trajectory than if our mission is to make earth more like heaven. So definitions matter because focus matters. And as Köstenberger says, "The church ought to be *focused* in the understanding of its mission. Its activities should be constrained by what helps others come to believe that the Messiah, the Son of God, is Jesus."[1]

Something Worse, Something Better

In the end, the Great Commission must be the mission of the church for two very basic reasons: there is something worse than death, and there is something better than human flourishing.

There's Something Worse Than Death[2]

We will never make sense of the Bible, the church's mission, or the glory of the gospel unless we understand this seeming paradox: death is the last enemy, but it is not the worst.

Clearly, death is an enemy, the last enemy to be destroyed, Paul tells us (1 Cor. 15:26). Death is the tragic result of sin (Rom. 5:12). It should be hated and despised. It should arouse our anger and mournful indignation (John 11:35, 38). Death must be defeated.

But, on the other hand, it must not be feared. Over and over, Scripture tells us not to be afraid of death. After all, what can flesh do to us (Ps. 56:3–4)? The name of the Lord is a strong tower; the righteous run into it and they are saved (Prov. 18:10). So even if we are delivered up to our enemies, not a hair shall perish from our head apart from God's ordaining (Luke 21:18). As Christians we conquer by the word of our testimony, not by clinging to the breath of life (Rev. 12:11). In fact, there is noth-

---

[1] Andreas J. Köstenberger, *The Missions of Jesus and the Disciples according to the Fourth Gospel: With Implications for the Fourth Gospel's Purpose and the Mission of the Contemporary Church* (Grand Rapids: Eerdmans, 1998), 219.
[2] This section originally appeared in a 9Marks eJournal, www.9marks.org. Used with permission.

ing more fundamental to Christianity than the certain faith that death will be gain for us (Phil. 1:21).

Therefore we do not fear death. Instead, "we are of good courage," for "we would rather be away from the body and at home with the Lord" (2 Cor. 5:8).

The consistent witness of Scripture is that death is grievous, but far from the ultimate disaster that can befall a person. In fact, there's something worse than death. Much worse.

Fear This

For the most part, Jesus did not want the disciples to be afraid. He told them not to fear their persecutors (Matt. 10:26), not to fear those who kill the body (v. 28), not to fear for their precious little hairs on their precious little heads (v. 30). Jesus did not want them afraid of much, but he did want them to be afraid of hell. "Do not fear those who kill the body but cannot kill the soul," Jesus warned. "Rather fear him who can destroy both soul and body in hell" (v. 28).

People often talk as if Jesus was above frightening people with scenes of judgment. But such sentiment exposes soft-minded prejudice more than careful exegesis. Often Jesus warned of the day of judgment (Matt. 11:24; 25:31–46), spoke of condemnation (Matt. 12:37; John 3:18), and described hell in graphic, shocking terms (Matt. 13:49–50; 18:9; Luke 16:24). You only have to read his parables about the tenants or the wedding feast or the virgins or the talents to realize that Jesus frequently motivated his hearers to heed his message by warning them of coming judgment. It was not beneath Jesus to scare the hell out of people.

Obviously, it would be inaccurate to characterize Jesus and the apostles as nothing but sandwich-board fanatics with vacant stares screaming at people to repent or perish. It flattens the New Testament beyond recognition to make it one large tract about saving souls from hell. And yet, it would be closer to the truth to picture Jesus and the apostles (not to mention John the Baptist) passionately pleading with people to flee the wrath to come than it would be to imagine them laying out plans for cosmic renewal and helping people on their spiritual journeys. Anyone reading through the Gospels, the Epistles, and the Apocalypse with an open mind has to conclude that eternal life after death is the great reward for which we hope and eternal destruction after death is the dreadful judgment we should want to avoid at all costs. From John 3 to Romans 1 to 1 Thessalonians 4 to Revelation . . . well . . . all of it, scarcely a chapter goes by where God does not appear as the great Savior of the righteous and the righteous Judge of the wicked. There is a death for God's children that should not be feared (Heb. 2:14–15), and a second death for the ungodly that should be (Rev. 20:11–15).

Steady as She Goes

The doctrine of hell, however unpopular it may be and however much we may wish to soften its hard edges, is essential for faithful Christian witness. The belief that there is something worse than death is, to recall John Piper's imagery, ballast for our ministry boats.

Hell is not the North Star. That is, divine wrath is not our guiding light. It does not set the direction for everything in the Christian faith like, say, the glory of God in the face of Christ. Neither is hell the faith wheel that steers the ship, nor the wind that powers us along, nor the sails that capture the Spirit's breeze. Yet hell is not incidental to this vessel we call the church. It's our ballast, and we throw it overboard at great peril to ourselves and to everyone drowning far out at sea.

For those not familiar with boating terminology, ballast refers to weights, usually put underneath in the middle of the boat, that are used to keep the ship stable in the water. Without ballast, the boat will not sit properly. It will veer off course more easily or be tossed from side to side. Ballast keeps the boat balanced.

The doctrine of hell is like that for the church. Divine wrath may not be the decorative masthead or the flag we raise up every flagpole. The doctrine may be underneath other doctrines. It may not always be seen. But its absence will always be felt.

Since hell is real, we must help each other die well even more than we strive to help our neighbors live comfortably. Since hell is real, we must never think alleviating earthly suffering is the most loving thing we can do. Since hell is real, evangelism and discipleship are not simply good options or commendable ministries, but are literally a matter of life and death.

If we lose the doctrine of hell, either too embarrassed to mention it or too culturally sensitive to affirm it, we can count on this: the boat will drift. The cross will be stripped of propitiation, our preaching will be devoid of urgency and power, and our work in the world will no longer center on calling people to faith and repentance and building them to maturity in Christ. Lose the ballast of divine judgment and our message, our ministry, and our mission will all change eventually.

Staying the Course

All of life must be lived to the glory of God (1 Cor. 10:31). And we ought to do good to all people (Gal. 6:10). No apologies necessary for caring about our cities, loving our neighbors, or working hard at our vocations. These too are "musts." But with the doctrine of hell as ballast in our boats, we will never sneer at the old hymns that call us to rescue the perishing, nor will we scoff at saving souls as if it were nothing but glorified fire insurance. There will always be soft cynics who eagerly remind us that the goal of missions is more than "mere" escape from hell. "Well," John Piper counters, "there is no such thing as a 'mere' escape from hell. Rescue from the worst and longest suffering can only be called 'mere' by those who don't know what it is, or don't believe it's real."[3]

---

[3]John Piper, *Jesus: The Only Way to God: Must You Hear the Gospel to Be Saved?* (Grand Rapids: Baker, 2010), 14.

There is something worse than death. And only the gospel of Jesus Christ, proclaimed by Christians and protected by the church, can set us free from what we truly must fear. The doctrine of hell reminds us that the greatest need of every person will not be met by the United Nations or Habitat for Humanity or the United Way. It is only through Christian witness, through proclamation of Christ crucified, that the worst thing in all the world will not fall on all those in the world.

So, to all the wonderful, sacrificial, risk-taking Christians who love justice, care for the suffering, and long to renew their cities, Jesus says, "Well done. But don't forget the ballast."

There's Something Better Than Human Flourishing

Just as there is something worse than death, so there is something better than the good life, something better, that is to say, than human flourishing. Every evangelical missional thinker agrees with this statement, but it is easy to forget. Sometimes we miss what the end of the story is all about. Yes, there will be a new creation. Yes, heaven will come down to earth. Yes, there will be peace and prosperity, security and abundance. Yes, this is all part of the coming kingdom that has already broken in on our world. But shalom is not the end of the story unless it's shalom with God at the center.

Or to say the same thing in different terms, human flourishing is not human flourishing without worship in spirit and truth. If we could somehow remake the world right now into a place with healthy relationships, meaningful work, adequate provision, and equal treatment for all, a place where the good guys are on top and the bad guys get their just desserts, we would still not have heaven. We'd have Bedford Falls at the end of *It's a Wonderful Life*—a great movie and a heartwarming story, but heaven rings out with better stuff than *Auld Lang Syne*.[4] The

---

[4] We realize the crowd sings "Hark! The Herald Angel Sings" right before this, but it's motivated by Christmas tradition more than Christ-centeredness. The movie is certainly

good life might be good, but without Christ it's not the goal of Christian mission.

Worship is the quintessential task of those who belong in heaven. The elders and the four living creatures in Revelation 4 are worshiping. Together with the angels they sing praise to God and to the Lamb in Revelation 5. The nations are gathered before the throne in Revelation 7 that they might cry out, "Salvation belongs to our God who sits on the throne, and to the Lamb!" (7:10). In Revelation, when all mission comes to an end, "it becomes clear that mission is in fact a means to an end, the end being a total focus on the worship and the glory of God in our Lord Jesus Christ."[5]

Worship is the end of the end of the story, not human flourishing, because a redesigned world is nothing without delight in God. This means that Christian mission must always aim at making, sustaining, and establishing worshipers. John Piper is right: worship is the fuel and goal in missions. "The goal of missions is the gladness of the peoples in the greatness of God."[6] And if this is our aim, our passion, our joy, then discipleship must be our task—the Great Commission must be our mission.

Aiming for the End

The beginning of the biblical story is about God with man. It is only secondarily about the perfect world they share. Likewise the end of the biblical story is about God with man. It is only secondarily about the renewed paradise in their midst. Heaven shines bright because the glory of God gives it light, and its lamp is the Lamb (Rev. 21:23; 22:5). If we want people to know heaven, we'll do what we can to get them to know God.

---

spiritual (what with the angel Clarence and all), but it's far from the vision of biblical heaven. Besides, the movie ends with *Auld Lang Syne* as its climax.

[5]Andreas J. Köstenberger and Peter T. O'Brien, *Salvation to the Ends of the Earth: A Biblical Theology of Mission* (Downers Grove, IL: InterVarsity, 2001), 262.

[6]John Piper, *Let the Nations Be Glad! The Supremacy of God in Missions*, 3rd ed. (Grand Rapids: Baker, 2010), 35.

We must never forget that if any are to enjoy cosmic re-creation, they must first experience personal salvation. Romans 8 must be read more carefully. Paul does not say individuals will be redeemed as the whole universe is redeemed. He says the opposite. Creation eagerly waits for the revealing of the sons of God, and creation will be set free from its bondage to corruption only as it is carried along in the freedom of the glory of the children of God (Rom. 8:19, 21).

Universal shalom will come, but personal redemption comes first—first in temporal sequence, first in theological causality, and first in missions priority. God will make all things new, but our job in the world is to help all peoples find a new relationship with God. We are not called to bring a broken planet back to its created glory. But we are to call broken people back to their Creator.

Our Responsibility

In 1933—in the depths of the Great Depression and in the heyday of theological liberalism—J. Gresham Machen tried to answer the pressing question: What is the church's responsibility in this new age? His answer was spot-on back then, and it is no less true three-quarters of a century later:

> The responsibility of the church in the new age is the same as its responsibility in every age. It is to testify that this world is lost in sin; that the span of human life—no, all the length of human history—is an infinitesimal island in the awful depths of eternity; that there is a mysterious, holy, living God, Creator of all, Upholder of all, infinitely beyond all; that he has revealed himself to us in his Word and offered us communion with himself through Jesus Christ the Lord; that there is no other salvation, for individuals or for nations, save this, but that this salvation is full and free, and that whoever possesses it has for himself and for all others to whom he may be the instrument of bringing it a treasure compared with which all the kingdoms

of the earth—no, all the wonders of the starry heavens—are as the dust of the street.

An unpopular message it is—an impractical message, we are told. But it is the message of the Christian church. Neglect it, and you will have destruction; heed it, and you will have life.[7]

It is not the church's responsibility to right every wrong or to meet every need, though we have biblical motivation to do some of both. It is our responsibility, however—our unique mission and plain priority—that this unpopular, impractical gospel message gets told, that neighbors and nations may know that Jesus is the Christ, the Son of God, and that by believing, they may have life in his name.

---

[7]J. Gresham Machen, "The Responsibility of the Church in Our New Age," in *J. Gresham Machen: Selected Shorter Writings*, ed. D. G. Hart (Phillipsburg, NJ: P&R, 2004), 376.

So You're Thinking of Starting a New Kind of Church?

Advice for the Young, Motivated, and Missional

MEET PASTOR CHRIS. He's not a real person (though I'm sure there are plenty of Pastor Chrises out there, so our apologies). His story is fiction, but it is not unfamiliar. Pastor or not, you may even hear echoes of your own story in this one.

Chris grew up in a Christian home, a loving, stable, somewhat stern home. His dad was the pastor at a medium-sized Baptist church in the South. When Chris was twelve, his family moved to a small city in the Midwest, where his dad took a job as the executive pastor at a megachurch in the suburbs. The new city was a little bigger—okay, *much* bigger—than Chris and his younger two sisters were used to. In fact, it was a bit intimidating. But the Christian school they went to was a nurturing place, which helped, and Chris's parents seemed happy.

All things considered, Chris was a pretty good kid. He broke curfew a few times and got caught drinking once, but he quickly learned his lessons and was usually eager to please his parents. His grades were decent. He was a good athlete and an unusually good guitar player. Over time, he began to feel at home in the 3500-person Riverside Community Church. Chris made friends in the youth group, went to church every Sunday, played in the youth praise band, and led, by all accounts, the normal, if not slightly better than average, life of an evangelical teenager.

Off to School

After he graduated from his Christian high school, Chris moved one state over, about two hours away, to a well-respected Christian liberal arts college. Initially, he wanted to go to the big state school, but his parents convinced him that he might get lost in a big university and he'd have to put up with a lot of anti-Christian bias. If he went to the small Christian college instead, he'd continue to develop a Christian worldview and might even be able to lead music in chapel.

Chris loved college. Through a freshman Bible study on campus, he quickly made friends with three other guys, all of whom were serious about their faith, more serious than Chris was at first. College was good for Chris's walk with the Lord in a lot of ways. He was consistently committed to personal devotions for the first time ever. He talked about the Bible and theology with his friends all the time. And he learned there was so much more to learn about the Christian faith than he ever imagined. At the beginning of his junior year, Chris decided to major in biblical studies. He was thinking of going to seminary to become what he never dreamed of becoming—a pastor.

But there were a few concerns too. For starters, Chris wasn't very involved in a church. He loved his classes, tolerated chapel, and went to church maybe twice a month. He figured he was learning so much in his classes and had to go chapel three times a week anyway, so a Sunday service was not a must. Chris also grew a little edgier. This wasn't all bad. Chris was a pretty quiet, compliant kid growing up, not wanting to disappoint his parents and all. But the new edge had its problems. Chris could be critical, especially of other Christians. He was self-confident to the point of turning people off. He was also smart, impressing his peers and professors with his love of learning and voracious appetite for reading. This, along with the popularity that came from playing guitar once a week in chapel, made him a little overbearing.

What Hath College Wrought?

Chris had grown up with the quintessential Sunday school faith. He knew a lot of Bible stories, asked Jesus into his heart at summer camp in junior high school, understood that he was saved by grace alone, tried to stay out of trouble, felt guilty for not praying and evangelizing more, and never really questioned anything. But a lot changed in college. Chris didn't completely reject the Christianity he grew up with, but he started to view it as simplistic and misguided—well intended but naïve. He became interested in environmental stewardship and in the plight of the poor, issues he'd never heard talked about in the suburbs. He also grew to resent some elements of his church background—the video games at youth group, the praise band that seemed too happy to be real, the squeaky-clean multimillion-dollar new facility that was completed just before he left for college.

What really impacted Chris was the semester he spent studying abroad during his senior year. Chris was a Spanish minor so he decided to go to Central America, where he took some classes, saw some historical sights, and enjoyed the Latin culture. During his four months abroad, Chris had several occasions to see real-life poverty in person for the first time. He was amazed by the vibrant faith these poor Christians had in the midst of so much apparent suffering. The little church he attended many times in

Central America seemed so much more alive than the churches he knew in the Midwest. The congregation worshiped with energy. The community was tight-knit. The church—with virtually no resources compared with his hometown megachurch—even ran an orphanage for abandoned children.

Chris returned to the States with a passion for a different kind of a church. He was tired of big churches, tired of the programs, tired of churches with so much doing so little. His passions and frustrations found a sympathetic ear with his professors. They encouraged him to pursue his vision and not let the naysayers get to him.

The Vision

Fast forward five years. Chris, now twenty-seven, has graduated from a seminary in the Northeast. He wasn't too keen on more schooling. It seemed like a waste of time with so many hurting, dying people in the world. But he didn't know any other way to become a pastor. It took him five years to get his degree because he spent every summer back in Central America and poured himself into the urban church he joined while at seminary. He never knew church could be so amazing. This little community lived a semimonastic life together in the rough part of town, and Chris loved every minute of it. In fact, this church was eager to send Chris out as a church planter to another part of town where he could reproduce what he had experienced for the past five years.

With this official call in hand, Chris was ordained by the denominational body he had been a part of as a young child. Five years ago, he didn't really know how to get ordained, nor did he care a whole lot, so he just went with something he knew. Now he was Pastor Chris, full of schooling, full of frustrations, full of ideas, and full of passion. A few months after graduation, Chris and five other singles from the previous church resettled in a regentrified part of town a dozen miles away. Here they would share most of their possessions, renounce the American dream, and pursue justice for the least of these. This church, *Missio Dei*, would be a different kind of church, one that would build the kingdom instead of building programs, one that would seek the shalom of the city and minister the whole gospel to the whole person. Their vision was to serve their neighbors and transform the community in Jesus's name.

A "Chance" Encounter

A month before the launch of their first public worship service, Chris decided to take a prayer walk through his corner of the city. After a dozen blocks or so he came across an impressive-looking building with a big steeple and massive front doors. Chris recognized the name of the church. It was a historic church with a good reputation in the community for faithful ministry. It was well known among Christians for its good preaching.

Curious, Chris wandered in and made an appointment with the pastor, hoping to build friendships with other churches in the area. At lunch the next day, Chris shared his church vision with Pastor Tim. He shared his past, his present, and his dreams for the future. For whatever reason, he really trusted Tim. Maybe it was the fact that he was more than twice Chris's age. Maybe it was the smile. Maybe the beard reminded him of his father. For whatever reason, Tim seemed different from so many of the big-steeple pastors Chris had met. Instinctively, Chris felt like he had something to learn from this pastor.

A Reluctant Conversation

About an hour into their long lunch, Chris decided to ask a risky question.

"I know we just met and you don't know me very well. But you've been doing this pastoring stuff longer than I have. Well, I haven't even started! So I was wondering if you had any advice for me as a pastor?"

"I don't know, Chris. You seem to have a lot of good ideas for your church. There are a lot of things I could say, but I'm not sure what would be most helpful."

"Then just say anything," Chris interjected.

"Well, I guess the first thing I'd say is that I'm really impressed by your passion and commitment. Twenty years ago it seemed like everyone was leaving the city. But now kids like you are coming back, or coming for the first time, I guess. I've seen more church plants in the last five years than in the previous twenty-five. I'm glad you're here."

"Thanks, I appreciate that, Tim. But what else do you want to tell me?"

"I'll tell you if you stop interrupting," Tim grinned. "I am encouraged to see your willingness to sacrifice and your compassion for hurting people. I also like some of your ideas about making church more focused on discipleship and less about gimmicks and games. Too many churches don't really seem to take God very seriously. I can see you're not going to make that mistake."

Chris liked the encouragement, but he wanted advice. "Okay, so you see some good things with *Missio Dei*. But I'm looking to learn. Most of the pastors I talk to don't have a clue, but you seem different. So give me some pearls of wisdom or something. I'm in my twenties. You're in your . . . whatevers. You've been doing this for decades. I haven't had my first day yet. So pretend you're me, just starting out. What do you know now that you wish you would have known way back when?"

The Floodgates Open

"All right, I'll talk," Tim quipped. "It's kind of you to ask my advice. I'm hesitant to get going on this topic because I probably have too much to say. This is actually something I've thought about a lot, partly because I've made a lot of mistakes and partly because I've seen a lot of fresh churches come in here and not last. Or worse, they become the sort of church we don't need more of. So if you're ready for the fire hose, I'll start unstringing my pearls."

"Strange metaphor, Tim, but I'm ready."

"I guess the first thing is, *deal with people, not stereotypes.* It's so easy when you're doing urban ministry like this to think city is good and suburban is bad, or bourgeois is lame and bohemian is cool. Don't get me wrong—people in the burbs misjudge poor people and black people and all the rest. I'm just saying, work hard to get to know real people and don't assume you know who the heroes are. There's good and bad in everyone—middle-class, poor, rich, you name it. Don't size up people or groups or demographics until you get to know them. And even then, be prepared to be surprised by how amazing and how awful people can be.

"One of the other lessons I had to learn was when to go big and when to go small."

"And that means . . . ?"

"It means *go big on the big principles and not as big on the specific application.* When I came here in the early '80s I wanted everyone to hear about the radical demands of Jesus."

"Yeah, and what's wrong with that? They're in the Bible. . . ."

"Nothing's wrong, of course, and a lot is right about this desire. But people need to hear the demands in the right way. We need to interpret Scripture with Scripture and not turn Jesus's hyperboles into Levitical law. So what I've learned is: go big and crazy with the broad principles—no holds barred, no caveats. But once you start talking specifics—in your sermons, in counseling, in discipleship—we ought to be a little more nuanced and careful.

"See, when Jesus speaks his most radical statements, it is to make sure that the people following him really understand what it means to follow him. He's trying to turn away the fickle crowds who haven't counted the cost. Christ's radicalism is about radical allegiance to himself. So whatever gets in the way of this radical allegiance is trouble, be it family, money, job, status, pleasure, rule keeping, whatever. So don't be afraid to tell people that

Jesus needs to come before all these things. But be careful not to overspecify what this looks like. You'll need to do some application, but don't insist the really spiritual people will automatically have lots of kids or no kids or do this kind of job but not that or live in this kind of community or give their money in this way.

"I know it feels more prophetic to lay down the law on lazy Christians. And some of them need you to do that. But don't give in to the temptation to tell everyone exactly what their life needs to look like."

"But shouldn't Christians look different from the world?" Chris asked. "Shouldn't we be an alternative community? I guess I'm afraid that if we don't challenge our people directly, they won't really turn from their materialism and individualism."

"You're right. There is a need for lots of exhortation. And Christians should form a counterculture of sorts. We should all be marked by love, joy, peace, patience . . . you know the list."

"But . . . ?" Chris knew more was coming.

"But," Tim took the bait, "we must allow that good Christian lives will not be identical. People have different callings and will pursue different vocations. The woman ardently concerned about immigration issues may go into the legal profession so she can seek justice in this area. The man who owns the corner grocery store may have different concerns. That's okay. Resist the urge to make the church body do everything you want the body parts to be doing."

"Wait—say that again?"

"Don't make the *church body* do everything you want the body *parts* to be doing. In other words, there's a difference between the church gathered and the church scattered. Some theologians call it the church as organization and the church as organism. Help people be faithful disciples and entrepreneurs and hard workers in their jobs, in their families, and in their communities. Your job is to equip them for ministry, but don't make a church program for every good deed Christians might do in Christ's name. If you have a church member who really wants to see better playground equipment at the downtown park, you could take this on as a church, or you could encourage this brother to spearhead this with families in his neighborhood. It might even make a good outreach opportunity, and it might save your people from ministry overload and from feeling guilty about not doing everything.

"While I'm spewing, let me say something else about guilt. One of the most important jobs of a pastor is to help people feel guilty when they are guilty and help people feel at peace when they are not guilty. Oftentimes, young pastors, especially passionate ones, are eager for their people to feel guilty about most everything. It's one of the ways we know we are getting through to people. Now listen, I'm not a feel-good-all-the-time positive-thinking preacher. So that's not what I'm telling you to do. I'm just saying don't confuse opportunities and responsibilities. Just because we *can* do something doesn't mean we *have* to. If you're thinking an afterschool program is the way to go, encourage your people that this could be a valuable ministry. Don't swing for the fences and try to convince them that they must do it or else.

"Like I said, people are called to different things. Their consciences are pricked in different ways. So don't expect everyone to be into whatever you're into, or against everything you're against. For example, I don't like most movies. I find the language, the violence, the bathroom humor, the sex and innuendo all very offensive. I feel dirty after watching most movies. So I gave up movies ten years ago. It's been a wonderful decision. Now, hopefully my convictions are based on some biblical principles. Certainly, many Christians watch trash and think nothing of it. But I've learned to be careful about projecting all of my entertainment choices on everyone else. I remember C. S. Lewis said something like, 'One of the marks of a certain type of bad man is that he cannot give up a thing himself without wanting everyone else to give it up.'[1] What I'm saying, Chris, is that if you take every last one of your convictions and all your idealistic passion and lay it over your whole congregation, you'll wear them out or tear them up."

"Okay, I get that." Chris was *sort of* getting it. Even though he wanted to be respectful and humble, he couldn't help feeling just a tad defensive. "But isn't it my job to help people change? And how will they change if I just let them worship their same idols?"

Tim worked hard to be patient, something he wasn't always so good at. "I'm not saying you leave them in their idolatry. There is definitely a time for throwing down rebukes. But as a general rule you'll be able to inspire people more by holding up grace. Motivate your congregation with optimism and grace and they will go farther and last longer. You're absolutely right that real discipleship is radical discipleship. But real discipleship, if it is going to last, must also be *realistic* discipleship. We need to guard against self-imposed exhaustion, against thinking we are never doing enough and things are always terrible. Likewise, we need to be careful the accent of our preaching—the flavor, the emphasis—is on the message of God's grace, not on the message of radical sacrifice. Radical sacrifice will happen, but only when your people are first caught up in Christ's radical sacrifice on their behalf. Help your people delight in God, rejoice in their justification, and understand their union with Christ, and they'll be much more effective in mission for the long haul. They'll be nicer to be around too.

"Again, as Christians, and as leaders, we need to call a spade a spade. We need to challenge the drifting. But don't forget that the justice and community things you're interested in are just one aspect of godliness. Sexual purity, forgiveness, kindness, joy, not taking the Lord's name in vain, not getting drunk, not indulging in gossip and slander—these things, and a hundred others, are also part of being holy as God is holy. Don't trade one

---

[1]C. S. Lewis, *Mere Christianity*, 3rd ed. (New York: HarperOne, 2001), 78.

imbalance for another. Be on the lookout for all sorts of idols, not just the ones twentysomethings can spot."

Round Two

Chris took a deep breath and ordered some more coffee. Tim delicately excused himself. When he returned, Chris was ready to go at it again.

He began apologetically: "I know you're busy and I don't want to monopolize your whole day. I'd love to hear more, but I don't want to keep you from your next appointment."

"I just made the only appointment I need to keep," Tim answered dryly.

"Nice."

"Let me finish my previous train of thought. The reason I keep harping on guilt and expectations and vocation and responsibility is that I care about the church, and I care about you. When I was your age, I could have used an older man telling me, Chris, you are not the Christ."

"Wouldn't it have been strange if he called you Chris?"

"Huh?"

"Never mind. Keep going."

"Anyway," Tim was trying to get his bearings, "you need to remember that you are not the Messiah. You don't have to build the kingdom. That's God's work. You don't have to atone for anyone's sins. Jesus has taken care of that. I know you have big plans and dreams. That's good. Really it is. But big plans are only accomplished after many days and years of small things. What I'm trying to say is, pray for the extraordinary, but expect the ordinary. Don't try to do too much right away. This is a big city in a big country in a big world. Get to know your neighbors. Invest in a few key leaders. Work hard at your sermons and don't fret about changing the planet.

"Practice patience. Lots of patience. And a day off every week. Don't forget that.

261

"And don't think too little of the people you're trying to help. It's all well-meaning I know, but sometimes we can be sort of patronizing toward people we perceive as weak or needy. Actually, we're all weak and needy, just in different ways. You don't have to be anyone's Savior. Just be their friend, their brother, their pastor. Sometimes, and this will sound counterintuitive, the best thing you can do for people is to expect more from them. I know you have a heart for the hurting here and around the world. I pray you don't ever lose that. But the issues are complex and the dynamic between giver and recipient is complicated. Sometimes it's better to help others learn to help themselves. I'm not trying to justify turning a blind eye to the injured man on the Jericho Road, but I learned the hard way that doing everything is not the antidote for doing nothing."

At this point Chris needed to get some things out in the open. "I really like what you're saying. It makes sense. One of my professors in seminary told me once that my ideas all by themselves made him exhausted. He told me I shouldn't feel so burdened with all the problems in the world."

"That's not quite how I'd put it," said Tim.

"But I knew what he was getting at. And I know what you're getting at. But here's my thing: I don't think most people get themselves in trouble because they try to do too much. It seems like most Americans, Christians as much as anyone, are lazy and apathetic. There's no sacrifice. There's no sense of urgency. There's no self-denial. Most Christians I've seen are just living up the good life. They live their life like vacation, not like war. They don't give a rip about anything except their kids and their retirement portfolio and next month's football party." Chris was getting fired up. "Most churches are failing because they are insular and couldn't care less about anyone else's problems. They're a bunch of holy huddles. They're country clubs only interested in taking care of their own members."

Tim struggled with how to proceed. Finally, he fell back on his preacher instincts. "I hear what you're saying. I'm sure you're right that a lot of churches and Christians are like that. But at the risk of launching into a sermon, can I give you three points in response to what you just said?"

"Sure, I guess. I've heard three-point sermons all my life! Preach away."

"First, you're right that some Christians are lazy and apathetic. Some of them are fakes, hypocrites, and cheats. And some are doing the best they can. And others are racked with guilt. And others have too many fears and worries to be thinking about freeing Tibet. I'm not asking you to go easy on the lazy. But as you get a little older, you'll see that there are different kinds of people in the world, and sometimes they need to hear different chapters of the old, old story. Be careful not to read your experiences or your personality into every text or every situation. Your take on the church is right, but so are other takes.

"Second, you probably know this too, but a huge part of the church's ministry is to take care of its own members. Think of all the 'one another' commands. These are commands for life in the church. Think about Paul's teaching on spiritual gifts. They're for building up the body. Think of Jesus. He said the world would know his disciples by their love—their love for each other. When I started out in ministry, I used to say things like, 'The church is the only institution that doesn't exist for the benefit of its members.' I'd often say to my congregation, 'The church doesn't exist for you. It's for the people out there.'"

"Exactly!" Chris interjected.

"Hold on. My heart was in the right place. I was trying to stir people up to evangelize and take an interest in their neighbors. But after preaching through most of the New Testament, I realized these statements weren't true. The local church is uniquely responsible for its own members. Elders have to keep watch over their flock, not over the whole city. The church is an army, but it's also an ark. People need safety, care, and teaching in that ark. It took me a long time to see that the way to get people to care about the world outside the church was not to chastise everyone for loving the church too much. We *are* a holy huddle. But we also break huddle and go out into the world."

"Okay, two down. What's left?"

"I'll try to be brief."

"I won't hold my breath."

"Yeah, probably a bad idea. But I'll try." Tim collected his thoughts. "One of the hardest things as a Christian is to figure out whether the good stuff in life is to be rejected or enjoyed."

"I'm not sure I follow."

"What I mean is that some Christians talk about how God gives us all these gifts to enjoy and how our lives should be wonderful. And other Christians talk about the dangers of loving things more than God and how we've gotten too soft and cushy. And of course, both sets of Christians are right. It's like G. K. Chesterton's line about the universe being at the same time an ogre's castle to be stormed and a cottage we come home to each night. The world is a fight and a gift all at the same time. Chesterton said God wants us to have a fiercer delight and a fiercer discontent with the world. So yes, we need to be willing to sacrifice everything for Jesus. But we also need to be ready to accept blessings from his hands. We don't want our people to think that the most serious Christians are always the most serious. We may be at war, but even soldiers get ice cream sometimes. I guess what I'm trying to say is that we must be on guard against affluence *and* asceticism. Both are counterfeit gospels."

As the Coffee Cools

By this point in the conversation, with more than three hours gone and too much caffeine, a few things were clear. Chris had gotten more than he bargained for. Tim had a lot to say. And a large tip was in order.

Despite a few tense exchanges, both pastors were thoroughly enjoying themselves. But both men were also getting ready to leave. You can only talk intensely with an until-recently-complete-stranger for so long. But Chris wasn't quite finished.

"I can't thank you enough for lunch and for taking time to talk. I'm sorry if I got a little pushy at times."

"I didn't notice. I was probably pushy myself. I'm just glad you ask so many good questions."

"Well then," Chris smiled, "I have one more."

"I have three minutes. Go for it."

"You've given me plenty to think about. I know I like some of what you're saying. And some of it I'll need to let simmer for a while. But I guess I'm a little confused after talking with you about the mission of *Missio Dei*. I've been telling people we are a different kind of church, one that builds the kingdom instead of building programs, one that will seek the shalom of the city and minister to the whole person. Our vision is to serve our neighbors and transform the community in Jesus's name. But it sounds like this is not exactly the way you'd put it. So what do you think the mission of our new church should be?"

"Great question. I have a revolutionary idea for you." Chris was all ears. "Are you ready?"

"I'm ready. But something tells me you're setting me up."

"Not a setup—just a buildup for something you already know. I believe the mission of the church—your church, my church, the church in Appalachia, the church in Azerbaijan, the church anywhere—is to make disciples of Jesus Christ in the power of the Spirit to the glory of God the Father."

"Wow, you got the whole Trinity in there."

"Thanks, I've been working on that sentence."

"So basically you're saying the Great Commission is the only thing that matters," Chris muttered.

"No, not the only thing that matters. But you asked me about your church's *mission*. And I'm saying this is your mission. Jesus sent the apostles into the world to make disciples of all nations. This is what God is sending *Missio Dei* into the city to accomplish. Discipleship is your priority. That doesn't mean you have to abandon all your plans for meeting people's needs. But it means that in a world of finite time, energy, and resources, your church, above all else, should be evangelizing non-Christians, nurturing believers, and establishing healthy churches.

"I know you want to make a difference. And in my experience the best way to make a difference is to teach the Bible and bear witness to Jesus in your sermons, on the bus, in your counseling, around the dinner table, and whenever you get the chance. Trust me: the Word of God is more than able to do the work of God."

Until We Meet Again

Then, just as they were getting up from the table to go their separate ways, Tim looked at his new friend one more time and spoke with a fatherly tenderness that surprised both men. "Chris, keep the main thing the main thing and you'll be all right."

"Thanks. That means a lot."

"I should be the one to thank you for such a pleasant and lengthy interruption. This was a great way to spend the afternoon."

Chris agreed and hoped there would be more afternoons like it. "So, Tim, would you be up for grabbing lunch again next week?"

"I'd be happy to."

"That'd be great. I think I can learn a lot from you."

"And I'm sure there are more than a few things I could learn from you too."

Bible Credits

Unless otherwise indicated, Scripture quotations are from the ESV® Bible (*The Holy Bible, English Standard Version®*), copyright © 2001 by Crossway. Used by permission. All rights reserved.

Scripture quotations marked HCSB are from *The Holman Christian Standard Bible.*® Copyright © 1999, 2000, 2002, 2003 by Holman Bible Publishers. Used by permission.

Scripture quotations marked KJV are from the King James Version of the Bible.

Scripture quotations marked NASB are from *The New American Standard Bible®*. Copyright © The Lockman Foundation 1960, 1962, 1963, 1968, 1971, 1972, 1973, 1975, 1977, 1995. Used by permission.

Scripture quotations marked NIV are from the *Holy Bible, New International Version®*. Copyright © 1973, 1978, 1984 Biblica. Used by permission of Zondervan. All rights reserved. The "NIV" and "New International Version" trademarks are registered in the United States Patent and Trademark Office by Biblica. Use of either trademark requires the permission of Biblica.

Scripture references marked NKJV are from *The New King James Version.* Copyright © 1982, Thomas Nelson, Inc. Used by permission.

Scripture references marked NLT are from *The Holy Bible, New Living Translation,* copyright © 1996. Used by permission of Tyndale House Publishers, Inc., Wheaton, Ill., 60189. All rights reserved.

General Index

Scripture Index

276

279

282

Also Available from **Greg Gilbert**

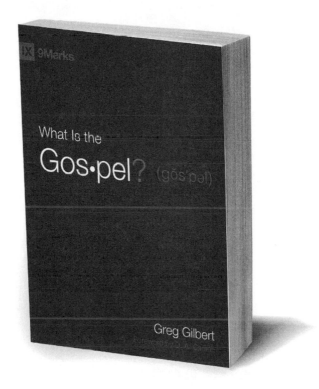

"*What Is the Gospel?* provides a biblically faithful explanation of the gospel and equips Christians to discern deviations from that glorious message. How I wish I could place this book in the hands of every pastor and church member."
C. J. Mahaney, Sovereign Grace Ministries

"*What Is the Gospel?* will sharpen your thinking about the gospel, etching it more deeply on your heart so you can share the good news of Jesus Christ with boldness. It will leave you pondering the extent to which the gospel has impacted your own life. It will cause you to cry out with thankfulness to God for what Christ has accomplished."
James MacDonald, Senior Pastor, Harvest Bible Chapel, Chicagoland Area; radio teacher, *Walk in the Word*

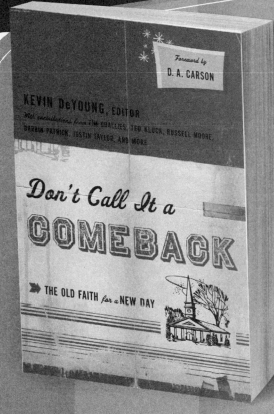